PRAISE FOR
PROVENCE, 1970

"A fascinating narrative."
—*NEW YORK TIMES*

"Required reading for anyone who fears a little life-upending change—even if they know change will bring happiness and *relief*."
—*OPRAH.COM*

"An enjoyable and perceptive group biography that reads as fluently as a novel." —*THE NEW YORKER*

"Barr's careful presentation of his characters' trajectories reveal[s] *Provence* as an important work of cultural history in the guise of a foodie treat." —*SLATE*

"The interplay of these four fiercely independent personalities makes this book a guilty pleasure."
—*WALL STREET JOURNAL*

"Delightful fodder for foodies."
—*PUBLISHERS WEEKLY*

"Brilliant conversation, dimmed lights, culinary intrigue, urchin mousse, a glass of Sauternes . . . Luke has written one of the most delicious and sensuous books of all time." —**Gary Shteyngart**

"Luke Barr paints an intimate portrait of the ambitious, quarrelsome, funny, hungry pioneers who brought about a great culinary shift—the ending of the classical era, and the beginning of a newly experimental, wide-ranging, ambitious cuisine, one that was inspired by France but was quintessentially American in style and flavor. *Provence, 1970* gives a front-row seat to the creation of modern American cooking." —**Alex Prud'homme**

"Luke has brought the icons of the food world vibrantly to life and captured the moment when their passion for what's on the plate sparked a cultural breakthrough. His graceful prose provides a thorough, affecting account of their talents and reveals how their disparate personalities defined the very essence of American cuisine." —**Bob Spitz**

"Luke Barr conjures the past and pries open the window on a little-known moment that had profound implications on how we live today. With an insider's access, a detective's curiosity, and a poet's sensitivity, he illuminates a culinary clique that changed the way we eat and how we think about food. *Provence, 1970* is a revelation." —Andrew McCarthy

"*Provence, 1970* is a lovely, shimmering, immersive secret history of an important moment that nobody knew was important at the time." —Kurt Andersen

"Luke Barr has written a wonderful, sun-dappled account of the pleasures of cooking and eating in good company. Both a meditation on the power of friendship and the uses of nostalgia, you will want to linger with *Provence, 1970* as long as possible." —Daphne Merkin

PROVENCE
⌒1970⌒

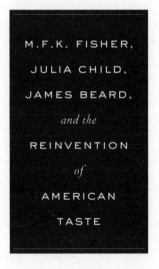

M.F.K. FISHER,

JULIA CHILD,

JAMES BEARD,

and the

REINVENTION

of

AMERICAN

TASTE

LUKE BARR

CLARKSON POTTER/PUBLISHERS
New York

Published in the United States by Clarkson Potter/Publishers, an imprint of the
Crown Publishing Group, a division of Random House LLC,
a Penguin Random House Company, New York.
www.crownpublishing.com
www.clarksonpotter.com

CLARKSON POTTER is a trademark and POTTER with colophon is a registered
trademark of Random House LLC.

Originally published in hardcover in the United States by Clarkson Potter, an imprint of
the Crown Publishing Group, a division of Random House LLC, New York, in 2013.

Grateful acknowledgment is made to the following for the permission to reprint
previously unpublished material:

Inkwell Management: Letter from M. F. K. Fisher to Paul and Julia Child, December
11, 1970, and letter from M. F. K. Fisher to Paul and Julia Child and James Beard,
December 16, 1970, copyright © 1970 by M. F. K. Fisher. Reprinted by permission of
Inkwell Management on behalf of the Trustee of the Estate of M. F. K. Fisher.

The Julia Child Foundation for Gastronomy and the Culinary Arts: Letters from Paul
and Julia Child to M. F. K. Fisher, December 12, 1971, Julia Child material copyright
© 2012. Reprinted by permission of The Julia Child Foundation for Gastronomy
and the Culinary Arts.

James Olney: Letter from Richard Olney to James Beard, October 1, 1970. Reprinted by
permission of James Olney, Literary Executor of the Estate of Richard Olney.

John Petersen: Letter from David Pleydell-Bouverie to M. F. K. Fisher, October 10,
1971 (M. F. K. Fisher Papers). Reprinted by permission of John Petersen on behalf of the
Audubon Canyon Ranch.

Library of Congress Cataloging-in-Publication Data
Barr, Luke.
Provence, 1970 : M.F.K. Fisher, Julia Child, James Beard, and the
Reinvention of American Taste / Luke Barr.—First edition.
pages cm
Includes bibliographical references and index.
1. Cooking, American—History—20th century. 2. Cooking, American—Philosophy.
3. Fisher, M. F. K. (Mary Frances Kennedy), 1908–1992. 4. Child, Julia.
5. Jones, Judith, 1924– 6. Beard, James, 1903–1985. 7. Olney, Richard. 8. Olney,
Richard—Homes and haunts—France—Provence. 9. Provence (France)—Biography.
10. Provence (France)—Social life and customs—20th century. I. Title.
TX715.B3417 2014
641'5973090'04—dc23
2013007782

ISBN 978-0-307-71835-8
eBook ISBN 978-0-7704-3331-4

Printed in the United States of America

Book design by Stephanie Huntwork
Cover design by Gabriele Wilson
Cover background photography by DNY59/iStock
Inset photography by Max Kim-Bee

6 8 10 9 7 5

First Paperback Edition

FOR YUMI

⌒CONTENTS⌒

PROLOGUE

ON A COOL AUGUST MORNING IN 2009, I drove up a sloping, narrow driveway in Glen Ellen, California, on my way to visit the past. Last House. This was where my great-aunt, the writer M. F. K. Fisher, lived the last twenty-plus years of her life, and where she died in 1992. I had not been back since then—none of us had. In the car with me was my grandmother Norah (M.F.'s sister), along with my father, my wife, and my five-year-old daughter. The house was set back a good distance from the country road, facing a dry, rustling meadow. I drove slowly, past a row of large walnut trees covered in extravagant drapings of moss. They were like something out of a dream, alien but beautiful.

The house was a fixture of my childhood: small and white, with a peaked tile roof, thick stucco walls, and arched openings over the veranda and entryway. M.F. referred to it with the barest note of irony as her "palazzo." Inside were two grandly proportioned high-ceilinged rooms, and the largest bathroom I'd ever seen, with a bathtub in the middle of it and a shower from which jets of water shot out in all directions. The bathroom walls were painted a dark, Pompeian red.

I called my great-aunt "Dote," which was her childhood nickname. We in the family all called her that, though she was M.F. or Mary Frances to friends. My grandmother was Noni or None—Dote and Noni, they called each other. M.F. was the older sister, by nine years.

In the 1970s, my parents, younger brother, and I used to come for lunch on our way to visit my grandmother for the weekend. Norah lived in Jenner, a bit farther north on the Sonoma County coast. I can still remember the pulsing, dry heat of midday, midsummer Glen Ellen, the pleasure of escaping the stifling backseat of the family car—a red VW Bug or white Toyota Corona, depending on the year—and entering the cool, dark interior of M.F.'s house. It always smelled faintly of cooking and even more faintly of vermouth and of books. The books were everywhere, and M.F. would have been reading while waiting for us to arrive, her glasses on a cord around her neck. As she rose to greet us when we walked in the door, her Siamese cat Charlie, never friendly, would retreat stiffly out of sight. The open kitchen was along one side of the large, square living room, and there was a long wooden table that looked out onto the terrace and the pasture beyond. The walls of the house were thick and solid, and the overall impression was completely different from that of the airy, open-to-the-elements glass-and-wood Joseph Eichler house my parents rented in Mountain View, in the Bay Area. M.F.'s papers were piled everywhere—on her desk, by her typewriter, in her bedroom.

I can still remember the dense and meaty grilled chicken drumsticks with watercress and homemade pickles she served for lunch when I was about ten years old. Or they may have been drumsticks from some other, smaller bird—I remember they were tiny and delicate, a little bit sweet. I loved them. Even more than the drumsticks, though, I remember my dawning sense of mortification as I heard myself say:

"This is exactly the same thing we had the last time we were here!"

The adults all laughed awkwardly. Needless to say, I hadn't meant the remark as any kind of criticism, but that's what they all thought, I realized too late. That I was suggesting she had a limited cooking repertoire. M.F. assured me she had made the dish again especially for me—since I'd liked it so much the last time we were there (which must have been months earlier; we visited three or four times a year).

I quickly agreed that I had, and still did.

Everyone watched me as I ate. I ate slowly at that age. This was another topic for discussion.

"Luke, you are a very slow eater," M.F. said, not for the first time. She approved of this character trait. One should stop and savor the food while eating, take pleasure in the moment. She, too, was a slow eater.

M.F. spoke to children as if they were slightly amusing adults. She took them seriously, though, I remember. Her voice was quiet and confiding. She looked me right in the eyes and listened when I spoke, and in her eyes I saw an impossible combination of intense interest and dispassionate, calculating judgment. There was no condescension at all, but she left no doubt that she was at all times taking note. Of what you said, and how you said it, what you ate, and how quickly. That look in her eyes is my most lasting memory of my great-aunt.

The adults drank wine. Wine with lunch was something that happened *only* up north, in Sonoma County, at Last House and at Norah's in Jenner. The lunches were correspondingly longer: leisurely hours spent around the table cracking crab and passing the salad and opening more wine. And there was dessert—an unusual and welcome luxury for a ten-year-old at lunchtime. After we cleared the table, M.F. served vanilla ice cream with baked nectarines.

The nectarines weren't hot, they were warm, and the same had been true of the drumsticks. M.F. always finished cooking long before her guests arrived, and then pulled dishes out of the cooling oven as needed, or left them on the counter. There was never a hint of effort or any last-minute flurry of activity.

"Did you bring your swimsuits?" M.F. asked after lunch. We had: in Jenner, we would go to Goat Rock Beach and wade in the surf, ice-cold even in summertime, or swim in the Russian River in nearby Guerneville, but at Last House there was a pool. It was just up the hill, behind the main house, which belonged to M.F.'s friend David Pleydell-Bouverie.

Bouverie was a debonair and idiosyncratic Englishman, an expat aristocrat—grandson of the fifth Earl of Radnor, a title dating back to the eighteenth century. He had come to America as a young man in the early 1930s, and eventually married Alice Astor, the heiress; they divorced after a few years, in 1952, and Bouverie went on to the life of a jet-setting bon vivant. He settled in Glen Ellen and built an estate suitable for the sort of grand entertaining he undertook, hosting dinners that mixed local characters, San Francisco socialites, and European royalty. The rooms were filled with art—paintings by Matthias Withoos and John Singer Sargent, among others—and dramatic pieces of overscale furniture. Trained as an architect, Bouverie had designed all the various buildings on his ranch, including a bell tower, a barn, and guesthouses.

M.F. and Bouverie met in the late 1960s, hit it off, and agreed to an unusual arrangement: he would design and build a house for her on his ranch, and she would pay for its construction; when she died, the house would revert to him or to his estate. She named it Last House, knowing that's what it was destined to be.

Bouverie's pool was round, lined entirely with tiny dark blue tiles. It was mesmerizing: the water was still, cold, and unchlorinated, glinting icily in the heat. My brother and I jumped right in, while my parents sat on the edge with their feet in the water.

◆ ◆ ◆

To a child, Last House always seemed a place of grown-up pleasures and writerly secrets, and it still does. Partly, of course, the mood here is that of any beloved place revisited years later: strangely different, yet somehow exactly the same, haunted by time and memory. But more than that, Last House embodies and represents a turning point, both in M.F.'s life and—as a consequence—in the life of American cooking. It was built during the fall and winter of 1970, after M.F. had sold her house in St. Helena, in Napa Valley. Her possessions boxed up and stored away while she waited to move into her new house, M.F. left that September for an extended journey to France with her sister, a journey that brought her into unexpectedly intense contact with many of her friends and colleagues in the world of food and cookbooks, including James

Beard and Julia Child. It was a journey that would challenge many of her beliefs about herself, and about France, which she had loved for so many years.

Looking back, I can see the story of that journey embedded in the shape of Last House itself, in the architecture, the Provençal colors and materials, even if, now, there is an enormous high-definition television in the living room and a small dog yapping in circles in front of it. The TV and dog belong to John Martin, an Irishman who was for years Bouverie's ranch foreman, and who now lives in the house. Bouverie left his land and all the buildings to a nature conservancy, the Audubon Canyon Ranch, and John Petersen, the director of the program, showed us around along with Martin, who now works for Audubon as a land steward. The barn functions as a classroom for visiting schoolchildren, with numerous bird's nests on display. No one lives in the main house anymore, and it's now used mostly for fund-raising galas and dinners. We walked around back, and there was the round, blue pool, still as ever: unchanged. From the veranda at Last House, too, the view was the same as it ever was, except there were no longer any cattle wandering around.

But if Bouverie Ranch and Last House seemed unchanged, the world of food and cooking over which M.F. for so many years presided has been utterly transformed. Within just a few miles of where we stood was a cornucopia of Michelin-starred restaurants, family-run organic wineries, self-taught goat herders and cheese makers, small-scale mushroom farmers, upstart Asian-inflected seafood cafés, artisanal salami and bacon producers, and too many farmers' markets to count—and those were just the people and places I'd encountered in the preceding *three days*.

Sonoma County is saturated with sophisticated flavors and ambitious cooking, and, more than that, with an unmistakable sense of craftsmanship and idealism. During the week we spent there I heard much discussion about ingredients, where they came from, who grew and raised them, and how; about what was in season and what was not quite yet but soon would be; about the importance of procuring organic hay to feed the goats who produced the milk for the cheese—and the fact that you could taste the difference in the cheese itself; about the farms and gardens that many of the restaurants operated, where they also sold produce. There was a moral dimension to the conversation about food in Sonoma, a sense that quality and refinement and taste were deeply connected to the land itself, to how one worked the land, and how one lived on it.

Sonoma County may be a particular epicenter of food, agriculture, and urbane bohemianism, but the way Americans eat and cook has changed significantly everywhere in the United States. You can see it in the quality and ubiquity of fresh produce, in the democratization and popularization of cooking knowledge and expertise, in our multicultural, internationalized recipes and menus. You can see it in the valorization of ethnic street food and gourmet food trucks; in the spread of Whole Foods, slow food, and "farm-to-table" restaurants; in Michelle Obama's organic White House vegetable garden.

Of course, the culture of food is always changing, but the starting point for so much of the contemporary story is the epochal shift that took place at the end of the 1960s, when previously unquestioned European superiority and French snobbery lost their grip on American cooking. No one sensed this change more keenly than M.F., who had for years made France—the idea of France, the philosophy of France—a recurring theme of her writing. It was in France that she had found liberation, license, and pleasure. And it was in late 1970, on her trip to France with her sister, that she would come to terms, finally, with her European legacy, and her American future.

She would not be the only one making such a reckoning at that time.

◆ ◆ ◆

Who can know how history actually happens, where or when exactly an idea takes root, or blossoms, or wilts away? In December of 1970, the seminal figures of modern American cooking—M.F., Julia Child, Simone Beck, James Beard, Judith Jones, and Richard Olney—found themselves together in the South of France. They could feel their world was changing. Indeed, they themselves had set many of the changes in motion.

The gathering happened more or less by accident, but at a particularly combustible moment. So much was shifting in the larger culture—the politics of identity and style, the parameters of taste, of what it meant to be a sophisticated person—and they would each be making choices about how to move forward. There was new energy and a countercultural ethic in the air, and their reactions to it, and to one another, would change the course of culinary history.

This book tells the story of that moment: a few weeks in the hills above the Côte d'Azur, weeks that were full of meals and conversations, arguments and unspoken rivalries. The small group gathered there was the tightly wound nucleus around which all others orbited in the insular, still-clubby world of food and cooking in 1970. And while it would be folly to argue that they alone determined the future direction and sensibility of American cooking, their encounters in Provence, in rustic home kitchens, on stone terraces overlooking olive groves, in local restaurants, and at the ubiquitous farmers' markets in the surrounding countryside, provide a unique, up-close view of the push and pull of history and personality, of a new world in the making.

✦ ✦ ✦

Of course, before there could be a "new world," there had to have been an old world, and for all of them, that was Europe. Each of these cooks and writers had been profoundly influenced by their experiences on the Continent, and had fashioned themselves in its glamorous shadows.

It was M.F. who led the way. Her writing, starting with the 1937 publication of her first book, *Serve It Forth,* had defined for a generation how to talk and think about food and wine and life; she projected sly, knowing worldliness and American-in-Europe sophistication, and she did it with a light touch. In the book's introduction, she describes various types of "books about eating," so as to explain how hers would be different:

> They are stodgy, matter-of-fact, covered very practically with washable cloth or gravy-colored paper, beginning with measurements and food values and ending with sections on the care of invalids—oddly enough for books so concerned with hygiene! They are usually German, or English or American.
>
> Or, on the other hand, they are short, bound impractically in creamy paper or chintz, illustrated by woodcutters *à la mode.* They begin with witty philosophizing on the pleasures of the table, and end with a suggested menu given to seven gentlemen

who know his wife, by a wealthy old banker who feels horns pricking up gently from his bald skull. These books are usually French. They are much more entertaining, if less useful, than their phlegmatic twins.

M.F. would navigate her own course, she wrote, finding a way to avoid both the dull and the decadent. She would write about meals she'd had, but they would most certainly *not* be the kind where "you sit, pompously nonchalant, on a balcony at Monte Carlo, *tête-à-tête* with three princes, a millionaire, and the lovely toast of London, God bless her!" Nor would *Serve It Forth* be the sort of book to discuss with "firm authority the problem of Bordeaux versus Burgundies, or when to drink Barsac"—that being the type whose authors, needless to say, "are young and full of intellectual fun and frolic," and are, of course, "making a gastronomic tour on bicycles."

"I am not old and famous," M.F. wrote, "with friends whose names sound like the guest-lists of all the diplomatic receptions held in all the world capitals since 1872. Nor am I young and intellectually gastronomic on a bicycle."

Actually, M.F. *was* young when she wrote *Serve It Forth;* she was still in her twenties. But already she had managed to invent a new voice in American literature, one that was irreverent but never acerbic, witty, feminine, casual, sexy, direct, impatient, the very opposite of stuffy—in a word, modern. It was both effortlessly authoritative yet confiding and personal. *Serve It Forth* ranged amusingly through history and gastronomy, from the honey of ancient Greece to the invention of the modern restaurant in nineteenth-century France, and then, without warning, presented the most intimate of scenes. A cold February morning in Strasbourg:

It was then that I discovered how to eat little dried sections of tangerine. My pleasure in them is subtle and voluptuous and quite inexplicable. I can only write how they are prepared.

In the morning, in the soft, sultry chamber, sit in the window, peeling tangerines, three or four. Peel them gently; do not bruise them, as you watch soldiers pour past and past the corner over the canal towards the watched Rhine. Separate each plump little pregnant crescent. If you find the Kiss, the secret section, save it for Al.

Al was Al Fisher, her husband, whom she had married at the age of twenty-one and then followed to France, where he was studying for a degree in literature. She described setting the tangerine pieces on a newspaper, which she placed on the hot radiator for hours and then, later, out on the icy cold windowsill. She ate them alone.

The sections of tangerine are gone, and I cannot tell you why they are so magical. Perhaps it is that little shell, thin as one layer of enamel on a Chinese bowl, that crackles so tinnily, so ultimately under your teeth. Or the rush of cold pulp just after it. Or the perfume. I cannot tell.

The writing was liberated and intoxicating—it was, at the time, even a little shocking for a woman to write this way. To embrace sensual pleasure so openly. But it was more than that. There was a streak of fearlessness in M.F.'s writing, a willingness to reveal herself. There is, for example, a chapter in the book describing a long dinner with her friend Dillwyn Parrish, an artist and young cousin of Maxfield Parrish, at her favorite restaurant in Dijon, Aux Trois

Faisans. She and Al had spent many evenings there six years earlier, when they lived in Dijon, and the chapter is ostensibly about her fear that Dillwyn will be disappointed in the place, that it won't live up to the glamorous, idealized version she has described for him. This would become a recurring topic for M.F.: the nostalgic past as viewed from the unsentimental present. And indeed, the first thing she notices when she is there with Dillwyn is a strange, faint smell (bad air), and her suspicions of degradation and decay follow her through the entire meal. Taking their order for glasses of Dubonnet, the old, favorite (and possibly drunk) waiter Charles remembers her of course. Dillwyn (called Chexbres in the book) says, "You are known, my dear! You should be much flattered—or I for being with you."

He smiled, the sweet-tongued self-mocker, at me and at the table, and I looked with less haste at the tall crystal tulips to hold wine, at the napkins folded like pheasants, at the inky menu big as a newspaper . . .

On the little serving board beside us, Charles fussed clumsily with a new bottle of Dubonnet. Finally it was open. He poured it with a misjudged flourish. Purple spread on the cloth. I looked quickly, without meaning to, at Chexbres, but he was watching the quiet color of his glass. Perhaps he had not seen, had not realized, the fumblings of my perfect waiter?

He raised his aperitif. His eyes were wide and candid.

"I drink to our pasts—to yours and mine. And to ours. The wine is strong. Time is strong, too." He bowed slightly. "I grow solemn—or sententious."

I laughed at him. "I'm not afraid of time."

"Don't boast."

"I'm not boasting. Really, I'm glad six years—oh, it's too complicated. But this tastes good. I'm hungry."

It was 1937 and M.F. was still married to Al Fisher at the time of this scene, and when *Serve It Forth* was published. But not for much longer. M.F. and Dillwyn had fallen in love.

The 1940s saw the publication of four more of M.F.'s books—*Consider the Oyster, How to Cook a Wolf, The Gastronomical Me,* and *An Alphabet for Gourmets*—as well as her translation of Jean Anthelme Brillat-Savarin's *Physiology of Taste*. It was in writing about herself, something she would do in all her books, by turns brazenly and obliquely, that M.F. found a way to the emotional core of her nominal topic, food and eating. The atmospherics of desire and betrayal, the seductive pleasures of a shared glass of marc, the fleeting ripeness of peaches and zucchini flowers: the human appetite for food and for love were one and the same in her writing. This was a philosophical joining, an alchemy, that could only have happened in France, where an anti-puritanical attitude about both prevailed. And yet as much as France was at the heart of her writing, it was her directness and humor that made it American, made it new. She had not invented Francophilia, but she'd come up with the mid-century modern version and made it her own.

M.F. had opened a door to pleasure, to a serious and literary consideration of everything from shellfish to freshly picked green beans to the pre-departure glass of champagne at the train station café, and Julia Child, James Beard, Judith Jones, and, later, Richard Olney, all walked through that door after her.

✦ ✦ ✦

"Why is it that each year our bread gets less and less palatable, more and more flabby and tasteless?" Beard asked in 1952. And bread was the least of it: the 1950s were a time of awful food in general in America. There was the convenience-driven rise of canned and processed foods to accompany increasing prosperity and suburban living—the "Station Wagon Way of Life," as *House Beautiful* referred to it. Quick and easy cooking was celebrated. There were time-saving gadgets, premade salad dressings, instant and powdered soups, and Swanson TV dinners. And there were, to cite the usual suspects, tuna casseroles, sloppy joes, fish sticks, and numerous dishes involving melted marshmallows, canned mushroom soup, and Lipton dried onion soup mix. The dominant cookbooks were vast, practical compendiums of busy-housewife-friendly recipes: *Betty Crocker's Picture Cook Book,* Poppy Cannon's *The Can-Opener Cookbook, The Good Housekeeping Cookbook, Better Homes and Gardens Cookbook,* and many more.

Beard's cookbooks, and then especially Child's, led postwar America to better, fresher, and more sophisticated cooking. Like M.F., Beard and Child had experienced France and Europe as a revelation of taste, and they would bring those flavors to America in their recipes. Beard published *Paris Cuisine* in 1952, at the age of forty-nine, and the seminal *James Beard Cookbook* in 1959. His books made the case, in an accessible way, for fresh ingredients and ambitious home cooking. Beard wrote about food for *House & Garden* and *Gourmet* magazines, appeared on television to demonstrate recipes, and in general embodied the idea of cooking as an art form, something that transcended mere home economics.

There was a growing interest in cocktail- and dinner-party entertaining, and in French cooking, both because people were traveling to Europe in larger numbers and because French chefs were setting up shop in America—most notably in the White House, where Jacqueline Kennedy had installed René Verdon in the kitchen. Classic French cooking was of course the very definition of *haute cuisine*, as prepared at the best restaurants in New York. Henri Soulé's Le Pavillon had long set the standard, and starting in the 1960s, so had André Soltner's Lutèce.

But it was Julia Child—with the spectacular popularity of *Mastering the Art of French Cooking*, published in 1961, when she was in her late forties, and the even more spectacular popularity of her TV cooking program, *The French Chef*, launched in 1963—who made the biggest change to the culture. The book, written with Simone Beck and Louisette Bertholle, was clear, detailed, and accessible. In the foreword, the authors wrote:

> We have purposely omitted cobwebbed bottles, the *patron* in his white cap bustling among his sauces, anecdotes about charming little restaurants with gleaming napery, and so forth. Such romantic interludes, it seems to us, put French cooking into a never-never land instead of the Here, where happily it is available to everybody. Anyone can cook in the French manner anywhere, with the right instruction.

Child demystified French cooking with her disarming personal style, and became a celebrity in the process. She also upheld a certain rigor in the face of the shortcuts and packaged foods popular at the time:

One of the main reasons that pseudo-French cooking, with which we are all too familiar, falls far below good French cooking is just this matter of elimination of steps, combination of processes, or skimping on ingredients such as butter, cream—and time. "Too much trouble," "Too expensive," or "Who will know the difference" are death knells for good food.

Mastering was a landmark, and *The French Chef* was a pop culture phenomenon. Nora Ephron (years later the director of the film *Julie and Julia*) described the scene in *New York* magazine in 1968. The so-called "Food Establishment" (as she anointed it in the piece) was an easy target for her amused sniping about its various camps and cliques, each more self-important than the next. Her larger point was that cookbook authors, food writers, TV cooking show hosts, and restaurant critics comprised a bona fide cultural movement, influencing how and what Americans ate. Ephron reeled off a litany of 1950s and '60s dinner party food fads—"the year of curry," followed by the "year of quiche Lorraine, the year of paella, the year of vitello tonnato, the year of *bœuf bourguignon*, the year of *blanquette de veau*, the year of beef Wellington." She went on:

> And with the arrival of curry, the first fashionable international food, food acquired a chic, a gloss of snobbery it had hitherto only possessed in certain upper-income groups. Hostesses were expected to know that iceberg lettuce was *declassé* and tuna-fish casseroles *de trop*. Lancers sparkling rosé and Manischewitz were replaced on the table by Bordeaux . . .
>
> Before long, American men and women were cooking along

with Julia Child, subscribing to the Shallot-of-the-Month Club, and learning to mince garlic instead of pushing it through a press. Cheeses, herbs, and spices that had formerly been available only in Bloomingdale's delicacy department cropped up around New York, and then around the country. Food became, for dinner-party conversations in the sixties, what abstract expressionism had been in the fifties. And liberated men and women who used to brag that sex was their greatest pleasure began to suspect that food might be pulling ahead in the ultimate taste test.

Food and cooking were now part of the popular culture, as much as fashion, art, or rock 'n' roll.

✦ ✦ ✦

Even as gourmet food and cooking gained broader acceptance and attained an air of chic in the late 1960s, even as a flotilla of cookbooks reached bookstores, more of them every year, even as Child and Beck worked on their highly anticipated sequel, *Mastering the Art of French Cooking, Volume II*—the ground was shifting once again. Indeed, the very same cultural impulses that had fueled American interest in authentic French recipes and fresh, high-quality ingredients (and had rejected *The Can-Opener Cookbook* and everything it and the 1950s represented) were now beginning to point people in a variety of exciting new directions.

The utopian idealism and anticommercialism that defined the moment led quite naturally to the organic food movement, to health food, to baking your own bread. Berkeley communes were planting vegetable gardens, natural food co-ops were opening. Rachel Carson's *Silent Spring*, published in 1962, had set in motion a new awareness and activism around environmental and food safety issues. Euell Gibbons's books on natural food and foraging (*Stalking the Wild Asparagus, Stalking the Blue-Eyed Scallop*, and others) had introduced a kind of romance to the topic.

The nascent changes in the food world reflected the politics of the era—they were taking place in the context of the Vietnam War; the civil rights, environmental, and free speech movements; and sexual liberation and feminism. But more broadly, it was the sense of freedom from the old ways, of creating something entirely new, that inspired cooks and connected them to the moment. Cooking was essential, elemental, and, increasingly, local. The sensuality that M.F. had long associated with food took on a new currency and meaning in the late 1960s.

It was a time of discovery. There was an expanding interest in ethnic food and international cooking—Chinese, Indian, regional Italian. Judith Jones, the editor at Knopf who had discovered and championed *Mastering*, was looking for similarly definitive books about other national cuisines.

All this was percolating just as M.F., Child, Beck, Beard, and Jones gathered in Provence in December 1970. They would be joined there by Richard Olney, a self-trained American cook who had long lived in France and had just published *The French Menu Cookbook*, outlining a bohemian version of the French ideal. Olney maintained an aura of authenticity—his recipes were uncompromising, pure, and exacting—yet he rejected Cordon Bleu formality and restaurant traditionalism. He was an outsider to the American food world, a position he treasured, and he was also a snob, sure of his ultimately superior taste.

During the time they all spent together, Olney's sharp-edged, angular personality would bring underlying conflicts to the surface: the democratization of taste versus the hard-earned judgments of snobbery; the new culinary freedom, informality, and experimentation versus doing things the old way; America versus France, in other words. Child and Beck had been increasingly at odds during the writing of their new *Mastering* book, over these very issues of authenticity and accessibility, tradition and innovation.

It was the question of France that loomed largest, and meant the most, for all of them. The very idea of transcendent cooking, of cooking as an art form, the rituals of haute cuisine, the luxury and decadence of a béarnaise sauce or mille-feuille pastry, the wit of the seminal gastronome Brillat-Savarin, the knowledge of chefs Marie-Antoine Carême and Auguste Escoffier—that was all French, and always had been.

But a seismic shift was in the offing. And there was no better place to see it coming, to feel the sudden, moving fault lines, than in the steep, rocky hills of Provence in late 1970.

✦ ✦ ✦

This book is a history, a narrow slice of it, but also a personal story. It is the story of my great-aunt, trying to decide at age sixty-two what to make of her life thus far, and what to do with the rest of it. And that had everything to do with the events in Provence that winter, and with the future of American cooking, its debt to France, and M.F.'s role in that trajectory. France had been her ideal for decades, and that was changing. *She* was changing.

I know this because I found her diary.

I had started my research at Harvard, at the vast culinary collection of the Schlesinger Library, to which M.F., Child, and Beck had donated their personal papers. Mostly, I read their correspondence. M.F., Beard, and the Childs (both Julia and her husband, Paul) were prolific, elegant, amusing, and all-around brilliant writers of letters, and wrote one another frequently. Beard's letters were archived at New York University; Olney's were stashed in a box under a bed in Provence. Taken together, the letters formed a resonant picture— immersion in an echoing, ongoing conversation—and they are the basis for much of this story. I also spoke extensively with the very few people who were there at the time and are still alive, including my grandmother Norah; Judith Jones, who edited M.F., Child, and James Beard; and Raymond Gatti, the French chauffeur they all regularly hired.

But it was in a storage unit in Hayward, California, where I found what turned out to be the most intimate record of the period. My cousin Kennedy is M.F.'s younger daughter, and it was she who drove me to the one-story warehouse attached to a strip mall where she keeps our family archive. It was a room filled with boxes, stacked all the way up to the ceiling. There were a few old chairs and, along one side, vertical stacks of paintings leaning against the wall, many of them by Dillwyn Parrish, who became M.F.'s second husband.

I realized immediately that I would have to open every box. There was no other way of knowing what might be inside: books, magazines, letters, family photographs, medical records, legal documents, M.F.'s passport. I spent a day sorting through it all, looking for material relating to the Provence trip of 1970. It was thrilling work, a kind of treasure hunt, and never more so than when I came across a pale green spiral-bound notebook with the year "1970" written on the front in ballpoint pen. It was stashed in a manila folder along with the page proofs and edits for M.F.'s book *As They Were,* published in 1982.

In the notebook was the story of M.F.'s time in Provence that winter, written during the final weeks of the year. It was a daily journal, but as I read closer, what I found was something else: a minutely observed account of her changing relationship with France, and, finally, a kind of existential reckoning and break with the place where it had all begun for her, the place of her own writerly self-invention. The diary was almost stream of consciousness at times; it was moving, and revealing, and I soon realized it was also an inside-out version of the very story I was researching, about American food and cooking finding its way from beneath the shadow of France.

As I read it, I knew: I had found the key to my story, and to this book.

~I~

ALL ALONE

December 20, 1970

M. F. K. FISHER WALKED INTO THE LOBBY AT the Hôtel Nord-Pinus in Arles trailed by a bellhop.

Famously beautiful in her youth—she'd been photographed by Man Ray and peered out glamorously from book jackets—M.F. was still a striking woman. Her long gray hair was pinned up in an elegant twist at the back of her head, her eyebrows were pencil thin, and she was dressed in a tailored Marchesa di Grésy suit and a wool overcoat. She made her way to the front desk to check in. The decor was Provençal rustic, almost cliché, with tiled floors and wrought-iron chandeliers. She'd been here years ago, and it hadn't changed a bit. Her heels made echoing noises in the empty lobby. It was the week before Christmas 1970, and the weather was unusually cold. She had the distinct impression of being the only guest at the hotel. The place was a tomb.

The tall man at the front desk was vaguely hostile. He was sullen, but then that seemed to be the default posture of French service personnel in general, at least when it came to Americans during the off season. Veiled contempt. He explained that the room she had written ahead to request—one facing the Place du Forum—would be too cold at this time of year. He did not apologize for the lack of heat, he simply stated it as a fact.

She asked to see for herself, and he was right: the heat was off in that part of the hotel, which was noticeably colder. And so she chose a room at the back of the building, on the first floor. It was named for Jean Cocteau (there was a small brass nameplate on the door), and inside was the largest armoire she'd ever seen. It must have been twelve feet tall. It was grotesque, she decided, but she liked it for the audacity of its scale.

The bed was comfortable, so there was that.

She unpacked her things, three suitcases' worth, clothes for every occasion and weather, multiple pairs of shoes, books, and assorted papers, all of which fit easily in the enormous armoire. There was a writing table and a chair, and a photograph of Cocteau on the wall. She sat for a moment in the silence of the suddenly foreign room, looking at the quaint toile de Jouy wallpaper, and then withdrew from her purse a new notebook—small, pale green, spiral-bound. On the inside cover, she inscribed the words

WHERE WAS I?

in underlined capital letters.

Where was she indeed? And why? She'd spent the previous weeks in the mostly pleasant company of family and friends, having traveled from Northern California to southern France with her sister Norah Barr, and then finding herself swept up in an epic social and culinary maelstrom, which seemed to involve everyone who was anyone in the American food world. Julia Child and her husband, Paul. James Beard. Simone Beck and her husband, Jean Fischbacher. Richard Olney. Judith Jones and her husband, Evan. Together they had cooked and eaten, talked and gossiped, and driven around the countryside to restaurants and museums and to the incredibly beautiful chapel that Matisse designed in the late 1940s.

She had left all that behind at the crack of dawn that morning. Raymond Gatti, the local chauffeur she knew well from a previous trip, had picked her up in his Mercedes and delivered her to the Cannes train station, telling her repeatedly that they would be far too early for the ten o'clock train. But she didn't care. She preferred to be early: she had a great fondness for leisurely hours in train station cafés. And most of all, she was eager to get away and be on her own. She needed to write, think, and figure out what she wanted.

In her new journal, underneath WHERE WAS I?, she wrote:

I am in southern France, and it is December, 1970 and I am 62½ years old, white, female, and apparently determined to erect new altars to old gods, no matter how unimportant all of us may be.

The "old gods" were French, of course. They were the gods of food and pleasure, of style and good living, of love, taste, and even decadence. M.F. had spent the last thirty-odd years writing a kind of personal intellectual history of these ideals in her books, memoirs, and essays. These works were her "altars," so to speak, and she was now embarked on a new one. This notebook would serve as the site of her daily communion with France.

France had long been at the center of her philosophy. She had made France a touchstone of her writing, in which she alchemized life, love, and food in a literary genre of her own invention. But she was suddenly keenly aware of the need to make new sense of the old mythologies. The events of the previous weeks had shown her the limitations of her own sentimental attachments—to the past, to *la belle France*—and confronted her with the too-easy seductions of nostalgia, the treacheries of snobbery.

She was alone in Arles for a reason. It was a reason she was still in the process of formulating.

✦ ✦ ✦

The next day, M.F. wandered the cold streets, pushing against the wind, looking for a place to eat. The town was closed for the season. FERMETURE ANNUELLE, read the signs on every restaurant, including, most unforgivably, the restaurant and bar in her own hotel.

The tall and less-than-friendly front desk clerk told her this without looking up. "Rat bastard," she thought. This occurred with some frequency: she would swear to herself, fuming at an irritation while outwardly maintaining an air of dignified, steely calm. There was the man at the American Express ticket office in Cannes this morning, for example, who had issued her a ticket for a nonexistent train to Arles. She'd returned to the office, and he had impassively explained that she was surely wrong, then looked at the schedule and discovered *he* was wrong, and blandly handed her back the ticket and said she could take the next train, in a few hours. "Too bad," he said, diffidently. "You rat bastard," she thought. "You damned rat bastard."

And now the hotel clerk and his closed-for-the-season restaurant and distinctly unsympathetic attitude. She asked where she might find something to eat. She spoke excellent French, but had an American accent; he replied in French.

"Oh, a dozen places," he said idly. "Jean will indicate them whenever you wish."

"I am hungry *now,*" she replied.

"*Jean!*" he said. Jean turned out to be a teenager in a thin, dirty white jacket whose long blond hair whipped in his eyes as he stepped outside and pointed the way.

"Go down to the big boulevard. Turn to the right. They're all there, quantities of them!" He ran back into the warm hotel.

The sidewalks were icy. M.F. passed by a couple of gypsies playing intense, dramatic guitar music and eventually made her way to a brasserie on the other side of town, after a half-hour walk. She ordered mussels, followed by *pieds et paquets*—long-cooked stuffed and rolled lamb tripes—and sat reading *Le Provençal* and drinking a gin and red vermouth. She watched the room, mostly young men in groups or older men reading the local paper and eating alone. None of them seemed to notice her presence. She felt perfectly invisible.

That night, she wrote in her journal, describing the Provençal locals:

They have a haughty toughness about them, with possible anger
and suspicion not far back of their outward courtesy. When I
go into a restaurant or a bar, I am given a table when I ask for
it, and I am brought what I order to eat and drink, and when I
ask for the bill, I am given it, but there is never even a pretense
of interest in whether or not I like my table, my meal, whether

or not I want to drop dead right there. Good evening, yes, no, goodbye.

M.F. herself had a haughty toughness about her. Indeed, she had embarked on this solo expedition to Arles as a kind of challenge to herself. To travel alone, to see Provence as it really was rather than as she imagined it to be, to compare her fond, nostalgic recollections of the place with its immediate, cold reality. And more than that: to make sense of her life, and what the future held. Her children were grown. She could feel the past slipping away. She wasn't quite sure what she wanted of the future.

She lay in bed unable to fall asleep, too aware for comfort—her mind racing, her perception over-keen, every distant sound amplified tenfold in the dark. The bells from Saint-Trophime; the sudden roar of a car engine on the road outside.

She watched the light and shadows on the ceiling plasterwork. There were no spiders or large insects to be seen in the half-light, thankfully. Only the other night, in the apartment she'd rented in La Roquette-sur-Siagne, near Cannes, a many-legged creature had dropped from the ceiling and landed on her forehead. She had flicked it onto the floor, then lit the lamp and watched it cautiously unwind itself and cross the tiles to safety under the couch. Even as her heart beat in her chest, she felt strangely sympathetic toward the thing—it must have been as shocked as she'd been to find itself stranded on her forehead. She was reminded of another night not so long ago at her friend David Bouverie's ranch in California. She'd been put in a little-used guest room, and one of the cats, accustomed to sneaking through the open window and onto the bed, leapt onto her, the unexpected human lying there under a sheet. She kicked intuitively in the pitch dark, and just as intuitively, the cat sank all its claws into her like wires and then leapt with a horrified moan out the window. She went back to sleep. In the morning, the sheets were streaked with blood from more than a dozen neat little pricks in her skin.

◆ ◆ ◆

Days went by.

M.F. took long baths and drank cafés au lait and set off into town through the pre-Christmas crowds and past shutters closed tight, behind them warmth and family life. She found herself carrying on interminable interior monologues, perfectly formed of sentences and paragraphs, often in the third person. "She looked into the glass-thickened air of the café," for example. Or she would give herself practical instructions: "Mary Frances, go to the toilet while you know where it is." She was detached: a ghost, observing the town, its people, herself. There but not there. She was hungry all the time, always in search of a decent, open restaurant, and never quite satisfied. She recorded everything in her notebook.

It was ironic. Here she was, the great chronicler of food and love, of appetite and longing, hungry and alone. And furthermore: hungry and alone *in France*, of all places. It made no sense. This was, after all, the place that had reliably inspired her to eat, and to love.

Again and again, M.F.'s thoughts returned to the lunches and dinners with the Childs, Beard, and Olney, and her friends Eda Lord and Sybille Bedford, whom she had been visiting at La Roquette: one feast after another, the wines, terrines, roasted chickens and *jambon persillé*, leek and potato soups, and apple tartes tatin. And the gossip, talk, and more talk, comings and goings, trips to town to mail letters and pick up baguettes and groceries, country excursions and impromptu lunches. In the background, all the while, had been a growing sense that they were all on the cusp of something new—a new decade, a new era. It was a moment of flux, of new ideas. But what that meant for each of them was less clear. For M.F., the very meaning of taste and sophistication was in question—as was the viability of the literary voice and persona she had cultivated for nearly four decades.

It was the arrival of Richard Olney, just before Christmas, that had crystallized the contradictions of the moment; he had spurred her sudden departure.

Now, in Arles, it seemed to M.F. almost comical, the sudden change in circumstances. From feast to famine, so to speak. And it had been entirely her own doing! There she had been, in the hills above Cannes, surrounded by warmth, friends, and sustenance, and here she was in Arles, cold and alone.

Why had she left?

~2~

TEN WEEKS
EARLIER ...

LATE IN THE AFTERNOON ON THURSDAY, OC-
tober 8, 1970, M.F.K. Fisher and her sister Norah Barr boarded the
SS *France* in New York City, bound for Le Havre, on the Atlantic
coast of France. It was a hot day for this time of year, an Indian
summer–like eighty degrees, and hazy. Just before five o'clock, the
ship's horn blasted, echoing across the Hudson River and signaling
imminent departure.

The *France* was one of the last of the great ocean liners—a fantastically elegant ship with nearly one thousand staterooms. M.F.
and Norah were in tourist class, sharing cabin number 304. The
room was tiny, but they were delighted. There was a view of the
water through the porthole; they were on their way.

The ship had inherited the mantle of the legendary *Normandie*,
the Art Deco flagship of the French Line (which had caught fire
and sunk in this very spot at the New York passenger terminal in
1942, as it was being refitted as a battleship for the war effort). Built
in 1961, the *France* was the longest ship in the world, and fast—it

would make the crossing in six days. But this was the end of an era: jet travel had now supplanted ships on the transatlantic route. (The *France*, in fact, spent much of the winter as a cruise ship in the Caribbean, to make money during the off-season.)

It was a deliberate and nostalgic choice, to travel by ship. M.F. and Norah had been planning this trip since the spring, and hoped to relive some of the glories of previous grand European voyages.

They were sisters of a certain age, and they were women of a certain class and generation. Of independent means. Unattached, husband-wise, at the moment, their children all more or less grown up, or out of the house, anyway—enrolled in grad school and starting to have kids of their own. The two women had been to France countless times over the years. In Dijon in the late 1920s and early 1930s, M.F. had studied French literature while her first husband, Al, worked on his doctorate. It was during this period that she offered to take charge of her then-fourteen-year-old sister for a year. Norah was far ahead of her class at her local California public school and "too dreamily sensitive to be put into any distant and probably hockey-mad private school," as M.F. later explained in *The Gastronomical Me*. So she brought her sister to France and enrolled her in a convent school. It was the beginning of their love affair with the country. Years later, in the 1950s, M.F. and Norah raised their children for a time in Le Tholonet, a small town outside Aix. They were by then both divorced, single mothers. Like M.F., Norah had been strikingly beautiful and strong-willed in her youth, and the two women remained so in late middle age.

M.F. was at the height of her powers then. It had been the 1954 publication of *The Art of Eating*, an omnibus collection of her earlier books, that cemented her reputation. In his introduction to the

British edition in 1963, W. H. Auden had declared: "I do not know of anyone in the United States today who writes better prose." Her latest book, *With Bold Knife and Fork*, had come out in 1969 to rave reviews. She was also a frequent contributor to *The New Yorker*, writing, most recently, a column called "Gastronomy Recalled." Now in the final stages of work on a book about her childhood in Whittier, California, she was looking for new inspiration about whatever her next project would be. And what better place for that than France? The house she was building in Sonoma County was not yet finished, while her previous house, in Napa County, had already sold. So she was for the moment technically homeless and in transition. "I'm about to make a real break in my life," she explained in a letter to a friend before the trip. "My time in St. Helena is up . . . I went there to make a good home for the girls, and they are both gone . . . and I find it literally impossible to work well there. And writing is just about my one remaining pleasure. *So . . .*"

She was looking forward to her vacation.

M.F. and Norah would visit old friends and familiar places— Paris, Aix, Antibes. They would be on a river barge in Burgundy for a week. Then, for the months of November and December, they had rented the ground floor of an old *mas*, a farmhouse across the street from Eda Lord and Sybille Bedford in La Roquette-sur-Siagne.

Lord, a novelist, was one of M.F.'s oldest friends—they'd attended boarding school together at Bishop's in La Jolla, California, in the mid-1920s. The formidable and sometimes forbidding Bedford, also a writer, was Lord's partner. She was at work on a massive biography of Aldous Huxley, and also wrote frequently about wine, food, and travel for British and American magazines

(*Vogue, Esquire,* and *Venture,* among others). She and Lord lived in London and the South of France and were connected to the food world. They were good friends with Elizabeth David, the well-known London-based food writer, and with Richard Olney, author of a just-released cookbook who lived in the tiny village of Solliès-Toucas, outside Toulon, a couple of hours west of their house in France. Lord was eager for M.F. to meet him.

M.F. hoped to see Paul and Julia Child in December, too. They'd written back and forth about their overlapping travel plans. "Say we shall not miss again!" Julia wrote. "The main thing is to see you both again and be *together,*" M.F. replied.

And M.F. expected that some of their get-togethers would also include Lord and Bedford. A few years earlier she had arranged for them to meet the Childs—they were practically neighbors, after all, as the Childs' vacation house in Plascassier was only a few miles from La Roquette—and the Childs often invited them to lunch or dinner when they were in town.

The truth was, M.F. didn't know the Childs all that well, though they'd been carrying on a friendly, bantering correspondence ever since they met in 1966 while working on *The Cooking of Provincial France,* a big-budget Time-Life cookbook, meant to be the first in a series called Foods of the World. M.F. had been brought on to write the text—vignettes about the food and cooking of various regions in France; Julia was a consultant, lending her prestige to the project; Michael Field, a concert pianist turned cookbook author, was the book's editor and impresario. The lavishly photographed and heavily promoted book would be sold via a book club subscription, for which five hundred thousand people had signed up.

Well, M.F. wrote the text, and then the trouble began. The edits were torture—M.F. at one point walked away from the project entirely, only to be talked back on board by Time-Life executive Dick Williams. Many of the recipes (which Field himself had written) were apparently not authentically regional or provincial in the least, as it turned out. The *New York Times* restaurant critic and food editor Craig Claiborne wrote a mostly vicious review— lauding M.F.'s writing as "lucid and enlightened" but attacking the recipe selection as "dubious." M.F. and Child had to agree that he was basically right. But what flummox and consternation the review caused, especially since it appeared on the very day of the book's publication party at the Four Seasons! No matter. The job had paid well, and more important, it had introduced her to the Childs, and to Simone Beck, Julia's coauthor on *Mastering the Art of French Cooking*. The Childs in turn introduced M.F. to James Beard, the original American icon of food and cooking, and also to Judith Jones, the editor at Knopf who'd discovered Julia, and who was now M.F.'s editor, too, working with her on her current book, *Among Friends*.

So M.F. was officially a member of the club now—or perhaps she was even its *founding* member, having written about these topics for decades. In any case, they were all now part of the "Food Establishment" that Nora Ephron described in *New York* magazine.

The Childs were a warm if slightly frenetic couple, M.F. thought. They were always on the move, organizing and filming the *French Chef* programs, preparing cooking demonstrations, wrangling recipes for the next edition of the cookbook. Just a few weeks before M.F.'s departure on the *France*, Paul Child had written, "Such a time we've been having . . . oh my, oh my! Not that it was awful, just awfully intense. The intensity was compounded of the final deadliney days of *Mastering the Art's Vol. II* overlapping, and sometimes even confused with, our new series of TV programs, their planning, their rehearsals, their tapings."

This was so different from M.F.'s style, she being the quietly observant sort, a writer, after all. And yet she found the Childs simpatico, amiable. M.F. liked the charming Beard as well, and it seemed he would be in the neighborhood, too. So would Simone Beck, of course—the Childs had built their vacation house, called La Pitchoune, on Beck's Provençal estate. Indeed, the fall and winter were shaping up to be a kind of impromptu gathering of the American food world in France. Judith Jones and her husband, Evan, were also coming, and Eda and Sybille were eager to introduce everyone to their friend Richard Olney. M.F. looked forward to a bonanza of expat gourmet socializing.

◆ ◆ ◆

M.F. and Norah were drinking brandies at the Bar de l'Atlantique, which was open to both first- and tourist-class passengers. They were smartly attired, in simple dresses and minimal jewelry. It would have been clear to any observer that they were sisters, both of them slightly regal in late middle age, but Norah the taller of the two. Veterans of a number of transatlantic crossings, they had been highly amused by the brochure the French Line sent them a few weeks before departure instructing them on how to dress on board. It noted that "while a lady does not wear formal dinner dress on either the First Night or the Last, she will *instinctively* wear cocktail or long robes." The brochure went on to discuss the many social events on board, when tropical whites were appropriate, and more. "Shades of my great aunts!" M.F. said. She and Norah could not bring themselves to buy clothes they would seldom use, and that was another reason, aside from the fare, that they were happy to be traveling in tourist class. They lived well—having inherited the proceeds of the sale of the newspaper their father had owned and edited, the *Whittier News,* in the mid-1950s—but they were not wealthy. Norah worked as a social worker in the Berkeley public schools.

It was the evening of their second day at sea, and they were enjoying the relative calm of the ship after their headlong rush across the continent from San Francisco, mostly by train, just as they'd traveled in decades past. They'd had a day of rough seas, but things were smoothing out, and the worst was behind them. Now they were talking and laughing quietly, which they seemed to do quite frequently, their relaxed intimacy with each other as much a clue to their relationship as their physical resemblance. The place was empty, except for a young couple at the other end of the bar, also drinking brandies.

As the sisters got up to leave for dinner and were making their way to the elevator, the couple from the bar came rushing after them.

"Excuse me," one of them said, slightly breathlessly, "but are you M. F. K. Fisher?"

This was a surprise. "Why, yes, I am!" M.F. replied. "But how did *you* know?" As it turned out, the couple had seen an announcement in the ship's *Daily News* about an unclaimed package for someone by that name and, overhearing some of the sisters' conversation, had decided she sounded like vintage Fisher. M.F. wasn't exactly a celebrity, but she did have a devoted literary following, including, apparently, these two, and she was rather pleased by the recognition. M.F. thanked them for telling her about the announcement, which she might otherwise have missed.

After inviting the young couple to join them for dinner the following evening, M.F. and her sister made their way to the dining room.

The restaurant on board was unnamed, but it was spectacular. The ship's enormous kitchen was state of the art, with a staff of 130, and the menus were designed to show off French haute cuisine. The *New York Times* food critic Craig Claiborne had recently published a long and hyperbolic treatise in the paper declaring the *France*'s first-class dining room "the finest French restaurant in the world." The chef, Henri Le Huédé, had been on the ship since its maiden voyage in 1961. Claiborne had taken a twelve-day cruise on the ship and had never been served the same thing twice; furthermore, he pointed out,

> if there is nothing on a given menu to tempt the palate . . . almost any dish of classic or regional cooking can be commanded a few hours in advance, and it will be made with brilliance and no particular ceremony. On a recent crossing it was not at all uncommon to see an unlisted rack of hare being carved in the dining room, or a venison stew being ladled out, or an intricately put together chartreuse of pheasant or a heaping platter of snails being served.

Claiborne seemed also to have been quite soberly impressed by the restaurant's silly menu for pets, which included items such as "La Gâterie *France*—Haricots Verts, Poulet Haché, Riz Nature, Arrosé de Jus de Viande et de Biscottes en Poudre" (The *France* Treat—Green Beans, Ground Chicken, and Rice, served with meat drippings and over biscuits). The article ran alongside a photograph of Salvador Dalí and his pet ocelot, Babou, on a leash in the dining room. Babou's "culinary preferences," according to Claiborne, were boiled fish and grilled meats.

It was all a bit preposterous, but the food was delicious. The decor was modern: an avocado green carpet set off the lime-, lemon-, and salmon-colored chairs. The wineglasses were small and stemless, for stability's sake. M.F. and Norah ordered some caviar and looked at the menu. They would begin with the salad with chervil. "You don't see chervil outside France," said M.F., approvingly. The herb was a sign of quality and authenticity—a rarity. Norah couldn't recall ever having tasted it until that night.

✦ ✦ ✦

The unclaimed package the young couple had mentioned turned out to contain magnums of champagne and sparkling wine—a Taittinger and a Schramsberg. They were gifts from Arnold Gingrich, M.F.'s long-distance lover, whom she hadn't been able to see during the very few hours they'd been in New York. Gingrich was the founding editor of *Esquire,* and he and M.F. had known each other since the mid-1940s, when he hired her to write a column for *Coronet,* an *Esquire* spin-off. The column was called "The Pepper Pot" and included M.F.'s take on everything from the oysters at Delmonico's to southern corn bread.

Gingrich was married, but apart from that, he and M.F. were almost the perfect couple—they epitomized a kind of postwar, grown-up glamour. He'd edited Hemingway and Fitzgerald, written elegant books about fly-fishing (*The Well-Tempered Angler*), and was an accomplished violinist. He wore fedoras and pinstriped suits. He had a gray moustache and a piercing glare. He was every bit the sophisticated New York literary man. M.F., meanwhile, was the arch and witty literary stylist, biting one minute and effortlessly sensual the next. Her books were about food and love. They wrote each other letters with great frequency. It was an epistolary love affair, and a mostly chaste one.

Needless to say, they lived apart, on opposite coasts. M.F. had great affection for Gingrich. But there was the fact that he was married, and that she had already loved (and lost, to an early death) the man who was the great romantic passion of her life, Dillwyn Parrish. He had suffered from a progressively debilitating and painful condition called Buerger's disease and committed suicide in 1941. After three husbands—M.F. later married Donald Friede, a well-known figure in the publishing world—and many lovers, she had raised her children and lived alone for some twenty years. She preferred it that way.

✦ ✦ ✦

M.F. and Norah arrived in Paris in mid-October, after landing at Le Havre and taking a train from there to the city. The weather was glum. You couldn't see anything in the fog—the Eiffel Tower was invisible from as close as the Place de la Concorde. It was beautiful anyway, they decided. They were staying at the Hôtel de France et de Choiseul on rue Saint-Honoré, a delightfully rundown place, with cracked tiles in the bathroom and dreadful café au lait, but a pleasant staff. It was just the sort of hotel they both loved. They'd been given a sprawling suite, with a salon, three bedrooms, and an enormous bath.

A day or two after arriving they had lunch with *New Yorker* writer Janet Flanner (who'd been writing the "Letter from Paris" under the pen name Genêt since the magazine launched in 1925) and then walked to the Musée de l'Orangerie to see the Goya show. The art was beautiful, M.F. thought, but there were too many *people* and there was not enough *air.* They planned to have dinner at Brasserie Lipp, a nostalgic favorite, but now it was late afternoon, and they "stopped in a small bar for a good drink," M.F. wrote in a letter to Arnold Gingrich.

"A small bar for a good drink": M.F. had a knack for finding just that sort of place. She was a connoisseur of tastes and small bites, of tidbits and flavors, an oyster here, a touch of pâté there, and a glass of wine. She knew, for example, that the first-class buffet at the Gare de Lyon—where several days later they found themselves while waiting to catch the "Mistral" to Dijon—was just the spot for a glass of champagne and some *jambon de Parme.* She'd been here many times over the years; stopping for champagne at the station was something of a tradition.

M.F. and Norah toasted their excellent adventure so far—their "watery spree," first on board the *France,* and soon to continue with a week-long voyage on the *Palinurus,* a small but luxurious canal boat that would take them from Corbigny to Auxerre. Travel had become more difficult, they both agreed: there was a general dearth of porters and taxis all around, compared with even just a few years earlier. But it didn't matter—they loved being on the road together, and in France in particular. M.F. declared herself a "relaxed philosopher" when it came to the stresses and inevitable long waits of contemporary travel. It was simply a matter of arriving early and ordering a glass of champagne to enjoy during the wait.

The Mistral left in the early afternoon; they had reserved seats. After arriving in Dijon a couple of hours later, they checked in at the Hôtel Terminus, where their room, like every room in the hotel, was outfitted with wine faucets, one for red and one for white, in the bathroom. It was a marketing gimmick, meant to promote the hotel and the local wine. Hanging beside the faucets was a pair of silver *tastevins*—wine tasting cups. The wine was on the house, according to the small sign, and it really wasn't bad. They could only laugh.

M.F. and Norah had a few days in Dijon, and these were spent retracing the steps of their long-ago 1931 sojourn. They walked to the edge of town, to the vineyards that were as blazing as they remembered. They saw the tiny owl carved in the foundation stone of the Notre-Dame, and the house that once made famous gingerbread. They stood before it and remembered the aroma. This was why they had come: to immerse themselves in the happy echoes and recollections of the past.

On the day of their departure, they took a hired car to Corbigny to meet the riverboat.

The sisters were on a Georges Simenon kick—those mysteries were the perfect light vacation reading, and a way of practicing their French to get back into the groove. So it was fitting somehow that when they boarded the *Palinurus* they discovered that the passengers and crew seemed to have stepped right out of the pages of an Inspector Maigret murder mystery. "One has to be a real nut to do a trip like this!" M.F. said, noting the close quarters and instant intimacy. There were eight other guests on board, including a charming Parisian career woman; an elderly, voluble upper-class

Englishwoman with her daughter and son-in-law; and a young and wealthy English couple. The crew included Captain Jim and his smashing blond wife, Dinah, both English; and various cooks and helmsmen, all French, all with fashionably long hair and flowing moustaches.

Fortunately, there was no murder. Instead, day after day there was mesmerizing beauty and excellent food. The October weather was clear, with temperatures in the fifties. All the food was fresh—fat ducks, fish, veal stews, and lots of vegetables. There were local cheeses and fruits and endless wines. At night, when they docked, the boat's batteries would stop and they'd go to bed in dimness—no reading, but who cared? There was not a sound anywhere, except when a frog fell off the bank. The trip was everything they had hoped it would be.

◆ ◆ ◆

M.F. and Norah traveled by train from Auxerre to Aix, which was the heart of Provence in M.F.'s opinion. The sisters wandered along the Cours Mirabeau, the grand avenue in the center of town, lined with a double row of towering plane trees and punctuated every block or so with another fountain. Some were ornate—grandiose, even—but the best were large, simple stones covered in moss: bastions of quiet solidity. Just off the Cours, on the rue du 4 Septembre, was the family favorite, the Quatre Dauphins. This was very different from the others—an exuberant and cheerful fountain with four dolphins, each spouting a stream of water from its mouth into the pool below. M.F.'s daughters and Norah's sons had loved this one when they lived outside Aix in 1959. The kids had been enrolled in the local French grammar school, where they spent months learning French, reading *Tintin* comics, and riding Solex-powered bicycles with small motors attached to their front wheels.

It was all more beautiful than ever, thought M.F., at least here in the *vieille ville*. There were interesting new shops selling housewares and clothes—things one could never find back in the States—lining the narrow streets. She bought a set of snail forks, which were the perfect size for California cracked crab. The Saturday open-air market was as sprawling as she remembered. They were staying at the Roi René, a gloriously old-fashioned hotel in the center of town. They ate vast quantities of clams, urchins, and oysters, all of which were in season. Another night, they ordered in: "Norah and I did our secret trick for strength-through-joy, and took long baths and ate in our room—a *pâté maison, haricots verts frais, sauce vinaigrette,* and a bottle of local rosé," M.F. wrote to Gingrich, describing house pâté and green bean salad. "Then we fell into bed with two Maigrets!"

There was an out-of-time quality to moments like that—and a distinctly French one, too. The dowdy yet proper hotel, the long baths. This was how they'd always traveled in France—they had stayed at this very hotel numerous times: back in the 1950s with their children, for example, watching the Tour de France zoom by from their balcony above the street.

But outside the Roi René, things were changing. Parts of town had been built up with high-rise apartments, and the traffic and noise and fumes were noticeably worse. And in addition to the construction and overdevelopment, there were hippies, another sign of the times, Aix being a university town. M.F. viewed the kids fondly. The girls wore midi or maxi skirts, and the boys had longish hair and Abe Lincoln chin whiskers. They were relatively clean-cut compared to the kids in California, she thought. Back home, the scruffy and stoned side of the counterculture had become apparent, and so had the dark and scary side—from Altamont to the Manson family. And then there was the dark and scary side of the police response to the counterculture: the Kent State shootings, to take just one example, had happened the previous May. Still, France was not unscathed; in Aix, the venerable Les Deux Garçons café had recently been shut down for six months for drug violations.

But if France was changing with the times, so was M.F. She was sympathetic toward the antiwar and student movements in Berkeley and San Francisco. She and Norah both reviled Nixon, and they had many friends who were active in politics, as were their own children. M.F. felt unsettled, ready for something new. Would she find it here, in France? Or was her attachment to this place a figment of her nostalgia?

✦ ✦ ✦

The sisters were headed east, to the hills above the Riviera, not far from Cannes. For the coming weeks, they'd be planted just across the way from Les Bastides, the estate in La Roquette-sur-Siagne where Lord and Bedford lived.

M.F. was eager to do some writing, and to see old friends and meet new ones. Just a few weeks earlier, Paul Child had written:

> You and Norah are officially forbidden to leave your cellar at
> Les Bastides until we have appeared at La Pitchoune! We hope
> to make it by the 1st week of December. It would be silly to miss
> each other by a few days. Don't you agree?

So—you are leaving St. Helena . . . We too are regretful we've never seen your house there, with you in it. A house without its occupant is a shell without its snail—nothing on which to dab one's personal garlic butter—and the new Sonoma palazzo will of course have your familiar delicious flavor.

I am slowly—and with delight—reading *With Bold Knife and Fork* aloud, to Julia, as she prepares dinner: a most fortuitous wedding of pleasures. Do try to stay at Les Bastides until we get to La Peetch. We must see you and touch you again. Letters are long-distance, once-removed, forms of companionship. Stay! Be seen, be touched . . .

～3～

EN ROUTE TO
PROVENCE

LA PITCHOUNE WAS AN ESCAPE FOR JULIA
and Paul Child, a place where they could really relax. In Cambridge, Paul wrote, they were "invaded by telephone, telegraph, and letter, by peeping people, news editors, food writers, television tipsters, photographers, High School Year Book interviewers, cooking utensil salesmen, almond growers, fish experts, oven salesmen, restaurateurs, orchardists." At La Pitchoune, on the other hand, they could forget their intense American life and be quiet and anonymous.

The Childs had built the house on the grounds of Beck and Fischbacher's estate in 1965, on a hillside in the South of France. They'd paid for it using the advance money Julia had received to write *Mastering the Art of French Cooking, Volume II*. In a handshake deal, they agreed that the property would belong to the Childs as long as they lived, and then revert back to the Beck family. It was a simple house surrounded by olive trees, with a large kitchen and three bedrooms. The closest town was a tiny village called Plascassier, and while the crowds and sometime glamour of Cannes and Antibes were only a half-hour drive away, life in the hills above the coast was pleasantly sedate.

Of course, the house and grounds required constant care and attention. In semirural Provence that meant maintaining contact with a long list of local purveyors and handymen. Things were always breaking and needing to be repaired. But then, that was all part of the pleasure of living like a local: making the everyday connections and setting down roots.

Julia and Paul would soon be headed to "La Peetch," as they affectionately referred to their place, but first came the launch of the new book, *Mastering II,* in New York. This was the long-awaited sequel to Child and Beck's definitive 1961 treatise, the book that had, along with Child's genre-defining television cooking show, introduced a generation of Americans to sophisticated home cooking—which, at that time, really meant French cooking. Of course, Child wasn't the only one responsible—no single person brings about such a large-scale cultural shift, and this was the 1960s; there was a lot of shifting going on in general. Still, she was the face of cooking in America, the one who'd appeared on the cover of *Time* magazine in 1966. *The French Chef* television program had been on hiatus while she worked on the book, but it was returning to the air that fall.

The book was a high-profile release, with a first printing of one hundred thousand copies, a second printing already in the works, and a number of glamorous parties to kick off the publication.

In late September there had been a Boston event at the Plaza Hotel, hosted by PBS, which broadcast Child's television show. And on October 22 was the official launch party in New York, at the Ford Foundation, on East Forty-Third Street. The twelve-story building had been completed two years earlier, designed by architect Kevin Roche, who had run Eero Saarinen's firm for years. It had a tree-filled interior atrium, the first in the city, and was the perfect place for a party.

Child made sure to tell Beck that only press and food people, and very few friends, were to be invited. This was just the sort of practical detail that her coauthor could sometimes fail to comprehend. Beck was a force of nature. She was a brilliant cook, but not always a master of social niceties and practicalities. She was tough and direct—imperious. French, in other words. Not only was she French, but in her partnership with Child, *being French* had become a key element of her persona. She saw herself as the guarantor of authenticity when it came to their cookbooks, the one who made sure that no stray, vulgar Americanisms snuck into their recipes. Child had dubbed her *la Super-Française*.

Beck, known to her friends and family by her nickname, Simca, charged through life like an overconfident whirlwind, bluffing and blustering her way into every situation. Paul Child, for one, had little patience with her, though he was the first to admit that she got things done. It was Beck and her husband, Jean Fischbacher, who had built La Pitchoune, finessing and cajoling the local contractors and craftsmen. And Paul appreciated that. But dealing with Beck in social situations was another story.

The Childs had driven down from Boston; Beck was flying in from Paris, where she was based. There were press interviews to be done, and a brief but intense book tour, with stops in Minneapolis, Cleveland, and Chicago, and then Philadelphia, Washington, and Boston. In each city, they performed a cooking demonstration (mayonnaise in a Cuisinart, every time) at a local department store and then attended to various local press opportunities. In New York, they were interviewed on the *Today* show, and Child went on the seminal David Frost interview show, newly imported from England.

Child was a reluctant talk show guest: "I am not an entertainer— I am a cook, that's it," she would say. "But cookbook über alles."

Volume II was an instant hit. In *Newsweek,* the critic Raymond Sokolov declared, "It is hard to conceive of a cookbook to follow this one. It is without rival, the finest gourmet cookbook for the non-chef in the history of American stomachs." Gael Greene lauded the book in *Life*. It was the talk of the town in New York, she said, at least among the gastronomic set. And of course there was the inevitable backlash, too. In the *New York Times,* Nika Hazelton complained that the book had been "heralded like the Second Coming" and said it reminded her of Versailles, "a noble structure, whose excellence is above suspicion." Though Hazelton was respectful, all her compliments were barbed: "The elegance and accuracy of the authors' recipes are not to be questioned, nor are the results if you have the kind of mind and temperament to follow their recipe writing—that of people who learn to drive a car by having the workings of the internal combustion engine explained to them in full detail." She thought the recipes were too complicated. "French bread alone takes 24 pages and 54 drawings," she noted.

This sort of sniping was par for the course in the food world, which was small enough that everything was always personal. Child would not forget Hazelton's swipe, and she couldn't help but notice that earlier in the same roundup of the season's new cookbooks, Hazelton had sung the praises of Richard Olney's debut, *The French Menu Cookbook*. It contained "menus and recipes that are the soul of French cooking, as practiced by the French and as evocative of French living as anything I've ever seen in print. This is the way La Douce France eats when still uncorrupted by expediency foods and methods—balanced, uncluttered meals that never pall."

Julia and Paul had met Olney the previous summer in France—he'd been introduced by Eda Lord and Sybille Bedford. Julia, always supportive of new culinary talent, was intrigued by his book. His recipes had a personal, passionate quality, in contrast to her and Beck's more formal *Mastering* style. She was sure she'd see him again upon her return to France. Meanwhile, she fumed at Hazelton's critique, and was happy to receive notes of admiration and applause from her friends. M.F. sent a postcard: "Wonderful job. Very proud of you." James Beard missed the launch party at the Ford Foundation; he had a cooking class to teach—"*Tant pis!*" she thought—but he adored the book and had told her so. Beard was also en route to Provence in the coming weeks. And Judith Jones, the editor at Knopf to whom Child and Beck owed so much, was coming to France with her husband, Evan, to celebrate the completion of *Mastering II*. They were staying at an auberge just down the road from La Pitchoune. Such was the nature of the food world. On the one hand, yes, it was small and could sometimes be catty and vindictive. On the other hand, these were Child's friends!

And the truth was none of the reviews really mattered. The book sold itself. Home cooking was bigger now than it had ever been—it was *happening*. "Gourmet" had entered the cultural mainstream in America. There were more cookbooks, cooking schools, chefs, and restaurants than ever, not to mention a growing national conversation about health food and organic products on the one hand, and fast food and the dangers of MSG, artificial sweeteners, and "coffee whiteners" on the other. There was new excitement about ethnic food. Most of all, there was the power of television to drive the national conversation about food. That was what Child had been doing with *The French Chef*, and what no one had done before.

Child was a new kind of celebrity: She was a woman in her fifties, and she played herself on television. She was *real*. She made mistakes. Of course she was a masterful cook, but when things went wrong, she embraced the opportunity to use her mistakes to teach—here's what *you* should do if this happens. Indeed, one of her key talents was the ability to roll with the punches and to improvise and explain. Her viewers loved these moments—the famous potato pancake scooped back onto the pan after accidentally landing on the counter ("Nobody's looking," she said) or the fallen soufflés ("Never apologize—nobody knows what you're aiming at, so just bring it to the table"). Her unflappability was her calling card. Her realness distinguished her. She embodied the infectious pleasure and sheer thrill of cooking. And most of all, she was fun to watch. It was almost bizarre, the swooping, careening voice and grand gestures, the plummy, patrician accent. It was riveting television, and by the late 1960s, Child was well on her way to becoming an American icon.

Now, after launching the new book and the new season of the *French Chef* television show, Child wanted nothing more than to stand on her Provençal terrace and admire her olive trees.

✦ ✦ ✦

Judith Jones had thrown herself into the production of *Mastering II*, making regular trips to Cambridge during the intense final months of work, sitting at the kitchen table with Child late into the night. She stayed in the guest bedroom, and then it was up early and back to the kitchen, testing, revising, and editing.

It was Jones who had encouraged Child and Beck to really delve into charcuterie. She and her husband, Evan, were enthusiastic amateur sausage makers. Evan was an accomplished writer, publishing books on history and magazine articles on food, and also a serious cook. They had met in Paris in the late 1940s.

Jones got her start at Knopf working on English translations of Sartre and Camus. When the enormous manuscript for the first *Mastering* book came across her desk in 1959, she had immediately taken it home and started cooking from the recipes, beginning with the *bœuf bourguignon*. She and Evan agreed: it was the best they'd had since leaving France.

For the new book, in addition to the sausages and pâtés, Jones had also proposed a recipe for bread ("such an integral part of a French meal") since good bread was still hard to find in America, even in New York. And thus began an epic series of bread experiments, mostly carried out by Paul, who baked more than sixty loaves, some of which he mailed to Jones in New York. The result was the astonishingly detailed bread recipe in the new book.

Like Child, Jones was ready for a break. She was looking forward to Christmas in Provence.

✦ ✦ ✦

This was Richard Olney's moment, too.

With his first book, *The French Menu Cookbook,* he was suddenly, at least briefly, in the limelight. He was getting good reviews—not only from Hazelton, but also from *House Beautiful* and *Gourmet*. In late October, his publisher, Simon and Schuster, wired from New York: Urgent. Craig Claiborne to be in Paris to interview Olney for the *New York Times*.

Momentarily irked by the fact that he was being *summoned* (Olney was an easy man to irk), he nevertheless made his way "obediently" to Paris and spent the day with the all-powerful food writer. They had never met, but they got along fine. They ate at Chez Garin. Olney had introduced the owner, Georges Garin, to the American woman who would become Garin's second wife. The Garins were Olney's close friends.

The resulting article was stiff, Olney thought, referring to him throughout as "the gentleman." "He is, by his own definition, a hermit," the article began.

> He is described by his French colleagues as 'pur, droit, épatant,' and is a man possessed of an uncommon palate for food and wine . . . Mr. Olney lives on a hillside near Solliès-Toucas in the southern part of France, about eight miles from Toulon, in a home without a telephone. The house, incidentally, has no heat except that which emanates from the fireplace and the kitchen range. It does have a sizable wine cellar, which the owner dug himself over a two-year period.

Claiborne explained that Olney had bought the house in 1961, and spent the next five years renovating the place. He was in his early forties. He'd used the money he'd been paid to write the cookbook to buy a new stove. It was a La Cornue, a fantastically solid, traditional French appliance, and fantastically expensive, too. He lived alone and cooked himself simple dishes—soups, grilled meats, and snails, which were abundant in his garden.

Claiborne was not the first of the American food establishment to recognize Olney's talent. Julia Child had written to Beard over the summer about how impressed she was by him: "It is high time we had some more French cooking types, and he is unusually well qualified, being American. I know he is very much respected among the French, which is rare indeed. We hope his book gets a good sendoff. Do you know him?"

Beard hadn't met him yet, but reviewed the book in his weekly syndicated newspaper column, which appeared in the *Los Angeles Times* and in sixty other papers across the country, in September. He loved it: "Offhand, I can think of only two Americans who have absorbed the essence of France and its cooking thoroughly," Beard wrote. "One is Julia Child. The other is Richard Olney, who has lived in France for 21 years." The book would surprise those who thought all French food was overelaborate, according to Beard, and had recipes ranging from "the simplest kind of Provençal luncheon of fresh sardines cooked in vine leaves, lamb tripe *à la marseillaise,* salad, cheese, and strawberries in orange juice to a fairly formal dinner of sole fillets with fine herbs and stewed cucumbers followed by a spit-roasted leg of lamb with buttered green beans, cheese, and peach melba."

Organized around seasonal menus in different styles—"Two Formal Spring Dinners," "Three Simple Winter Menus," "Four Simple Summer Luncheons à la Provençale," and so on—the book was one of the first of its kind. The emphasis on fresh, seasonal ingredients was groundbreaking, as was Olney's careful attention to

wine selection. The book offered recipes that were detailed, authoritative, and opinionated. "If rare or medium-rare meat is looked
upon with displeasure," he wrote, "roast venison may as well be
discarded from one's repertoire." The recipes were also superbly
well written: sensuous and evocative but always absolutely clear.

Olney's editor had word that the coming book review in the
Times would be "a rave," and his friend Eda Lord had intimated that
her old friend M. F. K. Fisher, who would be arriving in Provence
soon, might possibly write an article about him for *The New Yorker.*
(M.F. had no such intention, a fact that was bound to cause trouble
soon enough.) "Things seem to be stirring," Olney wrote of the
anticipated publicity in a letter to his brother. "I pray that a public
explosion occurs before the Christmas shopping period."

Olney returned from his meeting with Claiborne in Paris to his
house in Solliès-Toucas and planned his holiday calendar. He had
invited Eda, Sybille, and their friend M.F. to dinner at his house in
late November, and planned to visit them in turn in December. He
would also have the opportunity then to visit Julia and Paul Child
and James Beard, who were staying close by. He would pay his respects, somewhat grudgingly. Despite their warm embrace, he was
already wary of joining the American food clique.

He wasn't sure he really *liked* any of these people. Of course
he had yet to meet James Beard and M.F., but that didn't stop him
from being skeptical.

+ + +

James Beard was six foot three, three hundred pounds, and bald. He
occupied the kitchen in his downtown Manhattan brownstone like

a friendly bear, wearing an apron and cooking and teaching in an easygoing and precise way. In his plaid suits and brightly colored bow ties, he was a flamboyant figure. But these days he was not well. His legs were swollen, and his heart was weak. Doctors said his circulation was poor, and that it had all started with his weight.

He did need to lose weight, and slow down, take it easy for a while. He needed to get out of the city. He was teaching a full load of cooking classes to small groups in his brownstone, trying to finish his latest book, making appearances, giving demonstrations, and writing his column. It was too much.

And so he'd conscripted himself at the Clinique Médicale et Diététique in Grasse, with the renowned Dr. Georges Pathé. Pathé had a high-profile clientele (including Norodom Sihanouk, the king of Cambodia), and his methods were straightforward: you checked in and ate exactly what he told you to eat. Beard was expected to arrive in early December.

Needless to say, the irony of attempting a weight loss regimen in France was not lost on Beard. There was a certain contradiction in place and purpose.

Indeed, the clinic in Grasse was only a few minutes from the Childs' house in Plascassier, and Beard knew they'd be there for Christmas. They would be cooking. And he was happy to hear that M. F. K. Fisher would also be in the neighborhood. He had been introduced to M.F. by Child a few years ago and shared her expansive view of the significance of food. Beard had recently written a brief appreciation to introduce a new edition of M.F.'s *The Art of Eating*, the omnibus volume comprising her first five books, in which he described the "wicked thrill in following her uninhibited track through the glories of the good life," while also noting that she wrote about simple cooking and eating with a "pure, primitive enjoyment."

M.F. captured the drama of food, its emotional context. Beard, meanwhile, intuitively understood the theatrical nature not only of restaurants (with their romantic lighting and careful choreography) but of food itself, as it was presented on a plate. He had gotten his start in New York in the late 1930s, catering parties. He made cherry tomatoes (a novelty in those days) stuffed with jellied tomato aspic and deviled egg, and smoked salmon with horseradish cream. "Designing hors d'oeuvre is not different from designing sets and costumes," he said. "Food is very much theater. Especially cocktail parties per se."

Beard was the original modern American food icon. He'd been a public figure since the 1940s—a relentless popularizer, author, and columnist; a one-time actor and lifelong opera aficionado; a man about town and dinner party host extraordinaire. The beloved and lovable Jim was always at the center of things, bringing people together, well served by his essentially gregarious nature. He knew everyone in the business and used his connections (and his magazine stories and newspaper column) to bring attention to new restaurants, cookbooks, chefs, recipes, kitchen equipment—whatever he came across. Of course, Beard also unapologetically called himself the "biggest whore" in the food business (he was a consultant for major companies such as Pillsbury and Green Giant), but it didn't matter to his friends; his warm embrace and mentorship was what counted.

For the past few years, Beard had been working on what he hoped would be his magnum opus: *American Cookery*. It was to be *the* definitive compendium of the national cuisine—an American *Mastering the Art*. It was long overdue to his publisher, but he was now almost done, and hoping to use some of his quiet time at the clinic to do more work on it. And like the Childs, he was looking forward to his time in France not only to escape his hectic, over-scheduled life, but also as a chance to catch up with old friends. Perhaps he would make new ones, too: Although he liked her, he didn't know M.F. very well, and he hoped to spend some time with her. And there was Richard Olney, whom he'd never met, but who lived nearby and had sent him a letter in early October:

Dear James Beard,

I have just read your review of the *French Menu Cookbook*, which pleased me immensely. I felt, while reading it, that you were absolutely sincere. It is rather delicate to attempt to thank someone for having said what he feels—please accept the expression of my gratitude for feeling it.

The tight little world of American gastronomic journalism is, as I understand it, highly competitive and newcomers are not always welcomed with open arms. In view of that, I feel that I may, indeed, thank you whole-heartedly for your generosity in expressing publicly those thoughts that others might have jealously guarded for themselves. . . .

I hope that, the next time you are in France, we may meet.

Sincerely,

Richard Olney

And so, over the course of a few weeks in 1970, they all arrived in Provence.

As planned, M.F. and her sister set up house in early November in the tiny town of La Roquette-sur-Siagne. At the beginning of December, James Beard checked in at the diet clinic in Grasse. Simone Beck returned from the book tour in the United States to her family estate in Plascassier later that month, and Julia and Paul Child, also in Plascassier, prepared to open La Pitchoune to their many guests. Their new book was already a hit, but Child and Beck were tired, their friendship fraying. Over in Solliès-Toucas, meanwhile, the brilliant and reclusive Olney had come back from his brief trip to Paris. And finally, just before Christmas, cookbook editor Judith Jones and her husband, Evan, arrived.

During the late fall and winter of 1970, they all lived together as neighbors in the most beautiful place in the world. Provence was where it had all started. It was a place that epitomized the food-centered culture and philosophy the group stood for, a place where life and cooking and style all intertwined so easily. The farmers' markets, the heat and sun and abundance all around, the wild and slightly disheveled gardens and fantastic sproutings of rosemary, thyme, and lavender. The elegant but simple outdoor entertaining. The old tumbledown farmhouses.

Provence was also the place, not coincidentally, where American cooking would first break with France, where its modern character would begin to reveal itself.

4

AN EPIC DINNER
with RICHARD OLNEY

RICHARD OLNEY WAS PREPARING A FEAST.

He sat at the kitchen table with a small, pointy knife, painstakingly piercing each large piece of beef stew meat and inserting small strips of pork fat into the incisions. The strips of pork belly had been covered with a paste of chopped parsley and garlic, and would add flavor to the meat from the inside out. He put the larded meat in a bowl, poured a bit of olive oil and cognac and then a bottle of dry white wine over it, and left it all to marinate.

This was the beginning of his *daube à la provençale,* a slow-cooking and unimpeachably moist and tender stew, with a rich sauce to accompany the macaroni he planned to serve with it. Eda Lord and Sybille Bedford were coming to dinner the next day, and they were bringing their friend M. F. K. Fisher.

It was late November and raining outside. He was alone in the kitchen. He was happiest at moments like this.

Now he took on the terrine, a delicate operation. Laid out on the counter were two sole and a large bag of small sea urchins, all from the fishmonger in Toulon. The sea urchins were still alive, their black spines moving. He filleted the fish, and started a stock with the bones, pouring over water and wine. It would cook for hours, until it had thickened to a jelly-like substance he would use to coat the terrine the next day.

He used scissors to open up dozens of sea urchins, holding the sharp, spiny shells in a folded dish towel to avoid injury to himself, and spooning out the pungent and slightly spongy roe inside. They smelled of the ocean. He combined the vivid orange roe with a small amount of uncooked, chopped white fish, then pushed the mixture through a fine sieve, one tablespoon at a time. These were the first ingredients in what would become a mousseline, a very delicate foamlike mousse that would be surrounded by the sole fillets.

This was the sort of dish in which most of the ingredients were forced through a sieve—some more than once. It took time and patience.

After putting the roe and fish through the sieve, he chopped some pistachios, whisked together some cream and egg, combined everything in a bowl, then spooned the mixture into a heavy terrine dish, which he had lined with the fillets. He folded the sole over the mousse filling to create a loaf, and dabbed more of the mousse around the edges and the top. Now he lifted the dish and banged it on the counter to settle the contents, then put it in the oven, where it would cook gently in a bain-marie, half-submerged in water. When the sole was done, Olney would press the terrine under a one-pound weight as it cooled, then refrigerate it.

To accompany the sole and sea urchin dish, he had decided to make a second mousse, of sorrel. He sautéed the sorrel greens with jellied meat stock, forced the mixture through the sieve, added whipped cream, and spread it into a mold. This went into the refrigerator alongside the sole terrine, both of which he would unmold some hours before the dinner was to be served.

Olney was a classicist and perfectionist. He insisted on the freshest ingredients, many of which he grew in his garden. He had endless patience for the complicated, time-consuming processes of *la grande cuisine française*—witness the extreme refinement of the urchin roe mousseline he had just prepared, for example. Fewer and fewer cooks, even at the best restaurants, were doing these preparations anymore, at least not properly. And yet even as he remained committed to the canon of classical haute cuisine, he also embraced more rustic traditions. He grilled lamb on an open fire, and loved braises, boiled meats, and tripe—traditional provincial dishes. He had no patience for fussy presentations, food decorations, or the flavor-sapping trickery and shortcuts of many professional kitchens.

Take artichokes: he grew them in his garden—the small, purple Provençal variety called poivrade—and planned to serve them the next day as a first course, with a vinaigrette. The textbook preparation, aimed at producing perfectly white artichoke hearts, called for precooking them in acidulated water with a bit of flour and oil, producing a taste both banal and, to his palate, perverted—the actual flavor of the artichoke lost.

He would rub the easily discolored artichokes with lemon and cook them in saltwater with a branch of thyme. And yes, they would look a bit gray in the end, that's how it was. But they would taste like artichoke.

He poured himself a scotch and sat at the dining table smoking

Gauloises cigarettes, taking a few notes about the menu he'd serve the next day, including which wines would go with which courses. He planned to write about the meal for *Cuisine et Vins de France,* a small but influential culinary magazine to which he regularly contributed. He needed two whites and two reds, so he left the house and went to his wine cellar, hidden behind a door to what looked like a tiny garden shed, underneath a persimmon tree in his garden. He unlocked the metal door and walked down the narrow stairs into the dark. There was no light. He switched on a small flashlight to reveal the wines: row upon row of dusty bottles, set on the heavy wood-and-brick shelves he himself had built after he dug the cellar. It had taken him six years to complete the cellar.

It was his buried treasure, a growing collection of Yquems, Domain Tempiers, champagnes, and more—all wines he had written about and collected. He took his time choosing a white Burgundy from the Côtes de Nuits, a Sauternes, and two Bordeaux.

The next day, Olney layered the stew into an earthenware pot: bits of pork rind, the marinated beef, tomatoes, carrots, onions, mushrooms, olives, and herbs. After pouring the marinade and some beef stock over the stew, he carefully sealed the lid, using a long, thin strip of cloth soaked in water and flour, and put the pot in the oven, where it would cook at a low temperature for five hours.

As the daube cooked, Olney began the arduous process of covering the unmolded sole and sea urchin terrine with the fish jelly, which involved painting the terrine with layer after layer of the gelatinous fish stock, putting the terrine back in the refrigerator between each coating of the jelly, to let it set into an aspic, and then repeating. The key was for the jelly to achieve a trembling, just-solid consistency that would melt upon eating.

He picked the small purple artichokes and rocket greens from his garden, and waited for his guests.

✦ ✦ ✦

At around four o'clock that afternoon, M.F., Lord, and Bedford arrived for dinner in Solliès-Toucas. The afternoon drive had been beautiful, two hours along the new Nice autoroute, passing through little towns with narrow streets and shady squares and stone fountains. They parked in the town square and made their way slowly up to Olney's house, which was on a steep ravine overlooking the village. The climb, along a narrow, twisting path and up a series of ancient stairs, was difficult. This had all once been a limestone quarry and they passed sheer rock cliffs, caves, and an abandoned mill on the way. It was slow going, the footing dangerous.

The house was magnificent. It had been built in 1859 and bought by Olney as an abandoned wreck for about two thousand dollars. In the early 1960s, he had repaired the roof, put in plumbing, and built an enormous stone fireplace. He constructed the wine cellar. He'd done most of the work himself. There was a wide tiled terrace and an herb and vegetable garden in front, and behind the house, a series of ancient walled terraces planted with olive trees.

The three women admired the view and caught their breath, and Lord introduced her two old friends, Olney and M.F. Olney took them into the house and poured glasses of white wine. The front door opened directly into a tall kitchen, at the center of which was a large fireplace. Cast iron, copper, and earthenware pots and pans lined the mantel and hung from the wall above the fire.

There were books everywhere, and a number of Olney's oil portraits and still lifes were on the walls. He was dressed in a loose, open shirt with the sleeves rolled up and had dark, swept-back hair. Dinner was simmering in the oven.

Lord had met Olney years earlier, in the mid-1950s, in Paris. He had moved to France after a few years as a painter in Greenwich Village, and taught himself to cook. He and Lord had in common a sense of being outsiders: they were both gay, for one thing, and expats, for another. Lord adored Olney in a protective and understanding way. She was more than twenty years older than he was, but it didn't matter, they were close.

M.F. hadn't particularly wanted to come, but was glad she had—she liked Olney immediately. They sat at a table in the kitchen, in front of the fireplace. It was set casually, with dish towels used as napkins.

APÉRITIF: MOREY-SAINT-DENIS "MONTS LUISANTS" BLANC
1966

ARTICHOKES *POIVRADE*

ROULADE OF SOLE FILLETS
WITH A MOUSSELINE OF SEA URCHINS IN ASPIC
SORREL MOUSSE
CHÂTEAU FILHOT 1962

DAUBE À LA PROVENÇALE WITH A *MACARONADE*
CHÂTEAU CARBONNIEUX 1966

ROCKET SALAD

SELECTION OF CHEESES
VIEUX CHÂTEAU CERTAN 1964

RASPBERRY SORBET

All the dishes were impressive and beautiful. When Olney cut slices of the two terrines onto their plates, the food looked like abstract works of art.

They raised their glasses of sweet and delicate Sauternes. And now began a long discussion about food and wine, and about how and when and whether they went together, or didn't. Olney was deeply knowledgeable on the subject. His just-released cookbook placed great emphasis not only on seasonality but on the proper flow of a menu, from course to course. It presented wine recommendations for nearly every recipe.

They all knew that Sauternes was traditionally a dessert wine, and sweet. On the other hand, it had the quality and complexity to stand up to foie gras, another traditional pairing. Olney was intrigued by the notion of serving Sauternes with something as delicate as the sole roulade. It worked, they all agreed; the pairing was inspired.

But the sorrel mousse, which he had served with the sole, was a mistake, Olney declared. Its sharp, lemony flavor was too strong: "It killed both the Sauternes and the marvelous, delicate, sweet flavor of the urchin mousse."

They debated this point and ate more of the sole, the urchin mousse, the sorrel mousse, and drank more of the Château Filhot. It was an excellent '62. Olney and Bedford compared notes on the various vintages they knew, which varied depending on how well the "noble rot" had taken hold that year. ("Noble rot" referred to the fungus that grew on ripe grapes, crucial for making certain sweet wines.) The year 1966 had been a bad one for the rot. The '64s were splendid.

M.F. listened to this conversation smiling and nodding, enjoying the wine very much, and the food, too. But she noticed in herself a growing impatience for this sort of talk, for the rarified and studiously opinionated banter about wine pairings and menu design, which at some level, to her ear, always ended up sounding self-congratulatory.

It was odd: Olney seemed on the one hand so unorthodox and bohemian, and on the other so beholden to the grand culinary traditions, the old order.

He dressed and lived like an artist, he talked like a snob, and he cooked like a genius.

Nevertheless, M.F. could tell that he was onto the beginnings of something *new*. Yes, he was a classicist and traditionalist—full of extravagant reverence for the old ways. And it wasn't as if he were an inventor of novel flavors or new techniques. But he was imbuing his cooking with what seemed a wholly new style, M.F. thought. It was evident in his person, his kitchen, his house—the unbuttoned shirt, the hard-won renovation of the building, the oil paintings on the walls, and of course the food on the table. Though the dishes were all classics, some of them were exceedingly refined and elaborate (the various mousses in aspic), others far more rustic (the stew in the oven), and he was not at all afraid to serve them in the same meal, a kind of high-low montage that was his signature. Each dish, no matter how humble, was given its due and presented as a paragon of craftsmanship, an object of veneration. Rejecting white tablecloth formality, Olney seemed to embody a kind of rough-hewn philosophy of taste—informal in presentation, rigorously seasonal, devoted in an almost religious way to the essential flavors of the ingredients.

Was it possible that only an American could have distilled the

French experience, and French cooking, in this way? M.F. wondered. She, too, had embraced France with the fervor of a convert all those years ago, and she, too, had arrived at something that was uniquely her own. Different from Olney's, but just as idiosyncratic and personal.

For Olney, cooking and eating were part of an expat-bohemian way of life. Indeed, the romance of the life Olney led infused his writing and gave it an almost hyperbolic sense of authenticity and authority. For every recipe, Olney provided the definitive, uncompromising version—obsessively detailed, brilliantly described.

So here he was, an American in Provence, preparing to serve what might possibly be the best *daube à la provençale* ever made, in a house he had renovated more or less by hand. This was a place and a life he had *willed* into being. He was also on his way, it seemed, to inventing a new kind of snobbery, based not on the prestige of rare and expensive ingredients but on the nuances of flavor.

Were his guests ready for the next course?

Olney had taken the daube from the oven and, using a knife, broken the seal he'd made with the strip of cloth, then removed the lid.

This sort of seal, he explained, was an old French country cooking tradition dating back to the days when the dish would have been cooked overnight, buried in hot ashes in the fireplace.

A quick rush of fragrant steam escaped. There was something inexplicably satisfying about this seal-cracking operation—it was one of those fleeting, thrilling cooking moments, like pouring wine on a hot pan to deglaze it. The smell was magical. He skimmed off the fat that was floating on the surface and then spooned some of the liquid over the pasta and let it simmer for a few minutes on the stove. He then layered it into a casserole dish with grated parmesan and Gruyère, and set it on the table, next to the daube, still in its *daubière* cooking pot.

He opened a bottle of Bordeaux—the Château Carbonnieux. For a moment, they were all transfixed by the wine. M.F. thought it was stellar. But Olney wasn't sure and said it tasted a bit off. This was a subtle point, though, and they continued drinking the wine as they talked about it.

The large pieces of beef stew were fork-tender and melted in the mouth. Every so often someone encountered a tiny pocket of the chopped parsley and crushed garlic Olney had carefully inserted the previous day. The *macaronade* (pasta) carried the faintest hint of nutmeg. This was perfection.

✦ ✦ ✦

It was getting late. Olney's guests ate a salad of the peppery rocket and other lettuces he had harvested from his garden just a few hours before. For the vinaigrette, Olney had used olive oil from a local mill and an aromatic vinegar cooked down with garlic and herbs and preserved in a jug. He made his own vinegar every so often and compared the vintages as if they were wines.

They opened another Bordeaux, this one indisputably excellent, a Pomerol from Vieux Château Certan. Olney brought out a selection of cheeses—a fresh goat cheese, a creamy Reblochon, and some Gruyère.

The conversation wandered a bit, and M.F. was glad of the change. She and Olney talked about his paintings—she admired the portraits and still lifes, which had "real radiance," she said (though she did inwardly wince at some of their visual clichés: the checked tablecloth, the mortar and pestle, the bottle of wine). M.F. had strong feelings about art, and was knowledgeable about it. Dillwyn Parrish had been a painter, his work hanging on the walls of her house in St. Helena. Now it was boxed up and ready to be moved to the new house being built in Glen Ellen.

Paul Child was likewise an accomplished painter, and M.F. adored his work, she told Olney. Had he seen it?

Olney was cagey when it came to the Childs. When he first met them, along with Simone Beck, the previous summer, he'd taken an immediate dislike to the couple. It was M.F., indirectly, who introduced them, as she'd suggested to Lord and Bedford that when Olney came to Les Bastides for a visit, as he occasionally did, they should bring all these people together. Olney and his brother James went to dinner at Beck's, and to the Childs' at La Pitchoune for a drink beforehand. Julia gave him a tour of the house that day: the kitchen with its Peg-Board and inked outlines of utensils; the bedroom with its pair of framed *Time* magazine covers, one of Julia (real), the other of Paul (a joking mock-up). They had drinks. "We enjoyed a few minutes of desultory conversation," Olney would later write; "she asked if she and Paul could come to Solliès for lunch, I said we'd be in touch, and we escaped to dinner . . ."

His feelings toward Beck were much warmer. Beck was French, and proud of it, and Olney admired her for that.

It happened that Olney had come to Plascassier on the same weekend that Child and Beck were being profiled for an article in *McCall's,* and the women seemed to have been fighting. He could sense the tension between the two coauthors, though he did not know the source. But it was clear to Olney that Child was the preeminent one in the partnership, and since he felt that Child was simply coasting on Beck's talent, Olney's sense of pride kicked in vicariously. This is how it was sometimes with Olney: his default mode was passive aggressive. A few months later, he took note of the way Beck disappeared from the many news stories about the newly released *Mastering II:* "All the articles I have seen are quite funny as they begin with a grudging mention of the co-authors," he wrote to his brother, "and from then on, only Julia is mentioned—Simca, who, as we know, owns Julia, must be furious." Olney possessed a refined sense of resentment; he was a man who cultivated grudges, particularly when it came to the rest of the food establishment, even when the grudges weren't his own.

But, for the moment, M.F. and Olney were getting along famously. She was wry and amusing, he was happy to be cooking for friends, and there was the possibility (unmentioned, of course) that she'd be writing about him and his cookbook for *The New Yorker.* Bedford was in an effusive mood. They finished the wine, and Olney served raspberry sorbet.

+ + +

It was well past midnight when M.F., Bedford, and Lord walked down the hill with a flashlight. The steep path was more intimidating now in the dark, particularly for the less-than-sure-footed M.F. She did not like heights. The many, many glasses of excellent wine didn't help, either.

Olney had found an old villa nearby for them to stay in, a dark and rather dirty place, but one that would do for the night. As they wandered the streets of Solliès-Toucas toward their waiting beds, Bedford insisted on stopping at each fountain in the village to taste and compare the waters. Each fountain had a unique taste, she claimed. M.F. and Lord took turns at the various spouts and had to agree—Bedford was right!

There was of course something more than a little ridiculous about this scene: three ladies, in the dead of night, discussing the flavor of water. And yet it was for M.F. emblematic of the evening, which had been filled from beginning to end with talk about food and wine, with judgments and discernments and pronouncements. They had talked as well as eaten with great seriousness—too much, perhaps, she thought. It was all too precious for her taste. There was a time when she might have reveled in such conversation. But no longer. Something was shifting.

The next day, with Bedford again at the wheel, they drove back to La Roquette. They had skipped breakfast; Bedford was testy and on edge, and drove with less than her usual finesse. But they all agreed it had been a tremendous dinner, and they looked forward to Olney's upcoming visit to Les Bastides a few weeks later, just before Christmas.

During the drive, they decided to do a potluck—what they were calling, a bit more grandly, a collaboration dinner—for him. Each of them would prepare and bring a dish. They would be hospitable in their own communal, casual way—creating a meal far less elaborate than the one Olney had prepared for them, but in the same gourmet and bohemian spirit.

When she returned to her rented apartment that afternoon, M.F. sat in pleasant solitude, drinking a vermouth rouge-et-blanc, writing a letter to Gingrich, and contemplating a simple dinner: a lamb's lettuce salad, bread, and cheese.

"Richard's house is fantastic. So is he, of course," M.F. wrote. "We ate the most amazing meal, with four wines."

"The M. F. K Fisher visit was fine—she is very nice." Olney wrote in a letter to his brother.

But M.F. and Olney's happy feelings for each other would not last.

FIRST MEALS IN FRANCE

THE VIEW FROM THE AIRPLANE WINDOW WAS thrilling, the horizon tilting this way and that as the pilot aimed for a runway somewhere below, in Nice. The glinting Mediterranean stretched off in the blue distance, and now the palm trees, beaches, and overbuilt coastline of the Côte d'Azur loomed suddenly into view: Cannes . . . Juan-les-Pins . . . Antibes . . . and then Nice. The airport was right on the water, at the western end of the Promenade des Anglais, the two-mile-long boardwalk fronting the sea. The plane sank ever lower, picking up speed along the way—at least that's how it felt. There was always something a little disconcerting about these last few minutes in the air, the changes in speed and air pressure. The Childs did not much like flying, but the landscape outside the plane windows was undeniably glamorous. Here was the Riviera, in all its seductive glory, spread out before them on a clear December day.

They were nearly there.

Once the small plane had landed and Julia had extracted her

six-foot-two-inch frame from the too-small seat and Paul had exhaled a sigh of relief at the safe landing (he suffered from vertigo), the couple made their way through the terminal to the airport restaurant. This was where they always went when they arrived in Nice. "This has become our ritual gear-shift from the USA," Paul wrote of the Childs' airport lunch in a letter to M.F., "because the difference between that kind of meal and anything even remotely like it in the USA is immense, and we only then realize we are in our second culture."

The restaurant was on the second floor of the passenger terminal, and had large windows overlooking the runways and sea, and in the other direction, views of the Alpes-Maritimes rising up in the distance. Some of the waiters recognized the Childs from their frequent previous visits, and greeted them like old friends. It wasn't a fancy place, but it was decent, upstanding in every way. The seafood was fresh, the bread was crusty, and the wine was a far cry from what they'd have been served at the bar at Logan, where their trip had begun.

There was no better cure for incipient jet lag than a glass of Riesling. They were finally free of the never-ending stress of travel: "While we are in the grip of airplanes, information booths, ticket counters, moving stairways, public address systems, money changing booths, surging, harried people pushing luggage strollers, and nine different languages bouncing off our eardrums, we could be *anywhere*, from Hamburg to Heathrow," Paul noted. But no longer.

"France—we are here!" he exclaimed.

They always ordered the same thing—this was part of the ritual. It was a meal that symbolized not only their arrival in France but *every* arrival, and all the memories of arrivals past.

PROVENCE, 1970

OYSTERS

FILET DE SOLE

GREEN SALAD

FROMAGE BLANC

It was more or less exactly what the two of them had ordered the first time they arrived in France together more than twenty years earlier, in 1948. They'd come over on the SS *America,* waited for their sky-blue Buick station wagon to be lifted off the ship by crane, and then driven from Le Havre toward Paris through the Norman countryside. They'd stopped for lunch at La Couronne, in Rouen. They'd eaten oysters, and *sole meunière.* They'd ordered wine—a Pouilly-Fumé, from the Loire Valley.

That first meal would eventually take on near-mystical qualities— a key entry in the Julia Child canon, which she described many times over the years, though not always consistently; sometimes the sole was a duck in the telling. But it didn't matter: it wasn't the fish or the duck; it was their experience, the fragrance in their memories, fleeting and indelible. Sitting in the dining room at La Couronne, Paul explained how butters from various regions in France had different flavors—the full-bodied Beurre de Charentes, or the fine, light Beurre d'Isigny. The sole was otherworldly, the salad vinegary, the coffee very dark. It had been the most exciting meal of Julia's life.

◆ ◆ ◆

It was food that signaled one's arrival in France, not only for the Childs, but for M.F. and her sister, for James Beard, for Judith

Jones, and for Richard Olney. They had all experienced that seminal mid-century American-in-France moment at some point during the preceding decades, the first epiphany of taste and promise of European pleasure. Something new, and better . . . and with lots of butter (or butters).

◆ ◆ ◆

M.F. had eaten her first meal in France on the five-hour "boat train" from Cherbourg to Paris with her first husband, Al Fisher. The transatlantic crossing had taken them to the port town some two hundred miles west of the capital, and the train took them the rest of the way. On the train, they had eaten the best bread she'd ever tasted, green salad, Petit Suisse cheese, gnarled apples, crude wine, and bitter coffee. "It sounds almost disrespectful to say it," she wrote years later, "but even the astonishing events of the past several weeks or so seemed but a logical preparation for this moment!" Falling in love for the first time, then getting married, crossing the Atlantic for the first time—"they all led irrevocably to 1:43 P.M., September 25, 1929, when I picked up a last delicious crust-crumb from the table, smiled dazedly at my love, peered incredulously at a great cathedral on the horizon, and recognized myself as a new-born sentient human being, ready at last to live."

Norah rode the same train a couple of years later, in 1931, when she was a teenager and had come to France to stay with M.F. and Al. She had eaten an unforgettable meal of roast chicken. Forty years later, in November 1970, when she and M.F. took the train again, they ordered the familiar *poulet rôti* and Petits Suisses with fresh fruit. Nothing, though, could equal that very first meal in

France, they agreed. The first taste of French butter, the demi-liters of white wine.

✦ ✦ ✦

As an aspiring opera singer in the 1920s, James Beard had moved to London for a year, and from there made his first trip to France in 1923. He stayed at a pension on the rue Jacob in Paris, not far from the Hôtel d'Angleterre, where Ernest and Hadley Hemingway were living at the time. The food at the pension was simple and good: pot-au-feu, *blanquette de veau*—boiled beef, veal stews, and so on. He soon discovered excellent hors d'oeuvres at a nearby boarding-house, and a few months later, he took an elegant acquaintance visiting from his hometown of Portland, Oregon, to the exceedingly chic Au Caneton restaurant. They drank champagne and ate caviar and blinis, among many other things. (Caneton was run by Russian émigrés.) "It was a dinner I have never forgotten," he later wrote. "Nor have I forgotten the bill. It was a hundred francs—the largest restaurant bill that ever was, I thought at that time."

It wasn't until much later, during World War II, that Beard became familiar with the food of Provence: In 1945 he was stationed in Marseille for the United Seamen's Service. The USS was a non-profit organization providing recreation, food, communications facilities, and other services to sailors, and the then-forty-year-old Beard volunteered to do his part for the war effort. Marseille was in bad shape at the time, having been bombed by the Germans, and provisions were in relatively short supply. But the city's food markets and vendors were still worth exploring, as was the food at Beard's hotel. He was staying at the Hôtel Continental, by the port, where the chef made stuffed eggplant with garlic and fresh rosemary and whatever small amount of meat he could find. Beard also ate bouillabaisse and *brandade,* garlicky *poulet aux senteurs de Provence.* These were the flavors that had stayed with him ever since.

+ + +

Like Beard, Richard Olney's first meal in France was in Paris. He'd been twenty-four years old. It was the summer of 1951, he had recently arrived from Iowa via New York, and he was eating in "a glum little dining room for boarders, in the Hôtel de l'Académie." He ordered the plat du jour: *gibelotte, pommes mousseline*—rabbit and white wine fricassee with mashed potatoes.

> The gibelotte was all right, the mashed potatoes the best I had ever eaten, pushed through a sieve, buttered and moistened with enough of their hot cooking water to bring them to a supple, not quite pourable consistency—no milk, no cream, no beating. I had never dreamt of mashing potatoes without milk, and in Iowa, everyone believed that the more you beat them, the better they were.
>
> The first few weeks, my days were spent mostly in museums and, for lunch, I ate as cheaply as possible. Good food was everywhere.

+ + +

A few years earlier, during the summer of 1948, Judith Jones had embarked on her own life-changing Parisian adventure—finding a job, renting an apartment, eating at inexpensive places. She'd grown up in New York City and had recently graduated from Bennington

College, in Vermont. In Paris, no one drank much, except red wine, she recalled, and her appetite was fantastic: "I am no longer content with a fish or meat course; it has to be both." She soon met a Frenchman named Pierre Ceria, a journalist and former member of the Resistance who taught her to make pan-fried *sole meunière,* and with whom she opened a *salle à manger* in the living room of her apartment. This impromptu restaurant was an immediate hit, but wouldn't last: the large apartment belonged to Princess Marguerite Caetani, an American married to an Italian aristocrat and living in Rome, where she published *Botteghe Oscure,* a literary journal. When she found out about the "restaurant" on the second floor, she very politely asked Jones and Ceria to leave. (The other tenant at the time was the painter Balthus, who didn't seem to mind all the cooking and entertaining.)

✦ ✦ ✦

Simone Beck was from Normandy, so the food of France was no source of astonishment to her. But she had always taken a more than casual interest in it. As a teenager in the late 1910s, she began to experiment in the kitchen, "mostly with cakes," she recalled, "for as a girl I had a very special fondness for sweets." She kept track of these experiments in a series of notebooks, the first of many over the years.

✦ ✦ ✦

These first meals and flavors were never forgotten—they became figments of Proustian memory that drew each of the Americans back to France again and again. They were idealized memories, certainly, but also a true record of a time when most great cooking *was* French cooking, simple as that, and when you could not easily find decent bread, fresh butter, let alone a transcendent *sole meunière* in the States. French food was a revelation, and they were going to bring it home. Which is exactly what they did, each in his or her own way.

~6~

LA PITCHOUNE,
COUNTRY RETREAT

AFTER THEIR LUNCH AT THE NICE AIRPORT, Paul Child lit up a Havana cigar. The lunch had been "perfect," he and Julia agreed, and so had the wine. They were in a celebratory mood—on vacation at last.

But if that first meal heralded the Childs' arrival in France, the drive from the coast up to the foothills of Plascassier revealed the less idyllic side of the country—being back in France meant driving on French roads, navigating French traffic.

It was murder.

The first problem was that the car was startlingly underpowered, in the way of all French cars of the era. It was a rented Renault, and required continuous and rapid gear-shifting just to keep it at speed. Even in Paul's state of tense vigilance, he found himself smiling at the competitive and really quite skillful style of the local drivers.

Paul relaxed as the roads became quieter, after they made their way past Antibes and Mougin, along the narrow streets of Mouans-

Sartoux, and then began climbing the hill up to Plascassier. The two-lane road passed through a lush and rather wild landscape of overgrown fields and clumps of forest, olive trees, hedges, and old stone walls. There were new villas going up here and there—most of them ugly, the Childs agreed—but it was beautiful neverthe-less, and now Plascassier appeared, on a hill overlooking the valley. They were close. They decided to stop at the local Casino super-market for some basic supplies—eggs and milk, that sort of thing.

La Pitchoune was on the slope of a small hill, a few miles from the center of Plascassier. The long driveway from the road was rocky and unpaved.

It was midafternoon when Julia and Paul arrived, and the house was cold; it felt like a dungeon. They turned on the furnace, and padded around the house in their sweaters, putting groceries into the refrigerator and unpacking their bags. They felt at home—and free. Back in Cambridge, they were "as tied down by television as though swarms of Lilliputians had cobwebbed us in our sleep," in Paul's words. Now, in France, whatever the shortcomings of their beloved La Pitchoune—the slow heat, the muddy driveway—none of that mattered. Indeed, it was all part of the charm of the place.

The floors were terra-cotta tile, the ceilings tall, with elegant plasterwork in the corners. There were multiple fireplaces, and most of all there was the large and excellent kitchen. It was a square room with light-blue Peg-Board walls and dark green trim, covered with a huge collection of pans, knives, sieves, and every utensil and kitchen device imaginable, each outlined in black ink, marking its particular spot. Paul and his twin brother, Charlie, had made the drawings in 1965. As in the Childs' Cambridge kitchen, the counters were higher than the norm, designed by Paul to suit Julia's height.

Julia had the same thought she always did when she came here: Why ever leave? It was so beautiful, the air so fresh. Paul checked on the olive tree on the front terrace, which he'd planted a few years before. Its roots weren't as deep as the big old trees on the hill and ran the risk of freezing in the winter or drying out in the summer. The tree was one of his many projects.

✦ ✦ ✦

The Childs had spent the year at a full gallop—finishing *Mastering II,* first of all. "I keep thinking THANK GAWD that dreadful book is done," Julia wrote in a letter to Beard, "and I don't have that driven feeling, that guilt of non-accomplishment always gnawing me." And then there'd been the new season of *The French Chef* to contend with—thirty-nine episodes to be planned, written, and shot. It had debuted in the fall, just as the book was coming out.

The show was now being broadcast in color, nationwide, Wednesday nights at eight o'clock—"primetime," Paul noted in letters to friends, using quotation marks to signal a bit of amusement at the breathless TV jargon he'd taken to using. The truth is, he loved it—not the jargon but the thrill and speed of the medium, the technical details. Going from black and white to color, he would explain, required the use of much stronger lights, which in turn required Julia to wear special makeup; the editing, incorporating scenes of Julia filmed outside the kitchen, required split-second precision. They had filmed many of these scenes the previous summer in France, at open-air markets, or visiting with butchers, bakers, and restaurateurs. Paul handled the logistics, as he always did.

Paul and Julia were a team. She was the unforgettable performer, larger than life, no-nonsense, and he was the elegant and articulate partner, an artist and photographer. They shared life in ways few couples do, from the planning of the shows and the cookbooks to the social swirl of Julia's celebrity. They had never had children, much to her regret, and so their emotional life together played itself out largely through her career.

France was at the heart of it all. The food they had discovered all those years ago—the sheer, stunning quality of it, the pleasure it represented—was what inspired Child to this day. She had taught Americans to cook, to appreciate the slow and careful simmering of a *bœuf bourguignon* or the proper composition of a vinaigrette. But the classic style of cooking that *Mastering I* and *II* represented had begun to hold less interest for her, and even feel a little constricting. In part, the sentiment was just a reflection of her impatience with Beck. It had been a long and contentious year for the two of them.

The final deadline for *Mastering II* had been in March, and for weeks leading up to that date, Child had shut herself in her office in her Cambridge house, writing furiously seven days a week.

She did all the writing, which meant that she did most of the work—understandably, since the book was in English, its audience American. Together, she and Beck worked out what recipes to include and tested them repeatedly, sending drafts and cooking notes back and forth across the Atlantic for the multiple revisions; but it was Child who made sure that, in the end, the recipes were replicable in America, that they made sense, and that they *worked*. Beck, on the other hand, felt it was her responsibility to ensure that the recipes were suitably French, and therefore authentic. She was a marvelous and intuitive cook. Indeed, many of the recipes originated with her. But Child knew that measurements, precise lists of ingredients, and clear explanations of timing were not Beck's forte. She didn't seem to understand just how time-consuming every revision turned out to be.

So there were inevitable conflicts.

There was, for example, the question of the Porc Braisé au Whiskey. Beck had sent Child the recipe and proposed adding it to the meat chapter, which contained only one pork recipe, for a roasted suckling pig. Beck had taught the *braisé* preparation at her various cooking classes and knew the recipe was a good one.

The problem was that they were out of time. This was another one of those things that Beck just couldn't quite understand, perhaps because she was an ocean away, in France: they were at this point already deep into the copyediting stage, with the schedule so tight that the text was being sent off to the printer for typesetting chapter by chapter, as soon as the copy editor finished each one and Child reviewed the copy editor's work. Adding a new recipe now would be insanity. And it wasn't just the pork recipe, Child knew: Given the chance, Beck would be adding and refining and arguing about recipes forever. She was the keeper and protector of French food. She would never be satisfied.

Child responded diplomatically, but firmly: "I have only 5 weeks before the final final deadline, and so much to do I am stopping bookwork (recipe writing) on March 15th, no matter what is lacking. I have just had enough of this seven day work week and no respite. No more books of this type, and that's final. Life is too short and we are getting too old!"

Beck then wrote a long letter in French to Judith Jones at Knopf, explaining her disagreement with the "adorable" Child. Beck asked Jones to please keep the letter a secret, and then described in great detail the precise merits of the pork recipe, the various people she had served it to over the years, how it was equally good hot or cold, and so on. The pork recipe currently in the book, she continued, was really "very poor." She proposed that Jones, if she agreed that the braise was worthwhile, should "say to Julia that you think the chapter with the tripe is a little bit short, and ask her if by any chance she has another recipe to complete it? See what she says."

Jones was the intermediary, soothing Beck and encouraging Child, and generally acting as psychologist, coach, sounding board, mediator, ego manager, and cheerleader. She understood the pressure Child felt as well as the frustrations Beck expressed. Beck had been sidelined a bit by Child's success as a TV star; she was the co-author of a book everyone thought of as Child's, and that had to be hard to take. So it was no wonder she kept poking at and perfecting the recipes—she was holding on to what remained of her authority.

Jones responded to Beck's charming and relentless scheming about the Porc Braisé au Whiskey with a charming and diplomatic letter of her own. "The recipe I must say looks tempting and I am dying to try it," she wrote. "But even if it were the most delectable thing in the world, it is too late at this point to hold up the chapter which is already in copy editing and due at the printers next week." She went on to ask a series of probing questions about the recipe, questions they did not have the time now to resolve—"How does ½ cup of bourbon and ½ cup of brown sugar make sufficient juice? You do say add bouillon, but how much?"—before concluding, "We could go on another year, but I think we all feel that would be foolish because there is plenty here for a fascinating book and you both want to get it out of your hair. It is hard to know how to help Julia because so much of the final burden does fall on her. But I am convinced one way we can both be helpful is not to argue about the details and specific recipes because it only uses up time and energy which she can't afford at this point. I hope you understand."

Of course she understood, Beck replied, she understood "parfaitement," and she thanked Jones for explaining Child's point of view.

Child, meanwhile, continued to receive recipe notes and revisions from the prolific Beck, but she had had enough. Never again, she swore, would she write a cookbook of this all-encompassing sort, and certainly not with Beck. Their friendship was forever, but the partnership was at an end. The rigidity with which Beck insisted on the most orthodox and tradition-bound aspects of French cooking had worn Child out. They had known each other since 1951, when they met in Paris and took cooking classes together, and almost immediately began working on a cookbook—the first *Mastering*. They had spent uncountable hours in the kitchen together over the years, but as a coauthor, Beck was simply impossible.

"Ma chérie," Child wrote,

> you have done *ta mauvaise habitude* of wanting to change
> everything in the recipe as soon as you have seen it again . . .
> you had this same recipe for *le success*, February '69, and you
> reported that everything was just fine . . . I am therefore not
> going to pay too much attention to this letter, because I am sure
> when you see the recipe again (were it changed as you have
> directed) you would say *NON NON NON—ce n'est pas correct,*

ce n'est pas français!—and as often happens . . . it is your very own recipe (that you have forgotten about) that you are now attacking.

No, there would be no further collaborations with Beck. Child would strike out on her own. What she would do, she was not yet sure, though she did have some ideas. . . .

◆ ◆ ◆

Child could feel a shift in the balance of the food world. Top American restaurants, French and otherwise, were getting better, while in France, the grand three-star icons—Véfour, Bocuse, Troisgros, Oasis—were now big businesses, but "not really temples of gastronomy in the old sense" anymore, as she had written to M.F. the previous summer. They had lost a bit of their magic.

Shopping for groceries in France, on the other hand, remained an unmatched delight. The open-air fruit and vegetable markets (even in winter) with their farm stands; the charcuteries, butchers, fishmongers, bakeries, and cheese shops—these were the places that inspired Child. She had made sure to include her favorites in the filming for the show, presenting tantalizing views of Old World food craftsmanship in full color. An olive oil press in Opio, just down the road from La Pitchoune; the fish market in Marseille; cheeses at Chez Androuet in Paris. She wanted to show her audience the authentic methods, products, and ingredients of good cooking. She knew this was no exercise in futility, for there were growing numbers of good markets, cheese shops, and specialty food purveyors back home in the States. There was even decent bread to be found, however rarely. M.F. had just sent the Childs a letter saying she had discovered the "best bread" in America, at a bakery in Sonoma, not far from where she was building her new house.

Now, in France, Julia could sense that some of the artisanal skills she and Paul had documented were slowly disappearing. There seemed to be ever more American-style supermarkets, for example. But she didn't want to worry about that now: they were here, where it had all begun, *la belle France*. In a letter to M.F., Julia described the feeling she always had, upon arrival, of being "re-imprisoned by nostalgia and present pleasure."

That line captured the mood, and not only of the Childs. M.F., Beard, Judith Jones, and Richard Olney had all been originally inspired by France, one way or another, and had changed American tastes with their passion. But this was a moment of looking forward as much as looking back. Change was in the air.

✦ ✦ ✦

The next day, Beard and M.F. stopped by to say hello. The Childs loved seeing their two friends together: it was the Childs, after all, who had brought them together a few years earlier. "And that dear Mary Frances, whom we have not seen for too long a time—she likes you very much indeed, we know, from her letters," Julia wrote to Beard earlier that year. "And wonderful you have met at last, the way you should have long ago. She is rather shy, however." To M.F., Julia wrote, "Indeed, Jim Beard adored you, said he knew he would, and felt that it was only fate that had kept you apart."

They were an odd couple: the effusive, gregarious Beard and the sly, acerbic M.F. They got along brilliantly.

It had taken Child herself a while to warm to M.F. During their collaboration on the Time-Life cookbook in 1966, Child thought M.F. indulged in a sometimes overly poetic, precious take on France and French food. "We who do not live in France might try adapting the good things in French provincial eating to our own potentialities, and our own conditioned hungers," M.F. had written. "We can find good salad greens and good bread, and good cheeses and meats and vegetables if we want to. We can try to reach the slower pace of older habits than our own new nervous ones, by serving a small, tasty course at the beginning of a meal, before the main dish, and then skipping the gelatin pudding or ice cream."

Child read the manuscript before publication and sent a letter to M.F. with her notes, expressing "an overall feeling that the French are over-romanticized and the Americans underestimated, as though France was seen with loving pre-war eyes, and America viewed from the super-highways, with every once in a while a meal with the TV-dinner set."

But M.F. was in fact far from saccharine, or fuzzy-minded, as Child soon realized. The two women struck up an affectionate, witty correspondence, and so did M.F. and Paul Child. M.F. immediately understood his importance to the entire Child enterprise, including the books and the show. Not everyone realized or saw that.

"One reason we are friends," M.F. wrote to Julia in late August 1970, "is that we both understand the acceptance of NOW. There is all the imprisonment of nostalgia, but with so many wide windows." The topic was France: its inevitable centrality in their lives, the site of their common awakening to taste and sensation. But they must not let the past overshadow the present, they agreed, for France was changing, and they both understood that they must, too.

M.F., a modern master of memoir, of the revelatory personal essay, was paradoxically but assertively anti-nostalgic, always looking for those "wide windows." This unsentimental toughness was in many ways at the core of her genius as a writer. It also bound her to Child, whose insistence on practicality and modern methods had led her into conflict with Beck's old-fashioned, this-is-how-it's-done-in-France (and how-it's-always-been-done) certitude.

The previous year, as she was working on the *Mastering II* manuscript, Child had read an article in a French magazine that included the line "Every Frenchman is convinced he is a connoisseur who has nothing to learn from the experts." She pointedly sent a photocopy of the article to Beck, and also to M.F., whom she addressed in a note in the margin, saying that this French trait was "exactly what has been bugging me in my collaboration, and why I can't take any more of it. I don't know why I have been so dumb, but it is something one can hear, but not feel viscerally because how can anyone (but the French) have such arrogant nonsense as to live by that conception."

❖ ❖ ❖

The Childs, M.F., and Beard stood on the terrace at La Pitchoune in the cool December air. There was a faint scent of smoke—leaves burning somewhere in the distance, the smell of late fall turning into winter. Beard was genial, as always, but he looked weak and unsteady. His stay at the Grasse diet clinic had yet to produce the desired results in his health—or his weight.

The four friends went inside, entering through French doors into the living and dining room. The high-ceilinged space was simply furnished—there was a large, round dining table by the window in the back, and a massive fireplace.

Paul poured glasses of wine, and they discussed plans for the coming week.

When were Judith and Evan Jones arriving, and wasn't Richard Olney coming to visit soon, too? M.F. described the elaborate dinner Olney had made for her, Bedford, and Lord a few weeks earlier, in his beautiful house on a very steep hill. There were more dinners to plan and excursions to look forward to. Simone Beck and her husband, Jean Fischbacher, had arrived the previous week, the Childs said—they were arranging an elaborate New Year's party at Le Vieux Mas, just across the way from La Pitchoune. M.F. and Beard had been tooling around the countryside together in recent days and had made a plan to visit Vence and Saint-Paul-de-Vence soon, to see the Matisse chapel and the Maeght collection.

Perhaps the four of them could drive over to Biot one day next week, Julia proposed. There was a nice little restaurant they could stop at for lunch on the way back. And M.F. and Beard must both come to dinner on Sunday, the Childs said, and bring Lord and Bedford.

There was a special pleasure in seeing friends in foreign places, out of context, away from America. M.F. sent the Childs a note the next day. She could have telephoned, but preferred the less intrusive intimacy of writing. It was in pencil, and scrawled across the top was an apology: "Sorry about the pencil—all 6 Bics have frozen at the same time!" The winter was turning cold.

Dec 11, 70

Chers amis—I am very happy and serene about having seen you yesterday, and *there*, and with that dear man. And it will be nice to come on Sunday with Eda and Sybille. I've never gone with them to another house! (And only once to a restaurant.) . . .

I'd like very much to have lunch with you and Jim Beard on Wednesday. Carpe diem. Would you like to come in for a vermouth or something? This is a pleasant little pad.

Love, MF

7

JAMES BEARD'S DOOMED DIET

CELEBRITY DIET DOCTOR GEORGES PATHÉ'S offices were in the discreet Villa Fressinet, on the outskirts of Grasse. From the windows, there were views of the valley below stretching into the distance—Grasse was set on a mountainside overlooking the rolling Provençal landscape. The medieval town was pretty, and had long been the center of the French perfume industry, with greenhouses and flower fields and numerous perfumeries.

In an examining room at the clinic, James Beard was having blood drawn. The doctor had noted his swollen legs, listened to his heart, and palpated his stomach. They were running every imaginable test, on every imaginable substance and molecule that might be found in his blood, urine, or anywhere else. There were electrocardiograms and abdominal X-rays. Pathé was an expert in diabetes and other endocrine diseases, and he was thorough.

Beard handed over a letter from his doctor in New York. It was typed on letterhead:

To Whom It May Concern:

Mr. James Beard requires reduction of weight and improvement in lower extremity vascular condition.

He is in good health except for mild cardiac disease for which he takes digitalis and hydrodiuril.

Sincerely,

John E. Sullivan, M.D.

Pathé asked Beard to step onto the scale. He weighed 138 kilograms—304 pounds. It was clear that Beard was significantly overweight, but Pathé took a holistic approach, knowing that the weight was only part of the problem. He asked Beard about his life and career, his work as a writer, his expertise in food and wine, the many long and exhausting trips he was obligated to take—consulting for restaurants, attending conventions, judging cooking contests, evaluating the in-flight menus for an airline client, and so on. Pathé tried to explain the relationship between Beard's weight and his health and well-being, his heart in particular. It would not be enough, he said, for Beard simply to go on a diet, to submit himself to Pathé's low-calorie regimen for a few weeks, and to lose a few pounds. No, he needed to change his life. It was a question of free will and choice, Pathé said—Beard alone could achieve a "moral victory" over his obesity.

Beard wanted this "moral victory"; there was no doubt about *that*. His weight problems were far from an abstraction, moral or otherwise: He felt terrible, worse than he ever had before. He was having trouble walking, and his legs were swollen and discolored. He was short of breath. But losing weight, he knew from long experience of failing at it, was hard. Success required superhuman self-discipline—not an area he excelled in—and there was the additional problem that his lifestyle was also his livelihood. Food and drink were what he did. Dieting, for Beard, was an existential problem.

Sixty pounds—that's what Pathé told Beard he needed to lose.

The doctor explained the principles of the diet he had devised for Beard. It was called the "Prudent Diet" and contained a total of two thousand calories per day, and no added salt or sugar was allowed. During the course of his stay at the clinic, Beard was meant not only to acclimate his body to this new diet—to eat *half* the amount he normally did—but also to learn to plan correctly balanced meals for himself once he returned home. Pathé handed him a sheaf of papers outlining various acceptable breakfasts, lunches, and dinners, along with detailed rules about what he must and must not eat. And drink: the doctor insisted he give up alcohol of any kind, and instead drink large quantities of noncarbonated mineral water.

Of course, for the time being, he didn't need to think about any of this. He just ate what they brought him. It was never enough.

Breakfast:
70 grams fruit
30 grams biscuits
10 grams butter
Tea

Lunch:
30 grams biscuits
10 grams butter
250 grams grilled tomatoes
150 grams leg of lamb
60 grams brown rice
140 grams fruit

Dinner:

30 grams biscuits	100 grams steamed potatoes
10 grams oil	150 grams artichokes
150 grams cold chicken	140 grams fruit

Everything was carefully weighed and excruciatingly bland. The portions were small: 150 grams of lamb and 60 grams of rice sat on the plate ever so primly, more *symbols* of food than food itself. A few bites, and they were gone.

There was some variation, but not much. Some days he got fennel or celery instead of tomatoes, or grilled steak instead of lamb. The second week, he convinced Pathé to replace the biscuits with a slice of bread, which was a slight improvement. But the diet was draconian, and it was hard to imagine eating this way permanently, when he wasn't locked away in a clinic.

For one thing, he was always hungry. For another, there was no wine.

✦ ✦ ✦

As Beard sat alone in his monastic room in Pathé's clinic, he looked over his manuscript. He was nearing completion, at long last, of his ambitious book, *American Cookery.* It would be the definitive statement on American cooking—the culmination of his years as the dean of the American food scene, a celebration of national heritage. He wrote his first cookbook, *Hors d'Oeuvre and Canapés,* in 1940, and much had changed since. Cookbook writers in the previous decade, and Julia Child in particular, had done much to popularize sophisticated cooking. But "sophisticated," in the popular imagination, still meant "French." His was the book that would codify and elevate the homegrown flavors of American food. He had collected recipes from many different sources. He had pored over two centuries' worth of recipe collections compiled by ladies' aid societies, missionary and hospital volunteer groups, and women's exchanges all across the country. He had looked to the legacy of the millions of immigrants who had arrived on U.S. shores from Europe and Asia to trace the evolution of the nation's cooking. He had even embraced what he called the "Polynesian school of cookery, a combination of American, Hawaiian and Oriental, popularized by Trader Vic and his imitators."

But it was the food of his own childhood that was most important to him. Beard had grown up in Portland, Oregon, and had an enduring love for the Dungeness crabs, razor clams, mussels, salmon, and trout of the Pacific Northwest. His mother, Mary, was a talented and opinionated cook—she owned a small residential hotel before she was married, and entertained often—and so was Jue Let, the Chinese man who ran the household kitchen. It was these two who taught him to cook, and looking back, he saw that they embodied the American culinary story, one of distinct regional traditions, embraced and transformed by generations of immigrants. (Mary was English and had come to Portland to work as a governess in 1882.) Beard's father was a distant presence; he was a customs official downtown. Beard's mother took him to spend weekends and summers on the Oregon coast, in Gearhart, where they prepared elaborate picnics and cooked over an open fire at the beach, and ate an endless variety of chowders, salmon, clams, and crabs. This was the food Beard would always love the most, and the new book would allow him to give it the prominence he felt it deserved.

In the book's introduction, Beard acknowledged that at that moment in time (1972 was the year it was finally published), French cuisine seemed still to be "the goal of every amateur in the kitchen." Giving credit where it was due, he said that "without a doubt it is a delight to follow the meticulously planned trail of Julia Child ... but we should also look into the annals of our own cuisine," for "we forget what distinguished food Americans have produced in several periods of our history." Bringing this cuisine to light was the goal of his book: "We have a rich and fascinating food heritage that occasionally reaches greatness in its own melting pot way," he wrote. "This book is a sampling of that cuisine, and inevitably it reflects my own American palate."

Beard had collected recipes for everything from creamed chicken à la king to angel food cake. He was a completist, a rigorous historian of iconic American dishes. There were eight varieties of stuffed egg, from Deviled Eggs to Roquefort Stuffed Eggs. There were numerous chowders: Mrs. Crowen's Clam Chowder, from 1847; Old Western Clam Chowder; Standard New England Clam Chowder; Mrs. Lincoln's Clam Chowder; and one he labeled My Favorite Clam Chowder. There were eleven recipes for fried chicken, including multiple versions of Southern Fried Chicken; Tabasco Fried Chicken; Bacon Fried Chicken; Maryland Fried Chicken; and Creole Fried Chicken.

He would not be eating deviled eggs, clam chowder, or fried chicken at Pathé's diet clinic, needless to say. All such delicious, decadent foods were now off-limits. (That favorite chowder recipe contained three cups of light cream. And fried chicken, well, it was fried chicken.)

His dinner came on a tray. He ate a cracker with some olive oil.

The cold roasted chicken was fine, and so were the potatoes and artichoke. The lack of salt was galling.

Beard looked over the documents Pathé had given him, at the long list of *aliments interdits*. No olives, nuts, avocados, fermented cheeses, cabbage, or onions. Eggs were to be eaten boiled or poached, but never in an omelet. Good-bye clams, scallops, and mussels—all shellfish, in fact—good-bye croissants and any sort of pastry. Nothing cured, smoked, spiced, or marinated was ever to enter his mouth: no salami, prosciutto, or goose liver pâté. There would be no sweetbreads, and no caviar, either.

Could he live like this? Forever?

And could anything be more ironic: the grand epicure, immersed in the sprawl of his monumental cookbook, conjuring the flavors of a lifetime's worth of eating, reduced to such meager provisions? Here he was, in Provence, surrounded by recipes and tasting notes, and he was starving himself.

Nevertheless, he forged ahead. He had been working far too long on *American Cookery*—six years!—and needed to finish. The entire enterprise seemed to have gotten away from him somehow. The book was too big. It was overstuffed, encyclopedic—a victim of Beard's voraciousness, his boundless enthusiasm, and his distractible nature (all the very same reasons he himself was too big— but he knew that). Did he really need to include recipes for cheddar cheese balls with pimientos; for chicken casserole with macaroni, corn, peas, breadcrumbs, and cheese; for sloppy joes? These were among what he conceded to be the "grotesqueries of American cooking," which he had included for the sake of making an accurate record of his native cuisine. And indeed he had a certain affection for such unpretentious, practical dishes.

But now he was trying to finish, to corral his unwieldy manuscript, hoping that he had managed to outline a distinct and worthy national cuisine—a cuisine he considered to be on a path to contend with that of France, as he said, for "after all, France created French cuisine over centuries," and of course America was still a country much younger than France. Yes, *American Cookery* had an everything-but-the-kitchen-sink quality about it, but the writing was modern and opinionated, full of personal anecdotes and insights. American food, in Beard's telling, was endlessly variable and always evolving. Although there were gaps in the book—for example, he had offered only a nod in the direction of the new vogue for health food and organic produce—he had made the case for the existence of a national distinct cuisine, and recorded much of its history, and he knew it was now too late for second-guessing. The book was long overdue. What he had would have to do.

This much was also clear: he was trapped in a French diet clinic with an unfinished American cookbook, and both facts weighed on him in unbearable fashion. He needed to escape.

Fortunately, escape was coming, in the form of M. F. K. Fisher.

◆ ◆ ◆

The small but rather pleasant apartment M.F. had rented in La Roquette-sur-Siagne was about a twenty-minute drive from Grasse. Lord had found it for her. It was just across the road from the grand estate, Les Bastides, where Lord and Bedford spent their summers. They lived in London the rest of the year.

The days there had stretched into weeks. The weather was sometimes rainy and chilly, but mostly windy, bright, and beautiful.

"Heavenly," M.F. thought. Birds sang in the olive trees, and now and then a frog would emit a pontifical croak. She rose early in the morning to write, while Norah went across the way to Les Bastides, to garden with Lord, the two of them planting bulbs under the trees around the big stretch of lawn and terrace behind the grand estate.

In their rented flat, Norah had taken the bedroom, and M.F. was set up in the living room. There was a small separate kitchen and a large terrace. M.F. hadn't quite known what to expect when she'd rented the place the previous summer, sight unseen, based on Lord's recommendation. "If you don't like being alone at night, simply lift your voice slightly and Sybille and I will hear you," Lord had written. The house was modest, clean, and quiet. It cost thirteen English pounds a week, including heat—a price in keeping with the genteel British atmosphere of the enclave. A local woman came three times a week to clean and do the laundry.

Lord was the "general handyman" for Les Bastides and for the rental apartment, too. It was rather embarrassing, M.F. thought, to have to ask for help so often, but it was a country house, and this was France. The butane ran out in the kitchen, for example, and M.F. and Norah did not quite remember how one went about replacing the tank, which, in any case, was locked in a cage to which Lord had the key.

Time slowed down. M.F. and Norah were reading and cooking, wandering into town in Lord's VW Bug to shop for groceries and mail letters at the post office. Les Bastides was only a mile from the center of La Roquette, but traffic on the narrow country road was heavy and precluded walking. Other days, they drove to Mouans-Sartoux, the next town over, and ate lunch there. Or they sat in a café with Bert Greene, a friend of M.F.'s who was in the area for a few days. A large, tall man in his late forties, Greene was exploring Provence with a friend. He laughed as he described his newfound love of pastis.

Greene had cofounded The Store in Amagansett on Long Island, New York, a shop that sold pâtés, salads, soups, roasted meats, side dishes, desserts, and other high-end groceries and gourmet prepared foods for takeout. It was one of the first shops of its kind, opening in the mid-1960s and catering to an increasingly sophisticated crowd—yet another harbinger of the changes in American taste. People were watching Julia Child, they were buying cookbooks, and they had an appetite, too, for "carry-out cuisine"— convenient, freshly prepared leek tarts and chocolate mousses.

Evenings, the sisters crossed the road to Les Bastides for cocktails with Bedford and Lord. The estate belonged to Allanah Harper, a wealthy and highly cultured Englishwoman who in the late 1920s founded the Paris-based literary journal *Exchanges,* which had introduced French writers such as André Gide and Henri Michaux to British readers, and W. H. Auden, T. S. Eliot, Gertrude Stein, and Virginia Woolf to the French. Harper and Sybille Bedford were old friends who'd been crossing paths in London and Paris since the 1950s. For years, Harper had loaned a converted garage on her Provence property to Bedford and Lord—"adjoining studios, a pergola, a terrace, jasmine and honeysuckle, night flowering climbers, tree frogs, set in an olive grove" is how Bedford described it.

M.F. and Norah had known Lord since they were kids in the mid-1920s. M.F. had idolized her—a fabulously glamorous high school student, the popular girl with the bob haircut—those many years ago, when they were classmates at Bishop's. Lord had also lived at M.F. and Norah's parents' house for a time, after she was expelled from Stanford for her wild behavior. Years later, in 1959, M.F. wrote a letter to Lord, recounting her teenage infatuation:

> If I believed, as indeed I did, that you were the most dazzling exciting human being I had ever met, it was because I was caught in one of the same mushy, ignominious, and disgusting "crushes" that so bored me in others . . . It seemed right and natural that girls would be swooning all over the damned silly neurotic hotbed for you, and I could only admit that I was as bad as any of them.

Not that anything particularly romantic ever happened. But it was a formative relationship for M.F., an early and intense connection that endured for decades, and one that tied her, however peripherally, to the London literary set.

Bedford and Lord were an odd couple. Bedford was the dominant, domineering one—moody, gregarious, irritable, loud, impatient, all depending on how her writing was going. She'd emerge from her room "like a bear with a sore head" (Lord's words), daring anyone to strike up a conversation. She was born in Germany and grew up in Italy and Spain, her father some sort of dissolute aristocrat and her mother a morphine addict. She wrote novels that were also memoirs, in a fragmentary style. *A Legacy*, published in 1957, was widely praised, including by Evelyn Waugh, although the *New York Times* reviewer Richard Plant decried the author's insufferable snobbery: "With breathless casualness, she tells us of the Merzes of Berlin (extremely wealthy, Jewish, and quite old school, you know), whose daughter marries a South German Baron von Felden (very French, very devout, *ma chère*) and a few scandals befalling the Felden family after that Merz girl (what was her name?) has died in Davos."

Such was the oeuvre: world-weary, aristocratic, dense with the romance of the interwar years, people dying tragically in Davos. Bedford was also a cogent and serious culinary expert, and proudly judgmental. She wrote about wine, and traveled frequently to attend tastings.

Lord, meanwhile, was frail and birdlike, with big eyes and hidden depths. She smoked nonstop but did not drink, as her doctors had forbidden it after years of alcoholism. She had a quiet voice and an ironical, faux-naïve way of putting things. She was also a writer—her new novel, *Extenuating Circumstances*, would be published by Knopf the following year.

She could be socially awkward: when Child met her a few years earlier, she wrote to M.F. afterward that she found Lord "strange and withdrawn. I remember asking her some innocent question about herself, such as where did she grow up or some such inanity—she just couldn't answer, after hemming and hesitating, we managed to get the subject changed. Very odd, and one suffers for her."

Nevertheless, Lord and Bedford had an active social life and saw the Childs with some regularity when both couples were in France, not to mention the rest of what Lord called the "closed cooking circle," including Richard Olney and, in London, Elizabeth David.

The food world was indeed a small one, both in Europe and America. Everyone knew everyone else—all of them drawn together by a shared reverence for "the good life," and there was indeed a sense of "closed-circle" exclusivity about it. With who else, after all, would it be worthwhile to discuss the merits of a particular preparation or vintage, if not a fellow connoisseur? But of course, petty rivalries and rampant snobbery were all the worse in such insular society. Nora Ephron's "Food Establishment" article had made that very point.

Elizabeth David and M.F. were considered rivals of sorts—both of them seen as competing for the title of the most literary of food writers—even though they'd never even met. (David's seminal *A Book of Mediterranean Food,* published in 1950, described the pleasures of garlic, olive oil, and Parmigiano-Reggiano, among many other things, for readers in postwar England.) Lord told M.F. a long anecdote about seeing David in London. "We had two dinners—at her house with superb wines which kept us sitting until the small hours, and another evening with her at a restaurant, on us but of her choosing," she said. "I like her enormously, but I'm always mystified how time drops away when one is with her."

Lord's description of those dinners amounted to a bit of subtle social gamesmanship—name-dropping couched in carefully inscrutable phrases that may (or may not) have been intended as insults: the restaurant "on us but of her choosing"; the mystifying way (was that good or bad?) time dropped away in her company. Indeed, Bedford and Lord were experts at this game, and M.F., when she wanted to be, was no slouch, either.

More uncomfortably, Bedford and Lord also asked after M.F.'s daughters, Anna and Kennedy, in an ostensibly affectionate but unmistakably disapproving manner. Not that they disliked the girls, exactly; they just expressed wonder at the general neediness of even grown children. They were aware that M.F. had struggled in recent years to balance her life as a writer with her role as a mother of two young women. Neither Bedford nor Lord had children, so how could they understand? They couldn't. Nevertheless, they had found a sore spot, and they poked at it.

M.F.'s patience with the two of them was wearing thin. It would not be long before she was chafing at the effort of navigating these complicated personalities and different-size egos. The arch, glittering commentary about mutual friends and their books, all the astute wine talk, not to mention the simple fact of being a guest, the constant calibration of deference, obligation, and reciprocation—it was all getting to be too much.

Norah had left on a brief trip to Florence by herself. From there she would return to La Roquette, and soon after that would board a freighter for the return trip to California.

It was odd to be alone, suddenly, M.F. found. But it was what she needed, because it would give her the time and space to confront the uncertainty of her future plans. She was currently working on revisions of *Among Friends,* her memoir of growing up in Whittier, California. She and Judith Jones, her editor at Knopf, planned to meet over Christmas while they were both in Provence. The book would come out next fall, but what next? Something about France?

M.F. continued to feel a little oppressed by Lord and Bedford, especially Bedford. "I almost never see Eda except through a dense Sybillian fog," she wrote to Arnold Gingrich. "Sybille is hard to take, actually"; she was self-serious in the extreme. Lord, meanwhile, was perpetually flustered and nervous. It had been much easier for M.F. to stay aloof when Norah was there, but now she felt as if she were surrounded by "too many neurotic females."

She had to get away for a day. And fortunately, liberation was coming, in the form of James Beard.

* * *

M.F. arrived at the Grasse clinic in Raymond Gatti's Mercedes.

Gatti was the best chauffeur on the Côte d'Azur, or the most famous anyway. He wore a dark blue suit and drove a dark blue Mercedes 300, a new one every year, and had been in business for himself since 1951. (Rental cars were not widely available in the immediate postwar period, and he had seen a market need and filled it.) Gatti drove the stars at the annual Cannes Film Festival to and from their hotels and out to dinner. His clients included celebrities and royalty of all sorts—Elizabeth Taylor, Gary Cooper, Pablo Picasso, the Duke of Windsor, Jack Benny, Sergio Leone, Anthony Quinn, and so on, not to mention Texas oil company chieftains, French politicians, and international pop stars. M.F. had met him four years earlier, in 1966, when she was working on the Time-Life *Cooking of Provincial France* book. The Childs had recommended Gatti to M.F. as they recommended him to all their friends, including James Beard. Gatti would drive them to La Colombe d'Or in Saint-Paul-de-Vence, or Le Moulin de Mougins, or the Hôtel de Paris in Monte Carlo—to the best restaurants. He was also sometimes hired for longer trips: one year, he drove the Childs to Venice and back again.

Gatti was in his forties, a compact man with a genial smile, and he loved to talk. His family was Italian, but he'd been born and raised in Plascassier. He was full of anecdotes about his exploits during World War II, when he fought the Nazis. He had been captured and made a prisoner of war in Frankfurt, escaped a Polish labor camp using his wits and expertise with cars, joined the U.S. special operations forces as they marched through Provence, and witnessed the liberation of Buchenwald. His nickname among the Americans was Frenchy.

Today, Gatti was taking M.F. and Beard to the Maeght collection and the Matisse chapel, the expedition they had both been looking forward to. Beard sat in the front passenger seat, where there was more room for his large frame, and M.F. sat in the back. Gatti navigated the winding country road to Saint-Paul with care: he was a controlled and conservative driver. He drove the speed limit, pointing out the sights along the way: there was Plascassier, in the valley below them, and farther off, the Mediterranean. "On a clear day, you can see all the way to Corsica," he said. Every once in a while he'd complain bitterly about French drivers, how they failed to look behind them when they drove, how they didn't pay attention.

M.F. and Beard chatted about this and that. They would be going to Plascassier for dinner with the Childs on Sunday night. Would Beard be allowed to eat or have a glass of wine? M.F. asked him. Beard lamented his diet. He had been asked by the doctors to name the single food he would want to subsist on if he could eat nothing else. He chose potatoes, which he thought of as "glamorous aristocrats among vegetables." He and M.F. laughed. They talked about potatoes for a while. She had once eaten, as a very young woman, the most delightful potato soufflé, she said, made with chives and parmesan cheese. She'd been sitting in the courtyard of a restaurant in Avallon, a town not far from Dijon. The dish had struck her as a kind of tribute to the potato. It was the first time she could remember having potato on its own, without meat.

Beard recalled his fascination as a child with the short-order cooks in diners and railroad cafés, making hash brown potatoes. They were not trained chefs, but they had an awe-inspiring speed and confidence, roughly slicing potatoes directly into the hot fat, shaking the pan and tossing the potatoes until they were crusty and brown.

"Few potatoes ever tasted or looked better to me," he said.

"It was a fine moment," M.F. said of the long-ago soufflé in the sunny courtyard.

The day felt like a jailbreak for both of them—Beard freed however briefly from the confines of Pathé's regimented clinic, M.F. from the claustrophobia of La Roquette. Saint-Paul was about a half hour's drive away, another medieval town, like Grasse but much smaller and prettier, and set on a hilltop behind ramparts. It had been a center for artists and writers, including Renoir, Chagall, Gide, and others, since the 1920s. The town was empty at this time of year, and beautiful. The weather was sunny and cool. They had the place to themselves.

First they were going to see the Matisse chapel, the Chapelle du Rosaire, in the neighboring town of Vence. It was a modest single-story building on the side of the road, plain and white with bright blue roof tiles. Matisse had designed it at the end of his life, in the late 1940s, and considered it his masterpiece.

Gatti parked the Mercedes in front, and M.F. and Beard made their way inside. The interior was equally stark, all white with deep blue, yellow, and green stained-glass windows and crude, late-Matisse murals rendered on tile—black line drawings of angels and clouds, a Madonna and Child, robed figures and crucifixes. They stood in the empty chapel watching the light in silence.

The chapel was "one of the most beautiful man-made things" she'd ever seen, M.F. declared, as they returned to the waiting car. Beard agreed.

Gatti now drove back to Saint-Paul, past the walled town and up to the Maeght collection, in a wooded area on a steep bluff looking toward the Mediterranean. The museum had been built a few years earlier, in 1964, to house the private collection of the seminal Paris art dealer Aimé Maeght and his wife, Marguerite. The striking modern building, designed by Spanish architect Josep Lluís Sert, was capped by a pair of inverted half-pipe shapes, and seemed simultaneously whimsical and brutalist, with lots of exposed concrete and brick. The grounds, by contrast, were green and wild, even now, in December. There were expanses of lawn, and large-scale sculpture on display everywhere you looked, works by Calder, Chagall, Giacometti, Chillida, Miró, and Braque. The umbrella pine trees had a Dr. Seuss–like quality—long trunks and dense, bushy tops—that seemed to complement the often abstract art.

Beard couldn't walk very far because of his circulation troubles and swollen legs, so they limited themselves to a few favorites: the Braque pool, with its blue fish mosaic; the many Miró paintings inside, and his outdoor labyrinth, full of surprising, not-quite-beautiful gargoyles. This was the kind of museum with numerous doors opening onto courtyards, a sense of welcoming the outdoors inside, and art into the wild.

"What a wonderful way to spend a fortune," M.F. said, as they stood on a terrace looking down at the Braque pool, and up at the purple stained-glass window also designed by the artist. They walked slowly back to the car, where Gatti stood waiting.

The afternoon had been most enjoyable, they agreed. And pleasure wasn't something to take for granted. Certainly Beard, suffering the indignities of his salt-, sugar-, and calorie-free diet, of his uncooperative legs, and of his ungovernable cookbook, had needed the break. And M.F., too, for she had begun to feel like something of a hostage at Les Bastides, ensnared in the unavoidable social politics of the guesthouse resident—all that needed to be said so carefully, all that was so carefully left unsaid. And beyond the petty irritations of being a guest, there was, stirring in her, a rebellion against the pretensions and pomposity that seemed to intrude on her every conversation with Bedford and Lord. Food, art, restaurants—every topic an opportunity for another discourse, another opinion that would establish one's superiority. But she knew she was as guilty as they were, and was glad of an opportunity to escape her own worst impulses.

It was different with Beard. He and M.F. had found themselves momentarily liberated, immersed in the innate beauty and inspired artwork of southern France. And wasn't that, as much as the food and wine they both so loved, why they came here again and again? The French dedication to pleasure, in all its various forms, was what spoke to both of them.

∼8∼

PARIS INTERLUDE

M.F. AND HER SISTER NORAH WERE GOING TO Paris. They had dashed through the city on their way to Provence in mid-October, seven weeks earlier, and now they were dashing back so Norah could make her ship to California. (Norah had returned from Florence only a few days earlier.) They would spend a night in Marseille, and then catch the Mistral, the Trans-Europ-Express train, this time going north.

Norah had a cabin on the *Michigan,* a French Line freighter bound for San Francisco out of Le Havre the first week of December. She would be at sea for about a month and arrive in California in early January. She had packed a large quantity of books for the crossing. It was a good thing Simenon was so prolific!

There was no need for M.F. to accompany her sister to Paris, except that she wanted to. The Kennedy sisters, as they sometimes still thought of themselves, had a close and complicated relationship. They were the two survivors: their beloved brother, David, had killed himself in 1942, the day before he was to report for service in the U.S. Army, and their sister Anne had died in her mid-fifties, some years ago. M.F. was nine years older than Norah, and had taken on her quasi-parental role when the two were young. These days, ironically, it was Norah who presided more directly over the extended family, including looking after M.F.'s daughters—both now in their twenties and having children of their own—at those times when their relations with their mother had become distant and strained. M.F. and Norah had raised their families as single women.

However often it had been left to Norah to bridge the gap between M.F. and her daughters, to take on the role of matriarch, Norah still looked up to her worldly older sister. M.F. in turn counted on Norah, her most intimate friend and relation, to absolve her of the sins of the writing life: the flights of fancy, the periodic absenteeism, the dark moods and "emotional climates," the necessary self-centeredness of the artist. It was Norah who bound her most closely to the present, who played the peacemaker, and who kept her anchored in her family.

Now Norah was leaving, leaving M.F. here alone in France. M.F. felt slightly unmoored. But the two women still had close to a week to spend together. They'd planned on two nights in Paris, and then Norah's sailing was delayed for a few days—par for the course for a freighter, but who was complaining? They'd had so little time in Paris when they first arrived; now they'd make up for it, resuming their revisiting of the past.

In Paris, they once again stayed at the pleasantly shabby Hôtel de France et de Choiseul ("a dream, a lasting bit of *les neiges d'antan,*" M.F. declared). They went on long walks around the city, shopping, sitting in cafés. One day, they found themselves passing by the Hôtel du Quai Voltaire, where they'd stayed in 1931, when Norah was fourteen and M.F. was twenty-three. The hotel looked out over the Seine and across at the Jardin des Tuileries and the Louvre. It was another genteel old place the sisters adored. They stopped in to take a look, reminiscing about that long-ago year in France when Norah went to the convent school M.F. had found for her in Dijon, when she and her first husband were living there. Norah remembered her sister telling her that Oscar Wilde had stayed at the Quai Voltaire, in a room with faded scarlet-striped wallpaper, upon which he'd written an illegible poem. Now the sisters stood in the lobby and surveyed the newly installed 1960s aluminum chic. Modernity had overtaken memory.

It was hideous, they decided.

The day before Norah's departure, they ate lunch at Prunier, on avenue Victor Hugo.

BELON OYSTERS AND PALOURDE CLAMS
CHAMPAGNE NATURE 1969

BROILED SCALLOPS EN BROCHETTE
CHÂTEAU CENIS POMEROL 1964

CAMEMBERT

Prunier was everybody's favorite Paris restaurant at the time, an art deco palace of seafood, totally calm and yet still buzzing with glamour. The Childs were frequent patrons and had filmed a *French Chef* segment there for the new season.

Norah had the oysters, M.F. had the clams, and they shared the scallops, which they agreed were beautiful. The Pomerol was superb and so was the cheese. The weather outside was a soft gray drizzle, and they were happy.

Norah set sail from Le Havre the next day. She wore M.F.'s old Eterna-Matic wristwatch, borrowed at the last minute to keep track of time during the long voyage.

◆ ◆ ◆

Richard Olney was also in Paris in early December 1970, attending one of the regular dinners hosted by *Cuisine et Vins de France* (*CVF*), the French culinary magazine. He had been attending these dinners for years. They were elaborate productions, meant to showcase chefs and winemakers for the gourmet elite. *CVF* also organized annual visits to the wineries of Bordeaux, among other places. It was on one such trip, in 1961, that Olney met and befriended the editors of the magazine, which led a few years later to his writing a monthly column: "Un Américain (Gourmand) à Paris: Le Menu de Richard Olney." These columns opened the door at Simon and Schuster and led to the *French Menu Cookbook*.

The *CVF* dinner was at the iconic Lucas Carton, on the Place de la Madeleine. It was a seasonal menu, with a focus on game.

CREAM OF PHEASANT SOUP

WHOLE ROAST PARTRIDGES

HARE À LA ROYALE

CUMIN SORBET

WOODCOCK PÂTÉ

SALAD WITH APPLES AND WALNUTS

CHEESE

PEACHES FLAMBÉ

This was French cooking in the grand, classic style. The preparations were pure and refined, distillations of the flavors of the season. The soup was elegant, the partridges were tender, the woodcock pâté was rich, but the centerpiece was the *lièvre à la royale*, an iconic haute cuisine dish, versions of which had been described by the nineteenth- and early-twentieth-century arbiters of French culinary tradition, Auguste Escoffier, Ali-Bab, and Prosper Montagné. In her *Book of Mediterranean Food*, in 1950, Elizabeth David had given the recipe for what she said was the original (and exceedingly complicated) version, invented by the French politician Senator Aristide Couteaux in 1898, after he'd spent a week hunting for just the right rabbit in Poitou, in western France. At Lucas Carton, the wild rabbit was boned, stuffed with a delicate mixture of chopped giblets, truffles, foie gras, and bread crumbs, and then poached very, very slowly in white wine. It was served in slices with sautéed cèpes and an intense, enriched reduction of the poaching liquid; the meat was so tender it could be eaten with a spoon.

The wine, too, was otherworldly: a 1964 Petit Village, a 1959 Mouton Rothschild, a 1953 Margaux, a 1962 Yquem, all preceded, of course, by champagne—Laurent-Perrier Grand Siècle.

Olney sat at the dinner with the editor of *CVF*, Odette Kahn, by now a good friend of his. Kahn was a dynamo, a bona fide member of the French food establishment. (A few years later, in 1976, Kahn would sit on the infamous wine-tasting jury in Paris organized by Steven Spurrier, at which California Cabernets and Chardonnays were shockingly declared superior to their French counterparts in a blind test. When the results were announced, Kahn demanded to have her ballot back.) Kahn congratulated Olney on the success of his cookbook. He told her he was taking the train to Cannes the following day to visit some of the preeminent American food writers, and that he hoped she and Beard in particular might one day meet.

Now, in the private upstairs dining room at Lucas Carton, they discussed the menu. The wine was "sublime," but the food was "too complicated," Olney declared—too many dishes, too many sauces, too many distractions. He had great affection for the classics, and for long and arduous recipes and meticulous preparations, but he was always suspicious of the taint of luxury. "There exists a bastard cuisine that is too often assumed to be real French cooking," Olney had written in the opening pages of his just-published cookbook:

> It patterns itself superficially on the classical *grande cuisine*, but, leaning heavily on the effects of spectacular presentation, it ignores the essential sobriety and integrity of the classic cuisine which becomes its victim. It is not *grande cuisine* but "Grand Palace"—or international hotel cooking. It has, however, many enthusiasts. Perhaps, having never encountered the genuine, they are nonetheless impressed by the presentation and complication of the false.

The *CVF* dinner at Lucas Carton was a far cry from "international hotel cooking," but Olney detected among the dishes an abstracted, overelaborate quality. He strived, in his own cooking, for a kind of purity; a dish should be simple and sublime at the same time. This was easier said than done.

In the early sixties, Olney had made what became a legendary pot-au-feu, described at the time by the Paris food writer Michel Lemonnier as the best he'd ever tasted. Olney explained his method:

> I prepared an oxtail pot-au-feu, discarded the vegetables and bouquet garni, put the oxtail aside for a future meal and, with the broth, prepared a pot-au-feu with a boned, tied-up beef shank, and another bouquet, adding little carrots, turnips and potatoes toward the end; a quartered, blanched cabbage was braised apart in some of the broth. The bouquets were bundles of leek, celery stalk, fresh thyme and bay leaf.

This was a rustic-seeming dish, the broth twice cooked, once with oxtail and once with beef shank. The process was laborious, and the goal was to highlight the essential, transcendent flavor of the meat and broth, presented in the earthenware cooking pot. Olney had served it in his tiny Paris studio, which smelled faintly of oil paint and turpentine. He wore "rags"—an unbuttoned shirt, paint-flecked pants. And so the Olney mystique was born. All the cooking was done in advance: he made it look easy.

9

A DINNER PARTY
AT THE CHILDS'

IT WAS A SUNDAY EVENING IN MID-DECEMBER, and Julia and Paul Child were awaiting their dinner guests, M.F. and Beard. They had urged M.F. to bring her friends Eda Lord and Sybille Bedford, too. So they would be six.

Why had she bought such an enormous chicken? Child wondered. It sat on the counter looking rather larger, somehow, than it had at the butcher's. She'd gone shopping that morning in Plascassier and Grasse, to the excellent Boussageon for meat and various charcuterie items, and to Madame Londi's, her favorite fruit and vegetable shop. She found Boussageon's pâté to be fine and carefully flavored. In Cannes the previous day, she and Paul had walked along the narrow rue Meynadier, with its many food and specialty shops selling cheese, chocolate, and macaroons; fish, game, and quiche; and of course an endless selection of Provençal dishware, gifts, and handbags. She ended up buying a smoked salmon that was the biggest she'd ever seen—almost three feet long!

She would roast the chicken and some potatoes, and set out some of the prepared dishes as appetizers, along with fresh bread. She would make a salad. This would be an easy dinner—a casual affair. There would be something simple for dessert.

James Beard arrived early and was soon poking around the kitchen with her. He would make a soup, he said. He began washing and chopping a large amount of chard he had found in her refrigerator.

Child and Beard loved cooking together, and had even given themselves a joint nickname a few years earlier: Gigi, a combination of their names (or at least, the *J*s in their first names, as pronounced in French). It was silly, of course, but that was the point. The Gigis are in the kitchen, they would say. She wore a bright flower-patterned dress, and he had matched her with an equally colorful bow tie.

Child trimmed the fat from the extra-large roasting chicken, ran it under the cold faucet, and then dried it off with paper towels. She and Beck had disdained this practice rather imperiously in the first volume of *Mastering*, but had recently changed their minds, deciding it was a necessary precaution against bacteria. She rubbed butter and salt inside the bird, and then began to truss it with a great length of kitchen string and a large needle. She was an elaborate trusser of birds, tying up the legs at one end and the wings at the other.

She rubbed more butter on the outside of the chicken and then arranged slices of fresh pork fat over the breasts and thighs, and tied them in place with more of the string. She set the very secure-looking bird in a large oval roasting dish and put it in the hot oven.

Beard, meanwhile, was sautéing leeks and garlic in a large pot,

for his soup. He was doing his best to keep up a cheerful counte-
nance, but Child could tell it was a strain for him. He sat down
frequently to rest his legs.

Child sliced potatoes for a *gratin dauphinois,* layering them in a
heavy dish with plenty of cheese and butter, and then pouring hot
milk over it. Into the oven it went, next to the chicken, which she
took out to baste and to turn on its side. Her method for roasting
chicken involved multiple shifts in the bird's position, so it would
cook evenly and brown all over, and lots of basting. She added carrots and onions to the bottom of the dish, to enrich the sauce.

Paul went to collect some wine for dinner. They had determined
that digging a proper wine *cave* would be preposterously expensive, so they kept their bottles in a cellar-like room beneath the
cabanon—the small, one-room stone structure across the driveway
where Paul had his painting studio. It had a window looking over
the valley.

The sun was setting and the sky was dark as Paul, bottles of
Bordeaux in hand, heard Eda Lord's VW Bug sputtering up the
steep unpaved driveway. He waved as Lord pulled in next to his
rented Renault. She emerged with Bedford and M.F., all of them
shutting doors and calling hellos.

Julia opened the side door directly to the kitchen, and she and
Beard welcomed them in. Paul took the corkscrew from its hook
on the Peg-Board kitchen wall and opened the wine. The kitchen
smelled wonderful, and they all offered to help—arranging some
of the smoked salmon and pâté on plates, setting the table, string-
ing beans. Dinner at La Pitchoune was a communal affair. Julia
presided in the kitchen in her apron, towering over her guests. Everyone pitched in.

Beard's soup was simmering on the stovetop, the improvised chard and tomato soup, with various other tidbits tossed in. Child gleefully dubbed it the "Soupe Barbue"—the "Bearded Soup," after its maker.

The mood in the kitchen was very different at La Pitchoune than it was at the Childs' house in Cambridge. At home, Julia ran a working kitchen: Recipes were tested, alternate ingredients and methods were tried out, nothing was left to chance. The contents of her two refrigerators were carefully indexed and posted on their doors. There was evidence of her rigorous process everywhere you looked—competing versions of the same dish cooling on the counter, recipe notes and annotations stuck to the wall. "Put it to the test" was the spirit of the place.

Provence, on the other hand, was a free-for-all. No one was overly self-conscious: "Will Julia approve of this vinaigrette?" was not a thought that crossed anyone's mind. The kitchen was a happy, casual, slightly tipsy melee—chaotic fun. Paul poured more wine. Everyone seemed to be talking at the same time.

◆ ◆ ◆

Was there a better smell in the world than a chicken roasting in the oven? The slowly crisping skin, the sizzling noises reaching a crescendo. Julia had removed the pork fat for the final browning, and now she proclaimed dinner ready.

PÂTÉ DE CAMPAGNE AND SMOKED SALMON

"SOUPE BARBUE"

ROAST CHICKEN

GRATIN DAUPHINOIS

HARICOTS VERTS

SORBET

The round table was set in the main living room, the pâté and smoked salmon at its center, and Paul was cutting up a baguette. There was a fire crackling in the large fireplace. M.F., Beard, Lord, and Bedford began to arrange themselves at the table, carrying their wineglasses. In the kitchen, Julia took the bird from the oven to let it rest a bit before carving. To make sure it was completely cooked, she cut into the leg.

Quel désastre! It was bloody!

"You'd think," Julia said, laughing, "that I'd know how to cook a chicken by now!" Well, it *had* been an exceedingly large chicken. It would go right back into the oven.

M.F. and Beard laughed. Paul pretended to be irritated—the delay meant he'd have to open more bottles of wine. He went out to the *cabanon* to replenish supplies.

♦ ♦ ♦

At dinner, half an hour or so later, they talked politics and food. Nixon's invasion of Cambodia was bemoaned. The quality of the local ham and salmon were celebrated. The wine was praised.

Bedford was mostly in good form, M.F. thought—thank God, as she could be boringly difficult sometimes, especially when it came to discussing wine. As for Lord, she was quiet and enigmatic, as usual. Julia and Paul were relaxed and happy, and Beard seemed cheerful, though his health was on everyone's mind. "We worry about him," Julia wrote in a letter to M.F. the following week. "The sight of those mahogany legs that one glimpses between pant cuff and sock are frightening. He seems depressed, although manages to hide it—and no wonder. What a dear and generous friend he is. One can only pray that he will manage."

Privately, Julia and Paul thought the situation was dire: "Our dear fat friend is on his way out," they said to each other. "We must steel ourselves."

M.F., meanwhile, found herself contemplating the design of a special chair for Beard, on small, silent wheels that would allow him to move around, upright, without burdening his overworked legs—"zipping deftly here and there behind the counters in his kitchens, still taller than anyone."

The "Soupe Barbue" was a hit—the rich sweetness of the chard and leeks set off by the acidity of the tomatoes. And it was healthy, too, Beard insisted, made with a minimum of olive oil.

He was allowing himself to eat dinner, despite the forbidden nature of certain items—Pathé would never know about the bites of pâté or smoked salmon, nor the glass of wine. Or two. Beard was nearing the end of his stay at the clinic anyway.

There was gossip, talk of mutual friends, of new restaurants in Paris, New York, and London. Beard's old friend Joe Baum had been ousted from Restaurant Associates, the struggling New York company that ran the Four Seasons, Tavern on the Green, and many others. But Baum had just landed a plum consulting contract to create the restaurants at the World Trade Center towers, currently under construction. One of them would sit at the very top of one of the buildings and be the highest restaurant in the world.

Bedford and Lord realized they and Beard had a London friend in common: Elizabeth David, who'd recently sent Beard a letter from Italy:

I thought of you today while having lunch in a real Tuscan tavern in a place called Colle Val d'Elsa, such good, authentic food, and perfectly delicious roast pig, very delicately flavored with wild fennel and cooked perfectly—how you would have enjoyed it, and how rare this sort of food and this type of restaurant have become in Tuscany. It's been disappointing this year. Indifferent wine everywhere and not very interesting food. But the countryside is divinely beautiful in October.

Was good, authentic food getting harder to find in France as well as Italy?

David certainly thought so, Beard reported, but then, she was a gloomy sort, her small London kitchen shop in perpetual semi-crisis, her writing slow and arduous. She was working on a bread book and making little progress, and referred to her just-released *Spices, Salt and Aromatics in the English Kitchen* as "a squalid little book." From London, David wrote that chef Bill Lacy's new res-taurant (called Lacy's) was getting great reviews: "I'm very pleased for Bill—but somehow I can't bring myself to go and eat there. The food is just restaurant French food—or perhaps it's improved by now—if only one could go to a French restaurant and get a cup of beautiful consommé followed by just one authentic dish not fussed up with a lot of extra vegetables—and above all not heated up. I wonder if I will ever get back to Lucullus in Avignon to eat that fish soup."

Bedford shared her friend David's attitude of dismissive hauteur toward banal "restaurant French food"—her term for what Richard Olney called "Grand Palace" and "international hotel cooking." She was a purist, and yes, she felt the same way about consommé. She, too, adored Hiély Lucullus, with its Art Nouveau–style, second-floor dining room near the Place de l'Horloge. It had been there since the 1930s.

This they could all agree on: Hiély was a classic place. Unchanged and unchangeable, and with an admirable fish soup. M.F. had eaten there countless times over the years.

But today, Bedford now continued, there were too many restaurants serving reheated roasted meats wrapped in pastry, sauces thickened with corn starch, and various ridiculous flambés. It was theater, not cooking—it was, no offense, the *Americanization* of cooking.

They all laughed.

But Child was quick to retort: there was mediocre food all over. And in fact it seemed to her that even many of the great three-star French restaurants had been overly commercialized, made to run like mechanized assembly lines, at the expense of some of the craft and skill—"hand work," she called it—in their kitchens. She strongly disagreed with the *New York Times*' Craig Claiborne, who'd recently written that no American restaurant could touch France's greatest. She'd been to all of those so-called "greatest" places—indeed, Paul had gotten food poisoning the last time they went to Le Grand Véfour in Paris.

"I have eaten every bit as well in New York," she declared.

Child liked and respected Claiborne, but he was a snob. Earlier that year, she and Paul had written him a letter to protest his veiled, smirking criticism of Henry Haller, the White House chef under LBJ and now Nixon, a president "widely reputed to have a predilection of some sort for cottage cheese garnished with catchup," as Claiborne wrote. The Childs had no love for Nixon, but the Swiss Haller, an acquaintance of theirs, had nothing to do with the food made in the private quarters of the White House. He cooked state dinners, and he was, furthermore, a damn good chef, "doing his best to show the world that this is not a nation of uncouth hicks gastronomically," the Childs wrote, with some feeling. Julia herself bore no small amount of responsibility for the 1960s democratization of taste and cooking in America, and she took her role seriously. Hence the letter to Claiborne.

Child's aversion to snobbery was deeply ingrained, reflected in her whole persona, her slightly comic, encouraging patter on television, her no-nonsense practicality, her warmth. The antipathy had only become stronger over the years, probably never more so than this year. The collaboration with Beck—*la Super-Française*—had exacerbated and magnified the feeling. It wasn't just her coauthor's repeated declarations about correct and proper French cooking traditions; it was the righteous, Olympian authority with which she delivered them that was so maddening. And the same was true of Claiborne, so sure of the superiority of the grand old French restaurant institutions, and of Bedford, going on about consommé and the Americanization of cooking.

Child was ready to turn the page on the retrograde attitudes and old-fashioned ideas.

American food was changing, and she was ready to embrace that change. She was finally done with *Mastering the Art of French Cooking*—two volumes were quite enough!—and preparing to move in a new direction, whatever that might be. Rather than pine for the old days of consommé, she welcomed the beginnings of a more globalized, international food world. She could see herself branching out to New England chowders and Indian curries, to Italian pastas and Chinese sauces and marinades. Like Beard, she understood that American food was starting to embrace more ethnic traditions, and she was eager to explore them. She was also eager to write in a more informal, casual way, freed of the *Mastering* books' cooking school master class style. Of course, her cooking would remain French-inflected, but the TV show and cookbooks would allow her to spread her wings.

Was it Beck who had held her back? With her distinctly French sense of superiority? Her unspoken jealousies? Beck could never quite believe that *any* American could cook French food properly, and Child's identity as the TV's French Chef seemed to Beck a moral affront.

M.F. was now recounting an amusing day she had spent with Beck a few weeks earlier. She had dropped by Le Vieux Mas, next door, for an afternoon visit.

"Simca: *quelle femme!*" M.F. said. Beck had been full of talk and authoritarian vigor, so "energetic-firm-bossy-bitchy-forceful that one is cowed by her!"

Child knew just what she meant.

"I liked her, at home," M.F. continued. "But I'd sure as hell hate to cope with her in Paris or New York. Sit here, eat this, drink when I say—not any choice. Ah well."

Paul and Julia nodded knowingly. Exactly. Simca and Jean were in Paris at the moment, so the Childs hadn't had to invite them to dinner tonight. They would see them soon enough, over Christmas.

+ + +

Child carved the chicken and carried the platter out to the table. It was most certainly done now—but not overdone—and they all laughed again at the delayed start of dinner. The chicken was perfect, and so was the gratin, and so were the beans. They passed plates and dishes, and poured more wine, toasting each other, good fortune, and France.

It was remarkable, M.F. thought, how different this dinner was in spirit to the Olney dinner a few weeks earlier. The food was far simpler, of course, something like a family dinner. This was Child's kitchen, but they had all helped cook, however haphazardly. It had been *fun*. M.F. had liked Olney, and admired and enjoyed his brilliant, meticulous cooking. But the priestly high seriousness of it all had worn thin that night. Having long ago escaped America in order to discover France, she was now wondering if she needed to escape France to find herself. On the other hand, was this not where she belonged? It was here that her philosophy had been born: her insistence on pleasure, on the significance of ephemeral moments. She drifted back and forth between her thoughts and the conversation going on around her.

Bedford, God help them all, was now droning on about wine, and Paul was nodding patiently.

M.F. and Beard were soon in the midst of a discussion about the intriguing appeal of fresh green peppercorns—*poivre vert*—the ingredient of the moment, they agreed. M.F. had bought a supply at a local shop, La Grassoise, to bring home, and Beard's friend and collaborator José Wilson was already scoping out possible recipes back in New York.

Lord was mostly silent.

As they ate, Child asked M.F. about her new house in Sonoma County. It was progressing slowly, but well, she said, and they must all come and visit when it was done. True, it was in California and not Provence, and she'd had to say a "sad, grim No" to her dream of terra-cotta tiles like the ones here at La Pitchoune; they were too expensive. She was having all her shabby but beautiful rugs cleaned, however, and they would look very nice indeed.

They all agreed to visit her in California—they'd come next fall, the Childs said. They'd be out in San Francisco at some point, certainly, and Glen Ellen was only an hour and a half's drive north. Julia and Paul's Cambridge house was also being worked on—the noisy and dusty work was happening now, in their absence.

Talk turned inevitably to the overdevelopment of the Côte d'Azur. Too many new villas and too much traffic, Paul decreed. Of course, the problem was money: there was too much of it! M.F. said she'd gone only yesterday to visit an old friend, Larry Bachmann, and his wife, in the hills high above Cannes. Bachmann was a successful movie producer (and long-ago lover), and the newly built house was the most stylized modern one she'd ever seen, she said—"amazing, quite beautiful, completely impersonal, just like its owners. Black living room ceilings about 30 feet high—walls of glass—bathtubs out in the middle of rooms, silent manservants slipping about."

The movie people were interesting. Fun to watch, anyway. Paul described them coming en masse in the spring, for the Cannes Film Festival—a fascinating mob of

cinema sycophants, actual stars, bosom-bouncing starlets, quite
delicate dressed-alike young men in pairs, hangers on, thick-
set, hawk-eyed promoters and money-men, poseurs, aging

actors warming their trembling fingertips at the flame of public recognition, and endless starry-eyed teen-agers, notebooks in hand hoping to get Big Shot autographs, swirling through the crowds and the hotel lobbies like schools of minnows in an ocean full of aquatic giants.

He had a novelist's eye for the spectacle of it all. He and Julia would sit at Le Festival restaurant and watch the passing scene. "It's very enheartening to one's sense of superiority," Paul said. Of course, Julia was herself a celebrity of sorts, a "Big Shot." Not that she acted like one, or put on airs. But among food people in the United States, she was the star around whom all others orbited, seeking her approval and respect. Here in Provence, on the other hand, she was just the tall American with the intrepid accent, ordering vast quantities of food at the local grocery stores, butchers, and fish shops. Provence was liberating that way.

Child's matter-of-fact personality and good humor tended to overcome any bad feelings—bruised egos, competitive cookbook authors, slighted chefs—but her position could occasionally cause friction. A new food writer on the scene, such as Richard Olney, might well nurture a sense of aggrieved, disgruntled persecution—always finding himself in Child's shadow.

He was arriving tomorrow. Lord was picking him up at the train station in Cannes, and he had made plans to visit both Beard and the Childs. Lord explained that she, Bedford, and M.F. would be preparing dinner for Olney tomorrow—the collaboration dinner they'd been planning since the sensational meal he cooked for them a few weeks earlier. It was their way of repaying his hospitality. Well, they would try, anyway, Lord said, half-smiling.

Not to worry, Bedford said. The wines would be superb.

M.F. felt a distinct inkling of dread at the thought of another endless evening with Olney and Sybille. She liked them both, but the rigors of their company were exhausting, their obsession with food and wine having made them too disengaged from the life of the world around them. Yes, she had always been in favor of educating the palate, but she herself had an inclination to the simple and the spare. "For my own meals I like simplicity above all," she had written in *Serve It Forth*.

Paul opened another bottle of wine and outlined his plans for "*le parking*," which is how he and Julia facetiously referred to the spot at the top of the driveway that they intended to fix up, by putting in some blacktop or gravel. It struck them as amusing to use French in this bastardized way, poking fun at the inherent pomposity of the language, and their own pretensions, too. Another improvement project at La Pitchoune that Paul was set on was the installation of a dishwasher—"*le deesvashaire*," they called it. Of course, this being France, that would require the combined efforts, Paul explained, of (a) a carpenter, (b) a mason, (c) a plumber, and (d) an electrician. All men Paul knew well, since there was always something to be fixed or improved at La Pitchoune.

In the meantime, there was no dishwasher, so after they ate their sorbet, they all helped clean up. "Everyone has been splendid about dish washery," Julia noted gratefully in a letter the following week, "and we have gotten along splendidly and happily. I did go a bit wild on food buying, but it is far better to have a bit too much than too little, *n'est-ce pas?*"

10

SEXUAL POLITICS

M.F. AND ARNOLD GINGRICH WROTE TO EACH other almost every day; letters were at the heart of their relationship. She would sit at the dining table in the house in La Roquette, eating cheese and cold boiled potatoes, or drinking a brandy and Perrier, reading and writing. "I wonder if you've heard from me lately," she wrote. "I hope so, just to keep the threads untangled in the web that binds us." The coming and going of their letters was on a postal service time delay—one was always catching up and circling back.

Gingrich wrote longhand, with news of his travels and travails, how his writing was going, and a lot of New York literary gossip. Who was up to what at *Esquire;* his book deal with Crown (for *The Joys of Trout*). He also sent numerous newspaper and magazine clippings, including, for example, an endless and earnest and somewhat fatuous Charles Reich article in *The New Yorker,* "The Greening of America." It purported to explain that this was an age of generational revolution, when a new, enlightened form of consciousness, which he called "Consciousness III," would emerge. The essay was a sprawling neo-Marxist theory of everything from civil rights to bell-bottom jeans to "Mr. Tambourine Man"—a grand summary of sixties attitudes. It was "more of the same, restated, re-hashed," M.F. wrote back. "Or are people simply hungry for some new kind of medicine?"

M.F. may have dismissed Reich's grandiose theories, but she had long been fundamentally sympathetic to the new movements of the 1960s. She opposed the war in Vietnam, and supported the civil rights movement. Norah, a social worker, was also a committed political liberal, and so were all their children. And of course M.F. had long ago embraced a sort of libertine philosophy, a sensualist's view of the world in which the pleasure of eating extended effortlessly to all the pleasures of life, and where straitlaced morality had no place. This was considered "continental" in the 1930s and '40s; by the 1960s it had begun to resonate with the politics of revolution and rebellion in the United States.

Sex was in the air. Indeed, she knew from the letters she received from readers, and the various requests passed along by her agent, Henry Volkening, that her own work was increasingly being seen in the new, red-tinted light of sexual liberation. She had made her literary reputation with her voluptuous, elliptical writing about food, but it had always encompassed much more than that. "It seems to me," she wrote in the foreword to 1943's *The Gastronomical Me,* "that our three basic needs, for food and security and love, are so mixed and mingled and entwined that we cannot straightly think about one without the others. So it happens that when I write of hunger, I am really writing about love and the hunger for it, and warmth and the love of it and the hunger for it."

In the same book, she described a scene between herself and the man she referred to as "Chexbres" (Dillwyn Parrish, who was not yet her second husband) with a seductive yet reticent portrayal of love and longing:

> There was a bottle of smooth potent gin, unlike any I'd ever tasted. We drank it in glasses Chexbres had bought for them, shaped like crystal eggs almost, and with the caviar it was astonishingly good. We sat whispering and laughing and piling the pungent little black seeds on dry toasted bread, and every swallow of the liquor was as hot and soft as the candle flames around us.
>
> Then, after we had eaten almost all of the caviar and drunk most of the gin, and talked as Chexbres and I always talked, more and better than we ever talked with anyone else, I stood up, thanked him very politely for the beautiful surprise, and walked toward the door to the stairs.

Sometimes, however, M.F. could be quite bold in expressing her desires, including the illicit ones. Writing of a time when she was still married to her first husband, Al, she says:

> In 1935 or 1936, I went back to France with Chexbres and his mother. The whole thing seems so remote now that I cannot say what was sea change and what had already happened on land. I know that I had been in love with Chexbres for three years or so. I was keeping quiet about it; I liked him, and I liked his first wife

who had recently married again, and I was profoundly attached to Al.

By the end of that trip, a few months later, the "profound" attachment to Al had loosened. "The world I had thought to go back to was gone. I knew it, and wondered how I could make Al know too . . ." This was a level of candor that was quite startling at the time she published those words in *The Gastronomical Me*— but much less so thirty years later, when the times were definitely changing, catching up to her.

Now, Volkening asked her, would she be interested in writing a book entitled *How to Cook in Bed—a Primer for Hungry Lovers*? She fielded such requests with some regularity. The answer was a firm no. Not that her writing wasn't explicitly erotic sometimes—it very often was—but context was all. She'd been infuriated when Little, Brown sold an excerpt from her 1961 book *A Cordiall Water* to a stud magazine. "M.F.K. Fisher writes about food as others do about love, only better," Clifton Fadiman had written in *The New Yorker* in 1942, but now a critic in an English newspaper had referred to her as "the past-mistress of gastronomical pornography." She rejected the "Sexy Fisher" label, and explained in a letter to her close friend Eleanor Friede:

> Perhaps Kip Fadiman started the Sexy Saucepan Syndrome
> with his often-quoted remark. But that English critic helped,
> with his often *mis*-quoted one. As you well know, our mores
> have changed since 1937! A renewed interest in Fisher as a
> pornographer, if it happens, can only be a symptom of our
> avid interest in overt sex right now. It is old hat! We just like

to read and talk about it more hungrily than we did twenty or forty years ago. I shall continue to be as straightforward in my voluptuous approach to the pleasures of life as I have been in the past . . .

I just wish my fellow-countrymen were more relaxed. They have been conditioned to believe that there is something basically EVIL about physical and moral sensuality. I cannot possibly agree with them. Therefore their titillation from some of what I have written over the past forty years is their problem, not mine! California girl raised in a Quaker town has managed to imply, and for many years into an almost void, that eating and love can both be fun?

Still, it was undeniably heartening to be recognized, to be in demand, particularly at this moment in time. Contending with challenges to the status quo from women's groups and gays and lesbians (the Stonewall riots in New York had happened in June 1969) and from the civil rights and anti–Vietnam War movements, America was changing for the better, M.F. thought. It was opening up in intriguing ways.

The anti-establishment mood was now filtering into seemingly nonpolitical areas, too, signaling new possibilities, bringing about an infusion of energy. Just as the 1960s had introduced more relaxed attitudes about sex, the same was true of food and cooking. Chefs were no longer necessarily professionally trained—skilled amateurs were beginning to open restaurants and to experiment. For restaurant chefs and home cooks alike, fresh seasonal ingredients were front and center. One bought what looked fresh and created a menu to suit the ingredients, rather than the other way around. Great food was no longer necessarily French, either; it might be American. The embracing, sometimes amusing tone of Child's *French Chef* television program suited the moment better than the classic, pedagogical approach of the *Mastering* volumes, and so did Olney's effusive purism and his seasonal recipes.

As for M.F., she was glad her writing had new currency and sex appeal. She liked fan mail. But she was also aware of a new challenge that the cultural and political landscape had gradually, implacably imposed on her, for how could she continue to write and reminisce about France as she always had? As food and taste were changing, would she blithely keep turning out her "Gastronomy Recalled" columns for *The New Yorker,* with their nostalgia-heavy descriptions of food and drink she had enjoyed, mainly in France?

France had always been at the center of her worldview, her primary source of inspiration, but now, here in France once again, she found herself confronting the seductions and limitations of Francophilia. Were not the poetic evocations of "Gastronomy Recalled" just another, gentler version of the very snobbery she increasingly deplored in Sybille Bedford? There was, after all, in both cases an unspoken assertion of privilege and taste, the source of which was undoubtedly French, and of a prewar vintage.

◆ ◆ ◆

M.F. and Gingrich's correspondence was easygoing and diaristic for the most part, but every so often he would raise the question of "them," their relationship, and what it all meant. He wanted more, he said. He was jealous of her friendships with other men, demanding to know who was gay and who wasn't. "As for Beard," M.F. responded, "he has lived for many years with a male friend, an Italian architect. He is a wonderful person to be with, and is always surrounded by genuinely loving females (like me!). Draw any or all conclusions!"

And "as for talking about 'us as us,'" she wrote, "What, really, is there to say, that we don't already know?" They loved each other, but for her, the connection was more romantic than sexual. Their flirtatious letters kept a sensual element in her life, and sensuality was the current that animated her writing, the very essence of her philosophy—the entwining of hunger and love. They would never really be together, but for M.F., that wasn't the point. The fact was that M.F. was set in her solitary ways, and happy to continue in them.

·11·

TWILIGHT
OF THE SNOBS

RICHARD OLNEY HAD NOT PARTICULARLY
wanted to come, but here he was, making his way through the
Cannes station early on Monday morning, December 14, 1970,
newly arrived from Paris on the overnight train after the *CVF* dinner at Lucas Carton. The trip had taken nine hours.

He looked around for Lord, who'd promised to pick him up. It
was she who had invited him to stay at Les Bastides and insisted
that he come. She had arranged a busy schedule for him. First there
was to be an early lunch with her and M. F. K. Fisher. Later that
day he was to pay visits to Julia Child and then to James Beard,
and that night he would be attending the collaboration dinner Lord,
Bedford, and M.F. were hosting. M.F. was, maybe, possibly, Lord
implied yet again, going to write about him in *The New Yorker*.

These were the grand titans of the American food world, and
Olney had come to pay his respects. That was Lord's unspoken
idea anyway—that he ingratiate himself so as to be inducted into
the rarified circle of the American food elite.

Lord meant well. She was an old friend and he loved her. She was right; the success of his book did depend in part on the good will of people such as Child, Beard, and M.F. It was through connections with them and those in their orbit that one arranged to teach cooking classes, write for American food magazines, and publish cookbooks. But he would not kowtow, or play the role of eager young acolyte, thankful to be included. For one thing, at forty-three, he wasn't exactly young anymore. And for another, he measured himself not by his professional success in America—the sales of his cookbook—but by his skill as a cook. He would never be much good at self-promotion. He was too proud to shill.

And so he would pay his respects, but he would demand respect, too. It was he in this group, and he alone, who lived in this country; who was a contributor to its preeminent food and wine publication; whose closest friend, Georges Garin, was a preeminent Paris chef; who had been embraced, in other words, by the French food establishment. More than that, Olney had managed to absorb at a seemingly molecular level the intuitions, knowledge, palate, and prejudices of French cooking, from rustic to haute cuisine, and to articulate the mythological essence of *bœuf bourguignon,* or *gigot d'agneau,* or bouillabaisse.

He was a better cook, he was quite sure, than any of the other Americans in the group. He was an artist. And didn't that count for something?

+ + +

In the small kitchen of her rented apartment in La Roquette, M.F. was deveining shrimp. She liked shrimp; they were pretty little creatures. She had written about them at some length in her latest book,

With Bold Knife and Fork, noting how Asian brush-painters liked to use shrimp as models, and that the best she'd ever eaten were in Venice, "caught in unmentionable locations in the canals . . . served peeled in a bowl with enough herbs to mask the dangers and enough wine in the glass to counteract them."

She was planning a similarly simple dish for the long-awaited "collaboration dinner" that Lord had planned for Olney. Shrimp, baked with parsley and garlic, butter and bread crumbs. She usually served this dish warm, but it would be room temperature today for convenience's sake. She wanted something she could make now and then carry across the street to Les Bastides when the time came.

With a small, sharp knife, she split a prawn down the back, took out the vein, and then placed it cut side down in a baking dish that was well covered with olive oil. She continued in this manner until all the shrimp were peeled, letting them marinate in the oil for a while. Then she turned them all over, sprinkled parsley on them, and put the dish in the oven.

She poured herself a vermouth. She was anticipating an awkward evening. She liked Olney—she and Lord had taken him to lunch in Mouans-Sartoux earlier in the afternoon—but he was a tightly wound personality. He seemed on edge. And in her own steely, quiet way, she was on edge, too. For one thing, M.F. had reached the limit of her tolerance for Bedford's unrelenting superiority and snobbism, her persistent reminders of M.F.'s ignorance and "American" extravagance. There were stern dissertations about decorum, the proper pronunciation of French words, and in fact almost everything.

Just the other day, M.F. had been subjected to an entire conversation about tipping. Bedford was opposed to tipping on principle, she said, though she did comply with convention as a matter of courtesy. The waiter at a restaurant was paid a salary to do his job—why did he also require a tip? He didn't. A few coins left on the table were surely fine.

Americans, on the other hand, were liable to leave extravagant and unnecessary tips. It was vulgar. Bedford herself was a notably meager tipper, M.F. had not failed to notice.

"Ah well," said M.F.

Bedford's comments were indirect, but unmistakably aimed at her. Had M.F. really been tipping far too much? She didn't think so. It was true that she would rather leave too much than too little. She liked waiters. She paid particular attention to their shoes, which were, for a waiter, the tools of his trade, since he was always on his feet. There was a line in Simenon somewhere to that effect, she remembered, about waiters treating their feet well.

She said none of this to Bedford. "Ah well," she said again.

Bedford got as much mileage as was possible to get from an English accent and European aristocratic bearing. She declaimed. She projected unimpeachable hauteur. She talked about wine with great vim and unstoppable vigor. And she had nothing but disdain for Americans. They had no taste. They tipped too much, M.F. had heard her say, for what must have been the fifth time that day.

More distressing than Bedford's pontification was Lord's apparent subjugation. She murmured and demurred, deflected, and then lapsed into silence. She seemed unhappy most of the time. M.F. wanted to tell Lord that if she ever needed a place to stay, to flee for a while, she was always welcome to stay with her in California. M.F. hadn't yet found the moment.

But it was more than Bedford and Lord that was bothering her, more than silly talk about tipping that had her on edge. It was a creeping, ominous sense of being hemmed in by the past.

It was her own doing. She and Norah had come to France in search of the scenes that had given them so many happy memories, and they had found them, in Dijon, Aix, Paris. . . . But since the moment Norah left for California, the spell had been broken. The sisterly intimacy, the shared memories, the Simenon novels and late afternoon glasses of wine had been a sentimental journey, and now it was over.

In its place, she was seeing the dark side of sentimentality, the fossilized remnants of outdated attitudes and ideas, in the form of Bedford's relentless enforcement of proper rules and opinions and behaviors. It wasn't that Bedford was tedious or stupid; she was formidably intelligent. But she had no discernible sense of humor, unless you counted sarcasm. Her every utterance reflected a world-view that seemed unchanged since the 1930s.

M.F. needed to escape, and soon, to move beyond both nostalgia and snobbery. She needed to write.

She took the shrimp from the oven and spooned bread crumbs and minced garlic on each one. She dotted them with butter. She would take them out when the bread crumbs were brown and the shrimp had started to curl.

✦ ✦ ✦

At La Pitchoune, Julia and Paul cleaned up after the previous evening's dinner party. It had been great fun, they agreed, as they corralled stray wineglasses and emptied ashtrays. (Lord smoked heavily, and had a disconcerting cough.) Seeing Beard and M.F. had been a pleasure, as always, though once again the Childs worried about the dire state of Beard's health, wondering if his swollen legs were a sign of heart trouble.

The Childs particularly enjoyed entertaining in Provence: the house was beautiful, and so was the countryside. The mood there always seemed a bit giddier than back home: everyone was on vacation. And now they were expecting another guest, Richard Olney.

Olney arrived at La Pitchoune in midafternoon, just as Lord had said he would. Paul greeted him politely and then retreated to his study. Julia offered him a drink, but he declined. She told Olney, first of all, how much she admired his book. He was obviously deeply knowledgeable about wines, but he wrote about them without too much detail, and in such an accessible, approachable way. The recipes, too, were very personal. She liked that.

Olney nodded. Of course she did.

Olney did not say anything at all critical to Child, but he was reticent, and gave the impression of not quite wanting to be there. Cagey but polite, he told her he thought her grated zucchini recipe was a "valuable innovation."

He was referring to *Courgettes Rapées*, in which Child and Beck describe grating, salting, and squeezing the water from zucchini, and then sautéing them with butter and shallots. This was the base recipe for a number of variations.

"I immediately tried it," said Olney. But he was unable to resist adding: "I do prefer the sautéed paper-thin slices that I eat about three times weekly when alone."

Child congratulated Olney on the rave review of his book in the *New York Times*. He should count himself lucky, she said, for Nika Hazelton, the *Times* food writer, was a "nasty, vicious old cow."

Olney immediately resented the word *lucky*. As if he hadn't quite deserved the acclaim. In fact, as he recalled, Hazelton had in the very same review pointed out the overcomplicated and not quite "Simon-pure French" nature of Julia's book, while noting of his: "The unfussiness of the recipes is remarkable, though Mr. Olney sticks to the traditional French kitchen techniques with very little compromise." His book was correct, demanding, and true.

Whereas Child was a mass-market phenomenon. Her TV show was seen by millions. Her audience was American housewives—nothing should be too difficult or complicated. Or, if it was complicated, it needed to be explained in painful detail—like the endless recipe for French bread in Child and Beck's new *Mastering II* book. *Absolutely hair-raising,* Olney thought. He would not think of trying to follow those instructions, and doubted anyone else would, either. "I am completely puzzled," he wrote in a letter to his brother:

> It seems almost as if, after having successfully cajoled the American housewife into an acceptance of French-type cooking—after having, in fact, single-handedly transformed the culinary face of America—the co-authors had decided to play a good joke on her and scare her out of her wits—all that stuff wrapped in paste, and the explanations about how to stuff a pig's gut are nearly as endless as for breadmaking.

The very idea of baking a baguette at home was nonsensical in France, as was the thought of homemade sausage. These were things one bought at the local *boulangerie* or charcuterie. Olney might not have known, or might have forgotten, since he had not lived there since the 1950s, that in America decent bread and charcuterie were quite hard to find. Child's goal was to make them accessible to

Americans using ingredients from their local supermarkets, even if, from Olney's perspective, her recipes were clumsy, inelegant, and inauthentic.

Child, meanwhile, was perfectly aware of Olney's not very well-camouflaged disdain, his sense that he represented the more authentically French approach. He had been far warmer with Beck when they met last summer, and no wonder. She was, after all, *la Super-Française*.

Indeed, Olney considered Beck the far superior cook. Now he asked after her, and Child explained that Beck and her husband had gone to Paris and were coming back the following week. Beck was planning a New Year's Eve *réveillon* dinner to which Olney was certainly welcome. Impossible—he would be in Italy, he explained, in Vicenza.

Their conversation continued this way for some time. Pleasant and polite on the surface, but full of veiled, barbed remarks and prickly personality, hinting at an argument about the soul of cooking, how French it was, or ought to be. Olney's lack of respect for Child boiled down to two seemingly contradictory points of authenticity. On the one hand, she catered to the American housewife, she appeared on television giving basic cooking lessons, and she focused in her cookbooks too much on the practical (full of "ahead-of-time notes" and the like) at the expense of the artistic. She wrote for beginners. And on the other hand, she was overly fond of the grandiose and dramatic, Olney thought—meats wrapped in pastry, ridiculously complicated desserts. Some of the recipes in *Mastering II* were not far removed from what Olney witheringly called "Grand Palace" cooking.

So Child was too American, and her recipes were too French, in the wrong way. Not that Olney said any of this.

But of course, Child could tell. And as she had with Beck, she decided she didn't really care what Olney thought, or what the proper "French" approach to cooking was presumed to be. She was moving on.

◆ ◆ ◆

Olney and Beard had never met, and Olney's first impression was of a "huge, gentle and benign creature—touching, sad, and very ill." It was a remarkable contrast to the persona Beard presented in his columns, of the eminently authoritative and insatiable gourmet. Their meeting later that afternoon took place at Pathé's clinic in Grasse, where Beard was staying for a few more days. Beard was happy to see his visitor—curious to meet Olney, and eager as always for any distractions: from his book and from his diet.

Olney thanked him for the positive review of his book, which is what had brought them together. He knew that Beard was the godfather of the American food world, and he appreciated the generosity Beard had shown to a first-time author. (Beard had done the same for Julia and Simca when they started out—he was always a great champion of new talent, new chefs, new restaurants.)

Beard was most amusing in his description of his "salt-free, alcohol-free, starch-free, food-free diet." He jokingly suggested that the doctors had some secret plan to administer shock treatments, which would turn him away from food and wine for life. Impossible, of course. In any case, he said, he was due to escape this nuthouse in a matter of days.

Olney described for Beard, by way of contrast, the elaborate *CVF* meal he'd had in Paris the previous weekend. It had in fact been *over*elaborate, but the wines had been stunning. The editor of

CVF was a good friend, he said—Odette Kahn; Beard must meet her. Beard knew the magazine, of course, and held forth for a while on the food business in America and France, his book in progress, his newspaper column, and gossip about chefs and restaurants.

He asked Olney if he was planning to write for any of the American food magazines—he knew all the editors and could make introductions. No need, said Olney; his literary agent in New York had already done so. "I have no idea if *Gourmet* magazine has accepted or will accept my socio-gastronomic study of the French lower classes," he said, describing his first commission. "Although they assigned it, I believe they wanted something else."

The article he'd written was about rustic cooking traditions, something he'd been thinking about more and more. Pot roasts, braises . . .

And what about his next cookbook? Beard asked. He would be happy to put in a good word at any of the publishing houses.

If Olney was meant to be impressed, he wasn't. As with Child, he felt secretly superior to Beard; he had almost no interest in the *American Cookery* book, for example. It sounded dreadful. Olney was entirely focused on the nuances of French cooking. He refused to be impressed with Beard's status in the American food world. He just didn't care about the inner workings of the New York restaurant business, or the New York food magazine business, or the New York cookbook publishing business. (Or at least Olney did not wish to *appear* to care about such things.) He held business matters at arm's length, and viewed them with a bit of scorn. This was why he pointedly did not have a telephone. His interest was the art of cooking and not the commerce of cookbooks.

And so Olney soon decided, in his uncharitable way, that Beard talked too much—all banal pronouncements and clichés. "He had arrived at the oracular period in his career," Olney would write of Beard, "when he expected listeners to bow in silence to his superior wisdom. I bowed in silence to nonsense as long as it did not touch me, personally."

Olney was a man given to resentments; he nurtured and tended to them. When Beard asked him, a little over a year later, to give private cooking lessons to his longtime partner, Gino Cofacci, Olney readily agreed, while privately bemoaning Beard's "selfishness and willingness to use friends." At the same time, Olney was making good use of Beard's connections and knowledge as he arranged to teach a cooking class (his first) in Avignon that summer, sending Beard incongruously affectionate, intimate letters all the while. He wrote about the menus he planned, who had enrolled in the class, his hopes that Beard would attend one of the dinners, and about his love life. "I continue to moon around dreaming of my baby," he wrote of a boyfriend. "He keeps writing how much he wants to return here without promising that it can be a certainty."

When Beard asked Olney to demonstrate boning a chicken for his friend and protégé Carl Jerome, Beard had said, "Of course, I would teach him, myself, but my hands are too big." To which Olney silently retorted, "Why are *my* hands not too big to bone a quail?" He resented the fact that Beard wouldn't openly acknowledge his superior skill with a knife, and in the kitchen in general.

Olney's ambivalence about the food world was partly just a reflection of his personality. Beard, generous as always, immediately judged him to be a "deeply introspective" person, uncomfortable with those he did not know well, very much the opposite of Beard himself. But of course Olney was also a snob—quick to evaluate and always self-righteous, always holding himself aloof. More fundamentally, though, his dyspeptic view of Beard (and Child, too) reflected his allegiance to a purist, artistic outlook on cooking. The ingredients were pure, the dishes were pure, and he, too, was pure. It was an outlook oddly well suited to the historical moment.

As Beard filled the small room in the Grasse clinic with a stream of talk and gossip, Olney smiled tightly and nodded politely. But in his reserve and silence were judgments. He found Beard wanting.

◆ ◆ ◆

The "collaboration dinner" was a slow-moving train wreck. It started off well enough. They poured drinks.

M.F. drank vermouth on the rocks with a splash of gin.

Olney drank scotch.

Lord smoked cigarettes.

Bedford was in her study, writing. It was late afternoon by now. Olney had completed his visits with the Childs and Beard, a gauntlet that left him feeling relieved and irritated in equal measure. He was happy to have acquitted himself well, to have charmed them as best he could. But he was also filled with quiet resentment at their complacency and self-importance. What he saw as his own obeisance—which anyone else might have seen as a simple courtesy, paid to people who had been generous to him—left a bitter taste in his mouth.

Lord had made a lamb *navarin*, which was cooking in the oven. It had at least an hour to go, she said. The smells were delicious—the meat stewing in a light tomato broth with carrots, potatoes, turnips, and pearl onions.

M.F. and Olney had greeted each other warmly, drawn together by their affection for Lord. They all sat in the dining room at Les Bastides, drinking and talking. Bedford emerged briefly and, in mock-regal fashion, explained that her contribution to the dinner had been to pour kirsch upon the fruit for their dessert. It was now macerating in the refrigerator. Then she returned to her manuscript, the biography of Aldous Huxley.

Olney poured himself another scotch and lit a cigarette. He said little about his visits to La Pitchoune or to Grasse. The Childs were fine, he reported, wonderful. Beard seemed quite ill, but they knew that already; they'd seen him at dinner yesterday. Lord and M.F. chatted about restaurants and art—they'd been to the Grimaldi Museum in Antibes two days ago, and stopped for lunch at L'Oursin, sharing a couple dozen oysters between them. It was a good time of year for mussels and oysters—they were "small and crisp." M.F. had been eating shellfish in great numbers, she said—dozens and dozens of them.

Olney showed polite interest. He was half-expecting (and half-dreading) the conversation to turn to him, that M.F. might show her hand as a journalist. Presumably she would tell him at some point if she was indeed working on a *New Yorker* piece on him, and would ask questions about his cookbook and his life in France.

But no, she was talking about Picasso.

The Château Grimaldi displayed mostly works Picasso had produced immediately after the war, while living in the South of France and using whatever materials could be had in the mid-1940s, including house paint. He'd also begun making ceramics. All of it was vigorous, bright, and joyful. "Picasso was a happy man in his 60s!" M.F. exclaimed. She had turned sixty not that long ago herself, and was acutely aware of the ebb and flow of creativity. The perennial question of "What Next?" was looming ever larger in her mind.

Olney glowered into his drink. Lord wandered off to the kitchen. More than ever these days, she seemed elusive, wan, enigmatic. M.F. continued to worry about her, withering in Bedford's shadow. Left alone with Olney, M.F. confessed that she was concerned about Lord, and what did he think? M.F. and Olney were Lord's oldest friends, so they owed her support, M.F. thought. A place to stay, for example, if she were to leave Bedford.

But Olney brushed her off. Lord was perfectly okay. Furthermore, he said coldly, he was "not into breaking up friends' love relationships." M.F. dropped the subject.

It was dinnertime.

SHRIMP TAILS

NAVARIN OF LAMB

MACÉDOINE OF FRESH FRUIT

The meal was simple, nothing like the grand feast Olney had prepared. But that was its charm. It was a potluck.

Bedford took charge of the wine. She opened a white to start. Olney told her about the wines he'd had at the *CVF* dinner. Petit Village, Mouton Rothschild, Margaux, Yquem—they had all been transcendent. Bedford asked about the vintages, and she and Olney were off and running: the Petit Village had been a '64, the Mouton Rothschild a '59 . . .

M.F.'s shrimp were piled on a platter in the center of the table.

The wine talk continued as they ate. The shrimp were sweet and delicious, although the cooking butter had congealed in the bottom of the dish as it cooled on the counter. Ah well. M.F. caught Olney's studiously disapproving look as he maneuvered a shrimp to his plate.

Bedford was assessing California wines as compared with French wines. The French were better, obviously. She and Lord had visited Napa Valley in the spring of 1969, and M.F. had taken them to a few of the local wineries.

"Some pleasant wines," Bedford decreed. "And some very very good ones; not great, but good."

This was just the sort of dismissive thing that Bedford would say, of course. And it was also, if she were completely honest about it, just the sort of thing M.F. herself might have said, not so long ago. Not about California wine, which she knew and loved, but about some other wine, perhaps. So why did the words rankle M.F. so?

Well, the opinion was wrong, first of all. There were indeed great Napa Valley wines—she'd had them! But Bedford's opinion, conforming as it did with conventional wisdom and French prejudice, sounded impeccably authoritative and true, and rankled therefore all the more. And her voice—that casually assured tone of definitive judgment, on something about which definitive judgments were elusive, if not impossible.

M.F. said she had to disagree about Napa wines. What about Beringer, and Beaulieu, and Inglenook? She'd been closely involved with the developing wine culture in Napa throughout the sixties, as a founding trustee of the Napa Valley Wine Library, a collection of rare books and historical documents related to wine. She was one of the original champions for the local winemakers, hosting dinners and tastings at her house in St. Helena. And some of the wine, by now, was spectacular.

Bedford nodded without seeming to agree. Then it was back to French wine:

The 1953 Margaux he'd had the other night, Olney said—now that was great. It had reminded him of the scintillating, filigree-structured 1924 Margaux. But gentler, somehow.

On and on the oenological conversation went until Bedford finally changed the subject. She and Lord had been invited to *four* masquerade parties over the holidays, she said. They were becoming a highlight of the expat social calendar. Their entree into this world was Allanah Harper, who was for Bedford a kind of patron saint of the arts—not to mention of real estate, as they were living on her property, Les Bastides. They loved it here.

"We were living in year's or half-year's snatches in rented houses or flats in Dorset, in London, in Portugal, in Essex," Bedford explained, describing her and Lord's peripatetic life in the sixties. "Then London again, then Italy: the Browning villa at Asolo, an intolerable mistake with a sudden recourse to where we should have started: the south of France."

The "intolerable" Asolo villa had been owned by the poet Robert Browning in the late nineteenth century, had later belonged to the Guinness family of Ireland, and was now a small hotel run by Giuseppe Cipriani. Bedford specialized in this sort of name-dropping. She did not explain what had been intolerable about the place, beautiful as it was. The "sudden recourse" had been Harper's invitation to stay in the annex at Les Bastides.

Harper had attended the masquerade party last year dressed as a prince, Bedford continued, and had brought her coiffeur from Paris to do her hair in Grecian curls of pure gold, to match her gold body paint and makeup.

The very thought of this scenario—the cross-dressing social-ite in gold body paint—had Bedford laughing. It struck her as the height of winking panache and audacity.

To M.F., the party sounded like one of the lower depths of hell, passé and a little embarrassing, decadent in all the wrong ways. What were these people thinking exactly? It was as if they were living in a tiny little bubble, self-satisfied and self-amused, putting on masks so as to see even *less*.

The party this weekend was at a hotel in Cannes, and Bedford had devised a brilliant costume of her own, she said; it was abso-lutely hilarious. She had rented a palanquin, and would be carried into the ballroom wearing a fantastic robe and holding a bottle of 1879 vintage port wine, which she would present to the hostess as a gift. Then she would reveal, opening her robes, that she was dressed as a "Limey sailor" from that same period.

M.F. really ought to come, Bedford said.

M.F. made noncommittal noises.

Lord brought the *navarin* to the table in an enameled pot. She had parboiled green beans and strewn them on the stew in the final minutes of cooking, a beautiful dash of color on the rich, still-simmering surface. Olney piled the stew into large bowls. Bedford opened another wine, and they toasted again. The *navarin* was ro-bust, warming—it was "admirable," Olney said. They ate in si-lence.

And now M.F. seized the moment. After the never-ending wine talk and the discussion of Italian villas and masquerade ball plans, steeped as it all was in retrograde snobbery and privilege, M.F. felt compelled to turn the conversation to politics. Left-wing politics. California liberal-radical politics. The civil rights movement, the free speech movement, the antiwar movement, the antipoverty movement, the student movement. Were they interested in these things in Europe?

A few years earlier, in the summer and fall of 1964, M.F. had gone to Mississippi to teach at a boarding school for black children called Piney Woods—this was during the "Freedom Summer," which saw the murder of three civil rights activists in the state. She taught literature and composition classes to high school and junior college students. She had gone because she felt the need to "do more than stand here," she said, as the struggle for civil rights was taking place. Piney Woods had made 1960s politics tangible and personal. She told the story, by way of illustrating the changing cultural and social atmosphere, of a lunch at her house in St. Helena this past fall, just before she came to Europe. She'd invited her friend Paul Cobb and his sister Mary over, and various other friends had dropped in, turning the lunch into an impromptu party. Paul was head of the antipoverty program in Berkeley, and a labor and civil rights activist. Charismatic and egomaniacal, he was frequently arrested for his civil disobedience. His sister—tiny, but with a big, exciting voice—had started to sing, and the songs had filled the air.

"We all sat there in the living room, hardly breathing," M.F. said. "She just put back her head and let it flow . . . a lot of freedom songs, and then several parts of *Le Nozze di Figaro*. I felt quite moved by all of it."

It's not that M.F. expected them to care about black activists singing protest songs and Mozart operettas at liberal lunch gatherings in Napa Valley, but she did want to get across the idea that there was more to life than masquerade balls and a 1953 Margaux. That America was changing, and like it or not, so was France, however slowly. She had felt it in Aix: the energy on the streets, even on the stately Cours Mirabeau. The aftereffects of the May 1968 protests could still be felt. The old order was giving way.

Still, it was in America that the changes could be felt more immediately, where a generational shift and numerous political movements were forcing the country to become its better self. That was why she'd gone to Mississippi.

With her soft voice and in a roundabout, anecdotal way, M.F. had driven straight to the heart of the moral problem of the evening, as she saw it. In Mary Cobb's searing, spine-tingling voice—M.F. could almost feel it now—was the sound of liberation and openness, the very opposite of the insular world Bedford represented. Could there be a greater contrast? There was Mary Cobb, "black as coal," singing freedom songs. And there was Allanah Harper, painting herself gold. There was the tangible, human desire for justice. And there were the corruptions of privilege.

Olney yawned.

◆ ◆ ◆

M.F. left soon after dessert. Lord went to bed.

Olney and Bedford poured more drinks. And a few more after that. And now the truth came out.

What Olney felt was nothing but disdain for the American

gastronomes he'd seen that day, he told Bedford. M.F.'s whining, liberal nonsense. Child's undeserved fame and stature. Beard's self-satisfied self-importance.

Olney held forth:

On Child: "The fact that she's a television star doesn't mean she knows how to cook."

On M.F.: "She remains sweet but is essentially empty-headed, has no palate (eats practically nothing and drinks great tumblers-full of vermouth all day) and her writing is silly, pretentious, sentimental and unreadable drivel."

On Beard: "A pompous buffoon."

And more on M.F.: "A pathetic creature."

And on Child: "Bitter . . . irrationally anti-French."

Olney and Bedford were enjoying themselves.

"I came away feeling rather unclean for having been such a bitch," Olney wrote in a letter to his brother later that week, "and, at the same time, feeling quite cleansed for having been forced into being verbally honest about what I felt."

It was as if all the lingering resentments of the day had found a sudden, cathartic outlet in Olney's late-night encounter with "mad old Sybille," as he called her, who was, not coincidentally, just as vicious as he. They brought out the worst in each other: cutting, cruel superiority and a sneaking and rather pleasurable misanthropy, all expressed in the form of bitter complaint and vindictive character assessments. They issued "critical, negative, destructive judgments about everything and everyone," Olney wrote his brother. "The terrible thing is that we agreed about everything."

He knew they were being petty and personal, but he did enjoy the almost camp theatricality of Bedford's snobbery. Her ruthless, aristocratic views appealed to his own resentments, his sense of un-recognized superiority. He was seen by the others as the newcomer and ingénue, and yet it was *he* who had written the more important and more sophisticated cookbook. Child and Beard represented compromise and commerce. Selling books and appearing on televi-sion was what mattered to them. They were vulgar.

As for M.F., her "interminable and pointless" stories about Cali-fornia politics were reviled, and her writing dismissed. It was clear enough that she was not working on any story about Olney for *The New Yorker,* as Lord had intimated, and that was just as well. Lord had piled M.F.'s books in his arms and asked him several times what he thought of her old friend: "Very nice, ever so sweet, I like her very much," he'd said. But the truth was he thought the books were terrible.

"Trash," he told Bedford.

The problem was he just didn't respect these people. They were not authentic. Indeed, they were frauds, with their American-accented French, their inability to cook with any kind of intuitive grace, their follow-the-numbers cookbooks for American house-wives.

Olney justified his vicious outburst with his belief in himself as an auteur. Cooking was something he had elevated to an art form. He had found a way to express the deep connection between French food and the French way of life—its insistence on only the freshest, in-season ingredients, its refusal to take shortcuts, its celebration of taste.

And it was true: he had indeed written an original and brilliant cookbook.

He viewed himself as uncompromising in his commitment to

excellence, and therefore entitled to his scorn for the other Americans, all of whom he found compromised in one way or another. But it was also true that he was someone who simply *enjoyed* feeling scornful, whatever the circumstances.

Olney circled back to Child, taking note of her penchant for wrapping meats in pastry dough, as evidenced by the multiple recipes for meat *en croûte* in the new *Mastering* book. (He blamed Child, not Beck, for everything he didn't like about the book.) "In Escoffier's *Guide Culinaire*," he said, referring to the 1903 classic, "out of forty-five recipes for roast filet of beef, not one is served in pastry." And what about all the recipes for various things being flambéed? Desserts and other dishes flaming dramatically, causing children and Americans to ooh and aah. "None of Escoffier's recipes for crêpes are flamed," he said, "including crêpes Suzette—whose distinguishing characteristic, after all, is the presence, not of flames, but of tangerine juice." Flambéing was ridiculous—it was a cliché!

Speaking of uncouth, unknowing Americans, Bedford said, they tipped too much. Had she mentioned that?

"I have a feeling," Olney said, by now quite drunk, "that I shall shortly break ties with the whole fucking business and run and hide (who knows, perhaps paint). I'm more and more surprised, in retrospect, that anyone accepted to publish my book."

◆ ◆ ◆

Of course, none of Olney's targets heard his bitter words. But the suddenly pressurized atmosphere surrounding all the food people at this time, on this very day, was something they all felt. The sparks were flying for a reason.

It was Olney who had set them off. His arrival on the train that morning served to crystallize the changes that had been developing over the previous weeks and months among this small circle of friends, particularly for M.F. and Child. So much was changing so quickly—in America, in France—and they could tell they themselves were changing, too, even if they weren't sure how. But the sudden, bracing appearance of the cantankerous Olney was a tipping point.

His cagey contempt for all of them, his insistent purity, his obvious talent. His relative youth.

Olney was a snob. And he was provocative because he was a new kind of snob—perfectly conversant in the authoritative snobbery of Old Europe, the unspoken but rigorous assertion of "good taste" above all else, as represented by "mad old Sybille," but just as likely to find fault with an overelaborate *CVF* dinner at Lucas Carton. Bound up in his unforgiving personality were claims on both French tradition and refinement, and Provençal kitchen-garden bohemianism.

It was a combination that propelled the others to continue to reevaluate their own devotion to France—to begin to move away in decisive fashion from their France fixation. Olney had arrived at just the moment at which M.F. and Child were losing their patience with snobbery, and at which Beard was in the final throes of writing his American cooking opus.

They were all contending with what amounted to a philosophical problem: a question of taste and style and authenticity, and specifically how those qualities were expressed in food and cooking—things they all cared deeply about. What was it, exactly, that they were doing? Teaching Americans to cook French food? No, that wasn't it, that had never been it. Child had always known that what she did was teach people to be fearless, unintimidated, to try and if necessary to try again, to cook, to taste, to enjoy, to have fun—although she herself had been having ever less fun with Beck. That was going to change. And M.F., too, had not simply been celebrating French food and hedonism all these years; she'd been writing about something more essential, about how to *live*, to find pleasure in the moment. But was she herself living too much in the past? She was determined to find out.

In some ways, this day marked an inevitable break, the moment of American disillusionment with the sentimental glories of France. It was a world that M.F. and Lord and Bedford had all preserved in their books, and one that could still be tasted in a bottle of 1924 Margaux. It was this world that had inspired Child and Beard to learn to cook, and M.F. to do much of her writing (and living). The glamour of the prewar Europe of their youth—of the 1920s and '30s—was a lifelong influence. They had all absorbed in some unconscious way the era's terms of art, the art of eating, a way of being.

It was a beautiful world, preserved in the amber of fiction and memory. A world of faded aristocrats and remembered vintages, of boat trains and small family-run hotels that never changed, of excursions to Switzerland and meals in French restaurants where the *sole meunière* was always impeccably fresh and perfectly cooked. The ethos and aesthetic of the period had survived all the way through the 1960s, a worldview held together with wit and irony, tone and inflection, unimpeachable taste, and finally, at bottom, enforced by the logic of money and privilege.

But the mood had changed. The easy authority of the cultured and discerning was not so easy anymore.

For M.F., who had invented the very tropes of the genre, there was no going back. She would not be writing about ocean crossings and excursions to Switzerland anymore. Or idealized recollections of *sole meunière*. Olney and Bedford's curdled snobbery was a sign of the end of an era.

Even Olney could tell.

When he saw Bedford again in London, some months later, he described her in a letter to Beard:

> Eda and Sybille were also there, the latter suffering from a knee infection and being very grand dame limping around, clinging desperately to her cane with lace white gloved hands, her sharp tongue in no way affected by her affliction.

Olney adored Bedford and her sharp tongue, and had an ironic appreciation for the comedy and cruelty inherent in her militant policing of taste. But, twenty years younger than she, he was also aware that she was an artifact of the old order—that she was clinging desperately not just to her cane, but to a way of life that had run its course.

During that same London trip, Olney met Elizabeth David for the first time. She had read his cookbook and, knowing he was a friend of Bedford and Lord's, sent him a letter asking him to look her up next time he was in London. Also very much in "grand dame" mode, David purported to be shocked when Olney pronounced *basil* with an American accent, using a long *a:* "You don't r-e-a-l-l-y pronounce it that way, do you?" she asked. She hated basil: "I have no use for it," she said. As for his cookbook: "Of course, your food is *much* too grand for the likes of me," she said, mockingly. And so it went over an afternoon bottle or two of white wine, the judgmentalism part real, part comic put-on. By the end of the day they were great friends.

"Her observations about people were often scathing, but only because they were so devastatingly accurate," Olney later wrote. About M.F., for example, they agreed entirely: "Of course I am not supposed to say this [muffled laughter] but I do find her writing to be *too* detestable," David remarked.

Both of these encounters—with Bedford and with David— were emblematic of what M.F. and Child knew they had to put behind them: the ancien régime clinging to its privileges with lace-gloved hands, issuing scathing insults interrupted by muffled, cruel laughter. As Olney himself recognized, in spite of his great affection for both women, there was an air of self-parody and incipient irrelevance in the hollow superiority they projected. And they seemed to know it, too, to know that their time was past, which was perhaps what made them so spiteful.

This was the twilight of the snobs. Snobbish as he was, Olney had no desire to disappear into the twilight with them.

~12~

ESCAPE

M.F. HAD TO LEAVE. SHE WOULD NOT SIT THROUGH another dinner like the one of the previous night. Nor would she be attending any costume balls. She'd had enough. Enough of Bedford and Olney, their insufferable snobbery and boozy one-upmanship, enough of her own polite, too-mild responses to them.

She had realized, thinking back on the evening, that the problem wasn't Bedford or Olney.

It was her.

If she felt trapped at Les Bastides by the stifling atmosphere, it was one that she had played a role in creating. She had been celebrating the good life in France in her books since her twenties, and she had never stopped. She had always been honest in her writing, and with herself, and she had never been a snob. She could write just as elegantly about a single ripe tomato, or the potato chips she ate at the bar at the Lausanne Palace, as she could about mounds of caviar. But she could see that her writing was now trapped in the past. The *New*

Yorker column she'd been writing for the past couple of years was called "Gastronomy Recalled," after all.

This trip, which had started out as a self-consciously nostalgic attempt to revisit the glories of France, had stirred in her a kind of elemental doubt. If there was one thing Bedford and Olney had caused M.F. to realize, it was that she could no longer keep telling the same stories over and over again.

She wanted to immerse herself in the present, to write about what she saw, now. She needed to move forward.

She would leave in a matter of days and travel to Arles, where she would spend Christmas, alone, and then go to Marseille. Judith Jones had called from New York, and they had agreed to meet in Marseille just after the New Year to go over edits on *Among Friends*. And so her travel plans were set.

She told Lord and Bedford that she needed to immerse herself in her writing and would not be staying on at Les Bastides. They were courteous enough, avoiding any prickly remarks, leaving much unsaid, as always. She did not see Olney, which was fine with her. He was staying at Les Bastides for the next few days.

She had never found the moment to talk to Lord—really talk to her. So that was another thing that went unsaid: M.F.'s fear that Bedford was grinding Lord down; her vague desire to rescue her old friend, to offer her sanctuary. Perhaps she hesitated, too, at the prospect of seeming sneaky or treacherous.

She called Raymond Gatti and arranged to be picked up and taken to Cannes in order to buy a train ticket and exchange money at the American Express office.

"I should be packing," she wrote in a letter to Gingrich, "but feel rather more fatalistic than usual about What Next."

What next: not only the trip to Arles, but the rest of her life.

When Gatti arrived they drove first to Grasse, to pick up Beard at the diet clinic. He'd called that morning and, hearing of her Cannes excursion, offered to join her.

M.F. was in a contemplative mood, but delighted to see Beard. He had an infectious laugh, and he laughed often. When they got to Cannes, Beard stayed in the car while M.F. ran her errands, reading his mail and a few recent weekly magazines from New York. When M.F. got back to the car, Beard handed her a story announcing that Craig Claiborne was leaving the *New York Times*.

Well, this was news—of the most intriguing sort! Why was he leaving? Who would replace him? Claiborne had single-handedly invented the position of the *Times* food critic, and made himself a power in the food world.

An old school Francophile, Claiborne was respected by all and beloved at the *Times*, but he was bored with reviewing restaurants. And now, apparently, he was branching out on his own and planning to launch a newsletter called *The Craig Claiborne Journal*. It would be serious food and restaurant journalism, and would free him from the daily demands of the newspaper.

M.F. and Beard discussed successors. Well, what about Michael Field? He certainly had the ambition. But could he put up with the grind? Or Gael Greene of *New York* magazine? She was young and irreverent. There was no obvious choice—it was like trying to find another Sheila Hibben for *The New Yorker*, M.F. thought—impossible. (Hibben was the original restaurant and food writer at the magazine and had died in 1964.)

The next day, M.F. bid farewell to the Childs and to Beard after they all went to lunch in Biot, a small town nearby. Julia drove them there through the hilly countryside, and Paul drove them back—it was a wild ride. Beard had been released from Pathé's clinic (no thinner than when he'd arrived) and would spend the next few days at La Pitchoune. They were happy in one another's company—Americans in France, perfectly at ease. And Americans who were all, in one way or another, rethinking their connection to France.

That afternoon, M.F. sent them a letter:

Dear Julia and Paul and Jim—it is only a few hours since I was with you, and I miss you very much. "Happy is he who can weep at a departure" is one of the two things Dillwyn Parrish ever quoted, and it took me many years to understand what it said. By now I do, and can agree!

Thank you for showing me the beautiful country, and taking me to that good little tavern (inn, pub, restaurant—). I loved every minute of it, and every bite and drop.

It will be odd to play the role, by now familiar and quite comfortable of course, of a ghost in Arles. I'll drift among the pre-Christian carvings, and hope to find a midnight mass where there will be the piper and drum, and a lamb bleating. Marseille will be wild and noisy . . .

All my affectionate greetings, d*e*r*e f*r*e*n*s *three*—
MFKF

At dawn the following day, Gatti picked her up in La Roquette. The streets were icy. She was on her way.

◆ ◆ ◆

Child, meanwhile, had a different sort of escape in mind: a clean break with Beck. Beck and her husband would be back just after Christmas, and Child dreaded the thought of her arrival. The success of the new book had not quite smoothed over their difficult year, the many arguments and lingering resentments. In fact, the very success of *Mastering II* had only highlighted the extent to which it was seen as Child's book, an extension of her TV show. Child wanted to preserve the friendship but end the partnership.

The point of no return had occurred the previous summer, in June. *Mastering II* was done, and she and Paul had wrapped up the French filming for the new series, and arrived at La Pitchoune for vacation. And then came word that *McCall's* magazine, which was producing a three-part story ("The Making of a Masterpiece") timed to the book's release, wanted Child to pose for more photos. The magazine had hired Paul, who was an excellent photographer, to take pictures for the story. But the editors had decided to send the legendary Arnold Newman to take pictures of the kitchen at La Pitchoune and of the food the magazine's editors had prepared— and to shoot a portrait of the two women for the cover.

Julia had felt put upon and said no: "I am finished working on the book," she announced. "My time and energies are now devoted entirely to television. Furthermore, my husband has already taken hundreds of perfectly good photographs of Simca and me, and I see no point in taking any more."

Thus ensued the "contretemps," as Julia later referred to it.

Newman and his team had set up shop in the kitchen at La Pitchoune. There were lights and photo equipment everywhere. Newman still hoped to convince Child to pose for some pictures, and when he saw her and Beck together, he thought he'd won her over.

"No!" she said to Newman.

"Fini les photos!" she said to Beck.

Beck burst into tears. She had her heart set on this portrait, she said. "How can you treat me like that?" she wailed.

So Julia relented, and the two of them stood smiling in various poses for the rest of the afternoon. But they both knew, then and there, that their days of collaboration were over. (That was the weekend when Olney had first met both women and had sensed, without knowing exactly what was going on, the great tension between them.)

Since then, Judith Jones had begun talking with Beck about a cookbook of her own, which was a terrific idea, Child thought. This was a book that Child, too, had been suggesting to Beck, though Beck was resisting it. She needed Beck to find her own way, just as she was doing. And she needed Beck to get out of *her* way. Beck just consumed too much energy at a time when Child was preoccupied with thoughts of what her future would be.

Yes, the future was very much on Child's mind. Even as she prepared for the legions of guests who would be arriving in the coming days—including Paul's brother, Charlie, and his family, and Judith and Evan Jones—Julia found time to work on the scripts for the next season of *The French Chef,* also noting ideas and recipes that would form the basis of her next book. As was clearly signaled by the title, *From Julia Child's Kitchen,* it would be her most personal yet.

She was ready to embrace her role as a pop culture heroine, to embrace pleasure, joy, knowledge, and style, without regard to the higher authority of the Cordon Bleu—or Simone Beck. She wanted to experiment with international cuisines and microwave ovens and pressure cookers. She might even tell stories about some of the recipes—about the best lamb brochettes she'd ever had (at a couscous restaurant in Paris), or her response to a viewer's letter about the most humane way to kill a lobster.

The result would be something entirely new, combining the *je ne sais quoi* and self-assurance of France and the open-minded, can-do accessibility of America.

"Now I don't have to be so damned classic and 'French.' To hell with that," Child said to Jones, contemplating her next cookbook. "I am French trained, and I do what I want with my background."

Child felt liberated.

～13～

THE GHOST
OF ARLES
AND AVIGNON

THE RESTAURANTS WERE CLOSED FOR THE holidays. The weather was grim. The Hôtel Nord-Pinus was un-welcoming. M.F. was alone. Was she the only guest in the hotel? It seemed that way.

She was looking for France: she wanted to see it in the intense light of a cold, clear December day, rather than through the fogged-up windows of Les Bastides, or the rosy tint of her own memories, which dated back to her first visit in 1929, over forty years before. She and Norah had joked about the nostalgic, time-travel quality of their journey—revisiting the cities and hotels of their youth. And why not? It had all seemed harmless fun. But M.F. was feeling a deeper purpose now, one that seemed all the more urgent after the previous weeks with Julia and Paul, Beard and Olney, Bedford and Lord. She wanted to bring France into focus, unvarnished and raw.

She would be relentlessly unsentimental. She was not looking for the past, or even for beauty. She was looking for the truth. What did France look, feel, and taste like in 1970? What did it *mean?* And how could she write about it in a way that captured the moment? Arles would be a test—a test of her ability to see and report and write, rather than reflect and remember. She would keep a journal, and maybe, when she was done, she would be able to use the material for an article in *The New Yorker*. But that didn't matter now. More important was the opportunity to use her observations to contemplate her future. She had often idly thought that she would live out her final years in France. Now that her children were grown, and she had packed up her things at the old house in St. Helena and begun building Last House in Glen Ellen, now was the time to put this dream aside—or not. And she was clearly wavering, this way and that.

"I know, at this far date in my life," she had just written in a letter to Gingrich, "that I was meant to live and if possible to die on a dry, olive-covered hillside in Provence. If only Last House were here instead of in the Valley of the Moon!"

Coming alone to Arles was a conscious test of M.F.'s strength and independence, of her will to move ahead. She had left the warm comfort of her friends and family. Norah was on a boat somewhere off the coast of Portugal. (She'd sent a letter the previous week from Lisbon: Rough seas. Bad wine.) M.F.'s daughters and their husbands and infant children were at their homes in California and Oregon. It had taken a certain single-minded fortitude to pack her bags and venture into the cold, alone.

And that fortitude was immediately tested.

At the train station on the way there she had called for a porter, and then waited and waited. She hadn't counted on this. She'd had to put her bags in two lockers, and was sure she would lose the keys, or jam the locks, or miss her train. She felt strange, stumbling, and momentarily incompetent. "I recognized too many of my failings, willy-nilly, in the cold insecurity of the morning," she wrote later that day in her journal.

This is what sometimes happened when she was alone—she could turn on herself. And now she was in danger of being swamped in a paralyzing tide, a slow-moving whirlpool of interiority.

The cure for such thoughts, she knew, was to write. To observe, to immerse herself fully in the world, in Arles. She planned to stay for two weeks. And so she walked the city streets, day after day. She ordered gin and vermouths and *pieds et paquets* and went to the museum of Christian art and to the theater. The play was a political piece, set in Haiti, called *Les Nonnes,* by a supposedly revolutionary Cuban writer named Eduardo Manet. She found it sophomoric.

Back in her room at the Nord-Pinus—the Chambre Jean Cocteau, with its enormous armoire—she took notes in her pale green notebook. She described the meals she ate, the people she observed in the streets, the churches that seemed to be inexplicably closed. All the *bar-tabacs* were closed, too, even the one supposed to be open on Sundays, so she could not buy a newspaper. She was approached by a gypsy who wanted to tell her fortune. She went to buy stamps. She examined the stands at the market, which were selling everything from olives to pheasants to potted plants. She wrote it all down in her journal. Every interaction, every scent, every fleeting thought.

She was turning her isolation into fuel for a jaunty, heroic, and ferocious reportage. The diary was intensely personal and precisely observed—an unusual combination of intimacy and dispassion. "Since I got into this report, I feel fewer of the qualms that I could not push out of my thoughts," she wrote, "it is good for me to be writing, instead of carrying on the formless silent mumbling."

◆ ◆ ◆

The maid at the Nord-Pinus delivered a breakfast tray every morning with a café au lait and two croissants, a small dish of butter, and a large bowl of apricot jam. Delicious. The café au lait was over-milky and oversweet, an innocent sensuality that always made her want to get back into bed and read awhile longer. Some days she indulged herself. On others, to prevent this from happening, she would get dressed before the tray arrived, and write at the desk. She skipped the second croissant. If she was going to gain weight, she decided, she'd rather do it with some good pâtés.

After breakfast she was on her own. And M.F. continued to be troubled by food. The lack of it. The constant search for it.

She planned her days as cannily as if she were organizing a state visit. The museums were all closed from noon until two o'clock in the afternoon, for example, and she could not simply sit outside, not in this weather. The few restaurants that were open were not yet serving lunch at noon, which meant she'd have to find a café and have a drink before embarking on the next search for a place to eat. And since she did not want to sit silently staring out the window, she had to remember to bring a book—an Inspector Maigret mystery.

It was precisely these interstitial moments that she usually enjoyed most when traveling—waiting for trains, resting between engagements, eating. But they were hard to enjoy in Arles.

One day she sat in a shabby brasserie and ordered crudités and a cheese omelet and a *demi* of rosé. The sign on the sidewalk was a cutout in the shape of a fat chef and had large clumsy lettering: ICI SE HABLA ESPAÑOL. It was an ugly room. Her table had a paper place mat. The food was bad, though the wine was decent, albeit flecked with shards from a broken cork. She read, as always. This was a French lunchtime brasserie from which all the magic and romance had been leached away.

Still, it was food that connected her to the world, she realized. Even a mediocre omelet and a glass of wine with bits of cork in it. Lunch was a period of rest and escape; she needed it to be more than a mechanical stoking of the furnace, more than "a quick gobble and then crash bang out into the world again to walk until another museum is open." In her journal, she wrote:

> I could live well, and perhaps more sensibly than I do now, on a piece of fruit from one pocket and a handful of nuts and raisins from the other. But where could I go to eat them? The park benches are deserted even by the birds, this time of year. My hands in mittens would drop every raisin. What is more, *I*—not another different person but *I*—would grow more and more away from the human race, further into my own tumbled, troubled ponderings. No, it would be unwise—for *me*, that is. I am determined to stay on the human side, perforce.

Suddenly, there was a strangled whimpering sound from the other side of the restaurant. A sort of rhythmical moaning. Then a scraping of chairs and people standing, leaning, looking. Someone was ill. The proprietor of the restaurant came out from behind the bar, surveyed the scene wearily, and called for his wife, who clutched her breasts in alarm. Some of the other customers got up to look and then returned to their seats with pale faces. M.F. stayed where she was.

The restaurateur's wife called an ambulance, and a few minutes later, a beautiful and very pale young woman was carried out of the restaurant on a stretcher. "Had she taken poison?" M.F. wondered. "Had her heart failed her? Was she dead?" No: she seemed to be breathing. Her crying had stopped. Her eyes were closed. M.F. took a sip of wine.

That night, describing the scene at the restaurant in her diary, M.F. wrote, "I returned to Maigret. I was not concerned. It was as if I were a fish in a bowl, watching another world through curved glass."

How had she ended up on the wrong side of the glass? It wasn't just this particular charmless restaurant that had left her cold: it was Arles. She had been here a number of times in her life, but the Provençal town's toughness and vigor seemed careless and violent to her now. She couldn't escape the lurking hostility of the place. She was ready to leave. She wrote in her journal:

> People in Arles do not have happy natures—at least not in the winter! They frown and scowl a lot. There is a kind of surly belligerency in them. They are, subtly, ready for a fight, looking for a slur, an insult . . . Yes, I think the place is filled with suspicion and haughtiness, over-defensive.

She was writing about Arles but in invoking its people's "suspicion and haughtiness" and their "surly belligerency," was she not also writing, inevitably, about Richard Olney? About Sybille Bedford? About continental snobbery? Had she given up on Arles, or had Arles turned its back on her? That was the philo-sophical question, one that encapsulated her uncertainty about what France meant to her now.

✦ ✦ ✦

That night, in her room at the Nord-Pinus, M.F. ate a cold sausage roll and a tangerine. She put the fruit outside on the windowsill to chill and warmed the pastry on the radiator. She drank three brandy and waters, and she wrote.

The next day, she picked up the telephone and asked the op-erator to connect her to the Hôtel d'Europe in nearby Avignon—another town, like Arles, that she had visited many times before. The Europe was a rather more luxurious hotel than the Nord-Pinus, and she felt ready for some luxury. Did they have a room, she inquired, and more important, was the hotel restaurant open? *"Mais oui, madame, nous sommes ouverts toute l'année,"* the man said. She made a reservation for the following day, December 22, and would stay there through Christmas.

She was looking forward to a more hospitable lodging. One with a restaurant.

"It's not the weather that stymies me," she wrote to Gingrich, describing the persistent cold and bitter wind, "but that I'm HUN-GRY. Almost every restaurant in Arles is tight shut!" She listed other cold European Christmases past: Nuremburg, 1930; Bern, 1937. "But then I was with people I loved. Now I am alone, and it is RIDIKLUS to be alone and hungry at the same time. So tomorrow I'll take a cab to Avignon."

She felt guilty for leaving, but why should she? In fact, now that she had decided to go, she felt suddenly confident. Her French seemed magically improved, both her accent and her grammar. She felt in control. She was hungrier.

In her notebook, she wrote about Arles, making a list of things she wanted to remember: The sound of the church bells. The gypsies and their music. The waiter with the bad shoes. The loud traffic in the streets. The mischief and boredom of the young men. The empty hotel, with its white china doorknobs with little flowers painted on them.

In the lobby at the Nord-Pinus that afternoon, she'd seen a fat older woman drinking coffee. "How does she do that with the kitchen closed?" M.F. wondered, before realizing the woman was the proprietress of the establishment. Indeed, the woman rose to her feet and began questioning M.F. about her stay. Did she like the hotel? How was her room? She complimented M.F.'s French accent and admired her clothes, reaching out to pick up the hem of her coat to see if it was lined with fur, and if it was real leather.

M.F. backed away, flapping her arms, saying the usual polite things. The old woman cackled and wheezed. She must be the mother of the unhappy, unfriendly man at the front desk. That would explain his hostility. (M.F. was reading far too much Simenon, she reminded herself—imagining the secret lives of strangers. The staff at the hotel, the waiters in the restaurants, the gypsies in the streets, the girl collapsed on the floor of the brasserie—they all resembled characters in a murder mystery.)

M.F. liked the hotel fine, she said. "But if I'd been warned about the closed restaurant, I'd have come later." This was probably untrue, but she was being diplomatic.

"Ah, but one cannot, in this business, maintain a proper kitchen for two or three customers in the dead season!" the woman replied.

M.F. held her tongue. "Then turn off the neon signs," she felt like saying, "and notify the *Guide Michelin!*"

The old lady continued, telling her about a charming American guest—"*Elle était Américaine, mais charmante—char-MAN-te!*"—who invited Madame everywhere with her, *everywhere*—and asked her to lunch, even.

"But how strange," the old woman said, suddenly, with a baffled look. "She has never written to thank me!"

M.F. could hardly contain her desire to flee.

✦ ✦ ✦

The taxi driver said it was the worst mistral he'd experienced since he came to France from North Africa in 1956. He was a good driver, but had to work to keep the heavy car on the road in the heavy seasonal wind. When he wasn't concentrating too hard to be able to talk, he rambled on about how much he liked Americans. But M.F. was not in the mood to hear it. "I do find myself bored," she wrote afterward in her journal, "by the old spiel of how fine the Americans are—about how many of his faithful clients, '*Même les juifs,*' remember him every year from as far away as Pasadena—about how some Frenchmen have forgotten the American help in 1944 but not *this* one, etc., etc. Yes, yes. Fine. Good. *Joyeux Noël.*"

✦ ✦ ✦

In Avignon, enveloped in the luxurious comfort of the Hôtel d'Europe, M.F. began to relax. Her room was small and had a large window overlooking a pretty courtyard; just below the window was a small fountain with a series of three basins and water flowing down from one to the next.

She liked that beautiful sound.

The hotel was expensive and historic. The building, originally the residence of the Marquis de Graveson, was from the sixteenth century and had been a hotel since 1799. The decor was discreet; unlike in Arles, there were no fake Provençal chandeliers or Camarguais tridents to be seen. The walls were hung with tapestries. The hotel restaurant was indeed open.

M.F. was glad to be there. By the second evening the barman knew her name and room number, and that she didn't want any ice in her half-gin, half-vermouth cocktail. "Somebody like me needs a good small hotel-bar," she thought contemplatively. A place to sit for a change of pace after a day of looking at Roman carvings and shop windows, and before a night of reading and sleeping.

These days, though, she was writing rather than sightseeing. It was too cold to do anything else. She wrote about Arles, mostly, how closed and wary it seemed, and about her own reactions to feeling shut out, shunned. She had felt more American than ever, she realized, alone in a foreign land, on guard in a way she'd never been before in France.

✦ ✦ ✦

"To hell with Noël," M.F. thought to herself, a few days before Christmas.

She didn't much like the holiday. She was not a religious person, for one thing, and she found the hopped-up commercialism of the season unpleasant. Churches could be beautiful, of course, but as she walked through the bitter cold in Avignon one morning, she found them tired and dark. Saint-Agricol, Saint-Pierre, and the Notre-Dame des Doms cathedral all seemed worn out. Crowds were sparse, and there was no feeling of holiday or excitement.

In Saint-Pierre there was a crèche, a nativity scene with old painted wooden *santons*—the traditional Provençal figurines—and little houses with blinking lights. She kept noticing ugly crèches: the previous week in Cannes she had seen a coin-operated mechanical crèche with a sign saying it was out of order. Once repairs were made, she realized, the lights would beam in the stable and in the houses, and the fisher by the little lake of real water would dip his rod in and out, and the wise men would hold out their gifts and then draw them back again. The very notion of a mechanical crèche, let alone a broken one, was disheartening.

This was the second year running that M.F. had spent Christmas alone. She had gone to New York last year and stayed at a friend's beach house in Bridgehampton. She'd been all alone, writing. It had been cold there, too, she now remembered.

Why did she leave again? For years she had been the impresario of the family holidays, directing everything from the menus and the decorations to when to leave for midnight Mass and when to let the children open their presents. They were grown now, with children of their own. And she was feeling the strain of trying to do so much, when she needed time for herself. This was at least in part why she had sold the house in St. Helena. "All I did was cook and care for a constant stream of people, and mop up their tears, and wait for more," she explained in a letter to a friend. "I could not finish a single thing. And not only do I earn a living with what

I write, but it is the only thing that fulfills my creative nature, now that I have finished child-bearing and, apparently, sexual life. I was turning into a vegetable."

Now, however, she missed her family. After the cold walk past the churches, she stopped at a bar and ordered a drink. One or two men came in and stood at the counter. A young couple kissed in a corner. The waiters and barmen were joking quietly about their girls, their children, their hangovers. M.F. sipped her vermouth and gin and felt her hands and face get warmer.

She missed Norah and she missed her daughters. She missed being near the people she loved.

✦ ✦ ✦

That night, M.F. listened to the little fountain underneath her window, and at some point she realized the music had changed. Strange, it had snuck up on her. There was a soft occasional dripping sound now, not the lively fall from basin to basin of the previous nights. She looked out her window through the bare branches of the plane trees and saw that the basins were hung with long, beautiful icicles, with fresh water barely moving down them.

Tonight, she thought with some excitement, she would listen to a fountain freeze! And so she did, not trying to stay awake for it, but aware much of the time of the diminishing music.

By about five o'clock, there was no sound. As soon as it was light enough, after seven, she looked down and saw that the basins were now linked by rows of icicles that were like solid white columns between them. Later, a little boy stood for several minutes looking at the silenced water. He tossed a small rock toward the glass columns, but nothing broke, and he went shivering into the hotel.

It was the morning of Christmas Eve.

Later that morning, M.F. walked on the sunny sides of the icy streets. The mistral was over. She noticed a corner stand selling *coquillages* (the first shellfish she'd seen in some time) and a small café next door where one could order them, according to a sign in the window. She would eat lunch here, she decided.

It was not a fancy place at all, but it looked pleasant, with high, bright windows and bunches of balloons and streamers for the holiday dinner that night. She decided to eat mussels. They could be ordered raw or *marinière*. She would have liked the latter, but the plat du jour was rabbit, and she wanted that, too. Wouldn't both be too heavy? she asked the waiter. He gave her a quick but warm smile and agreed that it would, so she ordered the mussels raw. She ate about thirty of them—they were very small *moules de Bouzigues,* almost crisp from the cold, and delicious. The bread was the best she'd had in ages. And the rabbit was very good, too. It tasted like *rabbit,* with only a little juice, no batter, a sprinkle of herbs. It was served with excellent, simple macaroni, moistened only with the rabbit sauce and some grated Gruyère.

She ate more for lunch than she had for the past several days, reading and watching the customers enjoy Christmas feasts—children, lovers, old men playing cards. Sitting here in this simple restaurant in Avignon, M.F. knew that it was the civilized meal that made her human. A meal with crusty bread and butter and wine at lunchtime. She had eaten in a hundred restaurants like this one over the years. There was an uncanny familiarity to the gruff waiters, the old men, the girls drinking espressos, the sounds and smells.

She counted on meals like this one to sustain her: the impersonal embrace of the room, the routines and traditions that surrounded the ordering, cooking, presenting, and then eating of her lunch. It could be in France or America, it didn't matter. When she returned to the hotel she meant to read a while, but she took a nap instead. She was sated and happy.

+ + +

M.F. dressed with special care for dinner and felt quite dashing in her invisible way. She ordered a bottle of Veuve Clicquot Brut 1964 at the hotel bar and had a glass before dinner. "What voluptuous treatment I can give myself!" she thought. Well, it was Christmas Eve, after all, and she was alone. To hell with it.

The champagne followed her into the dining room, where she ate fresh foie gras, a *sole à la normande,* and a dutiful slice of bûche de Noël. The food was pleasant, but the mussels in the rich Normandy sauce were nothing like the raw, exquisitely fresh ones she'd had at lunch.

In her room after dinner, she could hear the fountain again, trickling outside her window, and she was glad she hadn't forced herself to go to Mass at Saint-Agricol or anywhere else. She had another glass of champagne. "It is necessary to impose a certain amount of discipline on oneself, I find, in order to stay human," she wrote in her journal. "But why force things? Why lacerate, rub salt, twist knives, in the name of personal courage? Why try too hard to stand up straight all the time? Rubbish!"

And so she sat in her pajamas and peignoir, drinking champagne and writing.

More and more, her thoughts turned to home.

She had come looking for France and she had found it—cold,

hard, and real—but it was not home. It was not *hers,* not really. She was American. And this trip, which had begun months ago as a kind of sentimental immersion in the pleasures of France past, had turned into something quite different. Instead of the past, she had found the future. Hers. She had found a new way of seeing, a way past nostalgia. She was looking forward to California, and to writing about California, too. She had ideas already—about the Italian, Mexican, Japanese, Hawaiian, and Cuban fishermen on the West Coast, and the fish they caught and cooked. About chilies and enchiladas, about Sonoma County wines.

Was it any wonder this all struck her in some deeply existential way? France had for so long been her inspiration. She was, indeed, one of the modern inventors of American Francophilia, articulating its tone and ethic, its codes and allusions and seductive sophistication. France was at the very center of M.F.'s emotional and intellectual life. It was the emblem of glamour and good living, the repository of dreams, a place, both in the world and in her own interior landscape, where she had found beauty and solace.

And now she was saying good-bye. To the past. To France. To her dreams of France.

She was choosing family, and a new chapter, a new house. In her journal, she wrote:

> Always before, in France, I have fought a hard battle within, to
> return to America happily. I have wanted to stay here. But by
> now I have decided to end my life in California, as far as one
> can decide such things. My two children are American (and that
> was almost certainly my own choice and I shall never know how

right or wrong I was), and I have decided to stay as near them
as they wish to be, instead of establishing myself in southern
France, as I once dreamed of.

She had made up her mind. "I do know that I have, apparently,
turned my back on the old vague dreams of living in Europe."

But even in Sonoma, France would be with her, always: "I hope
I'll still hear the fountain below, with the slowing water in the icicles at night."

◆ ◆ ◆

Christmas Day: a milky sky. There were still long, thick icicles and
beautiful white ice on the mossy sides of the fountain basins, but the
pools of water were clear and limpid from above.

That morning, she walked through the gardens at the Notre-
Dame des Doms cathedral to the sundial, where she had often gone
with her children, and once with Norah's sons, the Barr boys.

Before she left, she drank the last of the champagne—it was just
right, just cold enough, still very lively.

~14~

CHRISTMAS AND
RÉVEILLON

JAMES BEARD LEFT JUST BEFORE CHRISTMAS.
He'd been staying in the guest room at La Pitchoune after leaving Dr. Pathé's clinic. He and Julia and Paul cooked and talked and read and relaxed; it was a low-key few days. Beard stuck to his diet, more or less, although he did not seem to be losing any weight at all. Well, these things took time. He felt weak, but he was happy to be with friends.

For the Childs, this was the calm before the storm. They had said to everyone they knew, "Do come!"—and quite a number, including siblings and nieces and old friends from England, had decided they would indeed come visit. So the Childs were shopping and planning for the many large dinners they would be hosting for the new arrivals.

In the meantime, they gossiped some more about Claiborne and who ought to replace him at the *Times*. This was an endlessly enjoyable parlor game, and one for which there were no right answers, only conjecture—at least until Beard got back to New York to ferret out the latest. What about Jon Winroth, Child wondered—he wrote about wine and food for the *International Herald Tribune* in Paris. Might he be grooming himself?

Who knew?

It was indeed a "gossipy profession," Child declared, "which is part of its charm. But thank heaven we love and trust each other!"

Beard had a difficult trip home: Gatti drove him to the airport, and he could already feel a slight sniffle in his left nostril. Before the plane reached Barcelona that slight sniffle had turned into a bad cold, and after they left Lisbon, the charming stewardess, a fan, was squeezing glass after glass of orange juice for him.

He described the scene most amusingly in a letter to the Childs.

He was a most unattractive passenger, that much he knew, between his running nose and the increased swelling of his foot. "I am certain Pan Am was happy to toss me off the plane," he noted. "They even arrived 40 minutes ahead of time so anxious were they to get me away."

Once he got back to New York, Beard was relegated to a chair that kept his foot elevated—he referred to it as his "red gout chair"—and used the enforced immobility to attempt to catch up on all the correspondence and other business that had piled up on his desk.

"Some progress has been made nasally, footwise and deskwise," he wrote to the Childs. "I trust no germ was left lurking in my room." The fevered discussions continued, he reported, about who was to be Claiborne's successor—Michael Field's name seemed to be mentioned more than any other. "Otherwise, life around New York seems calm and collected," he wrote. He hadn't heard much gossip: "I haven't circulated enough to collect any choice items."

He looked forward to a necessarily quiet Christmas. He would be sticking to his diet.

At La Pitchoune, meanwhile, the "Soupe Barbue" Beard had made the previous week survived like an old Madeira—Child added various ingredients as the days went by: more chard, a couple of tomatoes, some mushroom stems, leeks and potatoes, and Provençal pistou garnish for a bit of zest. The soup lasted many days. It had become a true "*Soupe de l'enfant Barbue*," she wrote in a letter to Beard—a "Child" of the "Bearded" soup. This was another of their running jokes.

◆ ◆ ◆

Child planned to roast two geese for Christmas dinner. She would stuff them with prunes, sausage, and chestnuts. Prunes and goose were an exceptionally fine combination, she believed.

They had a full house: Paul's brother, Charlie, and his wife, visiting from Maine, at La Pitchoune in the room Beard had lately vacated; a couple of English friends next door at Beck's; and Judith and Evan Jones and still other friends at nearby inns. The Joneses were at an auberge called La Maillane, which Child decided was a charming place. It had very attractive rooms, and the proprietors were obliging in every way. It cost fifty francs a night for two people, including breakfast—about ten dollars.

Judith and Evan came in the early afternoon to help cook. The weather was cloudy and cold, but inside was warm and festive, with a fire in the fireplace, a kitchen full of food. Julia had bought a large terrine of *jambon persillé* from Boussageon, in Plascassier.

Child and Jones had a long-standing and warm professional relationship. They had worked together many hours, going over recipes and page proofs, particularly on the second volume of *Mastering*, when Jones had spent days at a time in Cambridge with Julia and Paul. She had stayed in their guest room, waking in the early morning to the "thump-thump-thump" of her hosts doing their daily exercises. But this was different: a purely social occasion—a vacation!—and included her husband, Evan, himself a well-regarded author. He wrote about archeology, American history, and, increasingly, about food; he was an excellent cook.

"What a dear pair they are," Child wrote to Beard the following week. "She is so gay, and such fun, and we like him very much, although he is rather quiet and less easy to know."

Judith and Evan had rented a car, and spent their time exploring the area and tasting the local food:

> The *pâté de bécasse* in oval crocks with the woodcock's head
> and long beak emerging at one end and the two clawed feet at
> the other; whole *alouettes*, little larks embedded in jelly; terrines
> of hare, duck, pheasant; and whole stuffed piglets with "*joyeux
> Noël*" written in strips of fat along their glistening sides; and, of
> course, our sentimental favorites, *boudins blancs*.

They had eaten the delicate *boudin blanc* sausages at their very first lunch together, in Paris in 1948. In the years since, they had become experts at making their own charcuterie, including sausages; Judith was pleased that Child and Beck had included an extensive selection of such recipes in *Mastering II*.

It was frustrating for Jones to see so much beautiful food and produce in all the markets, but not have a kitchen to cook it in! So it was a great pleasure to join Child in the kitchen at La Pitchoune—

not to work, or to test or refine a recipe, but simply to cook together.

They prepared the geese for roasting. Child gave a quick lesson
on how to judge the age of a goose by pressing the breast bones. A
goose had to be under six months old to be any good, she said. And
it was important that the feet still be attached: this was how you
removed the tendons in the legs. Jones watched as Child cracked
an ankle bone, cut the skin, and located a tendon. Then Child set
the goose on the floor and straddled it, winding the tendon around
a broomstick, which she used to yank it out. The tendon came out
whole.

"Just like pulling the cork out of a bottle," Child said.

The process was repeated with the other tendons, and then Child
cut out the wishbones, chopped off the wingtips, and removed loose
fat from the necks. Jones, meanwhile, was peeling gizzards. They
would be chopped and sautéed with the goose liver, sausage, and
onions for the stuffing. This all went into a large bowl, where it was
mixed with cubes of dried bread, eggs, and a dash of cognac.

Child set out smaller bowls, in which she poured preserved
whole chestnuts in syrup and prunes steeped in brandy.

The birds were ready for stuffing. Child and Jones spooned
in layers, alternating the sausage stuffing, the chestnuts, and the
prunes. When they were done, Child sewed the vents closed, and
pricked the birds all over, so the fat could escape while they were
cooking. She trussed the birds securely with string and placed them
in roasting pans.

Would both geese fit in the oven? They made it work. The oven
was the massive La Cornue the Childs had put in when they built
the house. All other French ovens had seemed like rickety junk,

Julia thought, so they'd bought the classic, handmade machine. It was tricky to clean and a bit temperamental. Ah well. The new dishwasher had arrived, and was sitting out in the *cabanon*, awaiting the various workmen who would install it after the holidays.

Child was always interested in the latest devices and machines—mixers, blenders, electric super-blenders, microwave ovens—anything that could save time and effort without compromising quality. Quality, of course, was paramount. Indeed, she and Beard and all the other pioneers of cooking in postwar America had fended off 1950s "home ec" attitudes about convenience and speed—the idea that cooking should be fast, simple, processed, frozen, and prepackaged. But while maintaining her commitment to excellence, she had taken a key lesson from the "home ec" approach; she understood the importance of accessibility. She felt strongly that her readers and viewers needed to be able to replicate her cooking, not just admire it. Hence her interest not just in laborsaving devices but in clarity and precision, too. She explained recipes step by step. She measured everything.

It was a point of pride for Beck, by contrast, that she did not measure anything; she relied on instinct. Olney was the same way: "Precise measures bore me," he would say. "I prefer pinches, suspicions, splashes and handfuls." His recipes were brilliantly written and evocative, but they were not quite reliable or precise. Elizabeth David, too, was scornful of what she saw as the American need for hand-holding and pedantic explanations and measurements. Her recipes were notoriously vague. When Jones made suggestions to David to clarify some of the recipes for Knopf's edition of her *Italian Food* in the late 1950s (it had already been published in England), David sent a curt and condescending reply. "The implication was," Jones later wrote, "that you'd never be a real cook if you were so fussy about details like that."

Well, Child *was* fussy about details like that. In fact her next book, based on the new episodes of the TV show, would include a detailed appendix on weights, measures, and the metric system, correlating grams to ounces to cups and tablespoons for numerous ingredients. "Although a pint of water is a pound and can be contained in a 2-cup measure, a pound of flour is 3½ cups and a pound of sugar is not quite 2½ cups," Child wrote. It was indeed confounding, but she explained all.

Olney and David were dismissive. "Poor old Julia," David sighed with amused contempt when the two of them discussed her. "Now she is Minister of Measures."

But if Child preserved a teacher's sense of basic instruction, she jettisoned schoolmarmish pursed lips and disapproval. She embraced pleasure and fun. And unlike Beck, or Olney, or the tradition-minded French, she was open to change and experimentation. She was unorthodox, unafraid. And she wanted her readers to feel the same way.

As she sat at her desk in La Pitchoune planning upcoming episodes of her TV show, she did not limit herself to the standards, to classical dishes and preparations, or to French food. She wanted to go beyond that. Sure, there would be a pot-au-feu and a quiche Lorraine (the dough made in an electric mixer), but there would also be a pizza episode—why not? And a curry dinner, or lamb shashliks and chicken shish kebabs.

"After all," she wrote, "although my formal culinary training was entirely French, and while I am constantly building it during our months in France every year, I remain very American indeed. I always look at French cuisine from an American point of view."

On TV, the force of Child's personality carried the show. And as she started work on the new cookbook, she found herself growing into a new role. The writing drew more upon her life than her previous cookbooks; it was full of stories and reminiscences. Recipes were introduced with variations, tangential observations, anecdotes, and personal discoveries. In the poultry chapter, for example, she might tell the story of a dinner in the English countryside in the early 1950s, at a charming Tudor inn with a garden filled with roses. Paul had ordered the roast beef, and she the chicken.

> My fowl, on a very large, very white plate, was a leg and thigh combination, rather bony, and partially covered by a stark pale blanket of what turned out to be the famous English white sauce, through which poked a good half dozen long brown chicken hairs. We were both delighted with my fowl; it somehow represented what we had always heard about English cooking but had never quite believed before. It looked so perfectly what it was, a thoroughly boiled, quite elderly hen, and a sauce that was literally only flour and water with barely a pinch of salt to flavor it.

Child told the story as she worked in the kitchen, side by side with Jones, both of them laughing about that awful boiled chicken, so vivid in the description that Jones could almost see it. She thought it the perfect, comic story to lead into a series of stewed chicken recipes.

And now Child realized more clearly than ever just how constricted she had felt over the previous few years, working with Beck on *Mastering II*. There had been no room for the personal in that book, no room for humor.

She was filled with a sense of liberation. Not merely, as she had expected, freedom from the endless arguments with Beck, from the stress of trying to finish the book. It was more than that. She was liberated from France, and from the sort of self-serious snobbery she had seen in her encounters with Olney and Bedford during the past weeks. She had made the firm decision to spread her own wings, and now she felt the full force of what that meant.

She laughed again, long and hard, about that miserable boiled English chicken.

+ + +

The birds cooked for two and a half hours. Every fifteen or twenty minutes, Child opened the oven and poured boiling water over the geese, to help draw out the fat. She was a firm believer in regular basting. She also turned the birds first on one side and then the other during the cooking, to brown them all over.

Paul had invented a cocktail for the occasion. It was a mixture of French vermouth, Dubonnet, orange essence, and dark rum. He opened bottles of Burgundy for dinner, chatting with his brother, Charlie, who had arrived with his wife a few days before.

When the geese were done, Julia and Judith made a sauce in the roasting pan, spooning out the fat and adding the brandy that had steeped the prunes, cooking it down and scraping up the caramelized drippings. Off the heat, they added a few tablespoons of butter.

Christmas dinner was ready.

APÉRITIF: VERMOUTH, DUBONNET, ORANGE ESSENCE,
AND DARK RUM

JAMBON IN PARSLEYED ASPIC

GOOSE STUFFED WITH SAUSAGE, CHESTNUTS, AND PRUNES

BÛCHE DE NOËL

Paul carved the birds, and Julia poured the wines. The guests served the *jambon persillé* from a large dish on the table.

The mood was celebratory—this was a Christmas feast, after all, but it was also a time to rejoice in being together with friends and family. Judith and Julia toasted each other. It had been a long year, they agreed, and how perfect that they were now here together, in Provence. Judith and Evan had decided to come only at the last minute, at Julia's invitation. So here they were, admiring the roast geese and delectable stuffing, drinking Paul's sweet and strong cocktails by the fireplace, looking out over the terrace to the Provençal valley below, congratulating themselves on their extraordinary good fortune.

The geese were fantastic, rich and dark.

"They seem much less fat than the ones we get at home," Child remarked. "Why are our ducks and geese so fat?"

It was a good question. Maybe Beard would know the answer, they decided. Child would ask him in her next letter.

✦ ✦ ✦

New Year's Eve was to be celebrated at Beck's. She would be preparing an elaborate *réveillon* dinner.

Jones was on vacation, but she was working, too. She had arranged to meet with M.F. in Marseille, to go over the manuscript for *Among Friends*. They would meet just after the New Year, their paths crossing before they both returned home. Jones also planned to talk with Beck, once again, about a cookbook of her own.

In mid-November, a few weeks after the official release of *Mastering II*, the *New York Times* had published an article called "Simone Beck: The Cookbook Author without a Show on TV," describing Beck giving a cooking demonstration in Westport, Connecticut, to promote the new book. The article was flattering, though it made note of Beck's imperious and humorless demeanor ("There was no time for idle chatter, or even a smile. Cooking is a serious business with Mme. Beck") and the fact that she did not measure anything ("much to the consternation of some of the women who prefer the teaspoon-by-teaspoon approach"). She prepared three dishes: onion-cheese tarts; fish and chicken in a Provençal sauce; and Le Talleyrand, a flaming fruit and meringue dessert. None of the recipes was from the book.

"Julia's more scientific," Beck told the *Times*, "but I go further with the ideas." She seemed intent on establishing her superiority.

The following day, Jones had written Beck a letter, saying she'd read the article, which had reminded her that they should talk about Beck writing a cookbook of her own. It could include all her recipes that had not fit in *Mastering II*, and the many dishes she had developed for her cooking classes. "It seems to me that you would have almost enough to make a small collection that could have a strong personal touch (it might even be called something like *Simca's Cuisine*)," Jones wrote.

Beck's response had again been a firm no. She was not interested. She wanted a rest, she said. Child laughed when she heard this: Simca was not exactly the resting type, she said. But Beck was so adamant that Jones had dropped the idea, at least for a while. She figured Beck must be exhausted from the grueling book tour, and the many cooking demonstrations.

Jones would have the opportunity again to talk with Beck about a new book, later in the week. In the meantime, there were country roads to navigate, villages to wander through. Judith and Evan planned an excursion to Italy for a few days, but turned back when they ran into unexpected snow and treacherous roads. The weather had turned very cold.

Julia invited Judith and Evan to another dinner at La Pitchoune, along with Eda Lord and Sybille Bedford—she wanted them all to meet. Child roasted a turkey for dinner.

Bedford had that marvelous, regal bearing, Jones thought. She was very direct, self-assured, and liked to talk about wine. At some point, the conversation turned to their old friend M.F., and how she'd gone off on her own to Arles before Christmas.

Bedford turned to Jones: "*You* were the one who sent M.F. away," she said. Bedford was joking, sort of, but also quite serious. Her theory was that M.F. was avoiding her editor—she didn't want to deal with Jones. M.F. hated being edited.

Child was sure this wasn't true in the slightest. M.F. was quite fond of Jones, she knew. Child was also irritated at Bedford's stentorian proclamations, and the impugning of her friend's motives.

After a bit of back-and-forth, Child said, "Well, let's just settle this right now!" She knew M.F. was at the Grand Hôtel Beauvau by now (her favorite in Marseille), and she would call her. They had finished dinner and were still sitting at the dining table.

The phone had a long cord, and Child passed it to Jones. She heard M.F.'s whispery voice on the other end of the line: "Of course, dear," she told Jones, "I will see you in a day or two here in Marseille." They would meet at her hotel. She'd gone off on her own to write, and think, that's all.

During this brief conversation, the phone cord was stretched across Bedford's throat, Jones noticed with some alarm; Bedford was fending it off with her hands. It was a bit of inadvertent symbolism that she would not soon forget.

Child had been right. M.F. was not avoiding her editor. Bedford had been wrong, and Child had proved her wrong.

It was a small, seemingly insignificant moment. But for Child, the battle against self-satisfied, superior European "expertise" had become personal.

✦ ✦ ✦

At the New Year's Eve *réveillon*, lingering tension surrounded Child and Beck: Would they discuss their future relationship? Beck knew that Child was going her own way, embracing her television celebrity and working on books related to the show. Beck would not be involved. Of course it was a bit galling that her American friend had become "the French Chef," when it was she who was *actually* French.

For Child, the decision wasn't simply a matter of escaping Beck's unfailing certitude about her way being the right way (i.e., the French way); no, it was also a matter of respect. "It is a fact,"

Julia said, "that she has never considered me a cook worth bothering about."

✦ ✦ ✦

For dinner at Le Vieux Mas, Beck served a fusillade of dishes, culminating in her annual *potée normande*. Her husband, Jean, had personally killed their year-old hen for the dish.

CAVIAR

SHRIMP IN FLAKY PASTRY

SMOKED SALMON

PÂTÉ OF *GRIVES* (THRUSHES)

FOIE GRAS

POTÉE NORMANDE

Cooking the *potée normande* was a five-hour affair. It was an elaborate, long-simmering dish of beef, pork, chicken, and sausage in a broth with carrots, onion, turnips, parsnips, and leeks. Beck cooked it in an enormous copper cauldron while she prepared the other dishes. The caviar, smoked salmon, and pâté she'd bought; the shrimp pastries and foie gras she prepared herself. The pastries she called *demi-lune* (half-moon) after their shape. To make them, she rolled out *pâte brisée* and cut out four-inch rounds; she sautéed tiny shrimp with onion, diced apples, cream, and a bit of curry powder. This filling was spooned onto the pastry, which was then folded over, glazed with an egg wash, and baked. She arranged them on a large tray.

For the foie gras, Beck cooked the fresh goose liver in a terrine with Armagnac. Jean made the rounds among the guests with each new delicacy. Paul and Julia sat with their French neighbors, toasting the New Year.

In the kitchen, Jones raised the idea once again of Beck writing a cookbook. She would be eager to publish it, of course—she was a great admirer of Beck's instinctive talents and original recipes—and Jones also knew that if Beck were to begin work on a book, that would go a long way to clearing the air between her and Child.

Jones reminded Beck of some of the wonderful recipes they had not had time to fit into *Mastering II*—here was a way to use them. Like that pork, brown sugar, and whiskey braise they had corresponded about at such great length. And Child, too, Jones said, felt strongly that Beck should have a book of her own.

Beck nodded. She understood that this was a face-saving way forward, and she also started to see that it could be a good move for her. Soon her enthusiasm got the better of her, and they were discussing how the cookbook might be organized, other possible recipes to include, and so on. Beck proposed a series of menus organized by style: menus for informal occasions, for more formal occasions, and for special occasions.

Some of the meals, she said, might be inspired by regional cooking—"Autumn in Normandy," for example. Other menus might be suited to a particular moment—"After a winter walk in the woods," a "High Tea," or even a "Hunt Breakfast." Beck would write brief introductory sketches describing how she had prepared these meals, adding colorful recollections and bits of advice.

Of course, they would need to engage a coauthor, Jones said, someone who could translate Beck's recipes and stories. "Certainly I am able to read chapters in French and ask logical questions," she said. "But there should be someone who would do the dog work."

Jones had a few ideas about possible coauthors; in the meantime, Beck would write up six or eight recipes and send them along. This would not be a book for beginners, she said, but rather for those "who adore to cook and partake of *la véritable cuisine à la française*—the true French cuisine."

♦ ♦ ♦

When the *potée normande* was done, Beck made a sauce with some of the cooking broth and heavy cream. This was then served over the thick slices of beef, pork, sausage, and chicken, along with the carrots and leeks. Large bowls were passed around, steam rising from the fragrant meat and soup.

It was almost midnight when they finished eating. Jean opened the champagne, and everyone stood and toasted the New Year— 1971! To old friends and new adventures!—kissing one another on both cheeks. Someone put an old foxtrot record on the old Victrola, and they all danced and laughed.

Child and Beck never did talk directly about their split. "There was no need to," Child would later write. "After so many years of working together, we knew each other inside out. Now we were graduating from each other and going our separate ways."

♦ ♦ ♦

41 minutes into 1971, and only in this wild, violent vital town could the noise be so sustained—like a too-long concert of very

modern music for auto horns, old coronets and trumpets, guns, churchbells, sirens. In my room high above the *vieux* port I am in a kind of cocoon of sound. It is hypnotic.

M.F. was in Marseille. The noise was tremendous, exhilarating—liberating, somehow. She felt at ease. She had escaped a major storm by no more than an hour or so when she left Avignon the day after Christmas on what turned out to be the last train out. A light snow had begun to fall, and the driver she'd hired to take her to the station cursed and said it would never last, but soon enough the trains were stopping, thousands of cars were stranded on the road, and the Red Cross was hard at work.

But she had made it to Marseille, and to the Grand Hôtel Beauvau. This was a sentimental favorite, of all the hotels M.F. had ever known, the one she loved the most. Here, she did feel at home. She felt warm, released from the lonely quest in Arles and Avignon. She'd been coming here since 1932, and the same severe, all-knowing concierge had been presiding over the lobby since the beginning. He never smiled, but she sensed a certain warmth. "I came to think of him as unflinching, eternal, like Gibraltar but a little nicer," she noted.

The Beauvau was at the old harbor, with views of the fishing boats and all the urgent excitement of that environment. The hotel was not for everyone; indeed, though it was her favorite, she did not routinely recommend it to others. They might find it too loud, or too foreign. But as far as she was concerned, the good old Beauvau, which had been newly redecorated and refurbished in what she considered excellent taste, was better than ever. Yes, she was at home, but ready to *return* home, too. She had written what she needed to write in her journal; she had made her peace with France.

Marseille was enchantingly beautiful at this season—there were delicate garlands of pale gold decorating the harbor, and a fantastic arch with representations of eleven kinds of fish, and festoons of sea-blue lights like waves on either side. The whole town was giddy, and she had the best seat in the house.

And now it was a radiant blue New Year's Day, *very* cold, with a rough, windy sea. The storm was still coming. The noise of celebration in the streets had lasted all night. She listened in astonishment, and did not sleep at all—writing a letter to Gingrich and then reading until about four o'clock in the morning. Afterward she lay in bed, warm and relaxed. The noise continued until about eight o'clock in the morning. Such a vigorous outpouring could surely happen only in Marseille, she thought, and only on the *Vieux* Port.

Today, the first day of 1971, she felt unusually well.

⌒15⌒

GOING HOME

FRANCE WAS PARALYZED BY COLD AND SNOW.
The storm had arrived two days after Christmas and lasted a week.
The Associated Press reported on the aftermath:

Paris, Jan. 3—Helicopters dropped food today to some of the 72
communities in the Rhone Valley still isolated by a record snow-
fall, and the rest of France struggled out from under a week-long
freeze.

Elsewhere in Europe, there was treacherous ice, snow, heavy
fog, gales and rain.

Thousands returned to Paris after exhausting trips from holidays on the sunny Riviera. Planes and trains from the south were
booked solid, and on the Nice–Paris line many passengers spent the
night standing because all seats had been reserved days in advance.

The storm cut short the time Jones and M.F. had together in
Marseille: Judith and Evan's flight to Paris was canceled, so they

had to take their chances on one of the very crowded trains north. The women had planned a leisurely several days, including time to go over edits on M.F.'s manuscript, and lunches and dinners in several restaurants. They would have to do it all in a compressed schedule.

It was true, just as Sybille Bedford had intuited, that M.F. took no pleasure in being edited, and in fact hated to revisit, or even read, her own writing. On the other hand, M.F. really liked Jones, who was in her mid-forties: young, dynamic, and smart. They met at the Beauvau in the New Year and talked about *Among Friends.*

The book was a memoir of M.F.'s early childhood in Whittier, California, a series of vignettes that Jones proposed dividing into three sections: "The Family," "The Town," ". . . And Beyond." M.F. had grown up as the oldest child in a large and busy household, overseen by her reserved mother, Edith, and much-adored father, Rex, who ran the town newspaper. They were Episcopalians in a predominantly Quaker town, and the social politics of Whittier's religious and ethnic divisions was a thread that ran through the book. M.F. and her family lived mostly segregated from the town's Quaker majority, not shunned, but never accepted. The politics of Whittier in the early twentieth century still resonated today, M.F. explained:

> I think this way of life was a good introduction to the powers
> and also the weaknesses of human prejudice, if not of love itself.
> It taught me a lot about why people must turn other people off.
> They seem to press an invisible button that says "No" or "Jewish"
> or "Garlic," and something mystical goes dead. Well, with chil-
> dren all the buttons can be pressed, but if the little human beings

are healthy in their spirits, the life flows on, innocently, irreversibly. It did with me, and I'm thankful for this plain fact.

M.F. also wrote about food and cooking: the Victorian and rather puritanical sensibility of her maternal grandmother Holbrook, who lived with them, she credited with nurturing, by counterexample, the family's "latent sensuality and gourmandise." Her parents and she and her siblings all loved eating together boisterously, especially when the strict Holbrook was absent: "We had a fine time when she was not there, mostly in the dining room," M.F. wrote.

M.F. learned to cook at her mother's side, standing on a footstool, beating eggs for the occasional Saturday cake and licking the bowl afterward as a reward. Later, she filled in for the family cook on her day off: "It made me feel creative and powerful," she wrote, "and that is possibly the truest reason for my continuing preoccupation with the art of eating."

I had to fight for my place on stage, and I soon discovered, no matter how melodramatically now and then, that almost everybody smiles passing beams of pleasure if a little girl, or even a jaded old one, can turn out good scrambled eggs and a commendable oyster stew, a crisp well-seasoned salad, even a cupcake. That was my way to show that I was there *too* . . . and perhaps it still is.

When she was six, her mother took her to a restaurant for the first time, along with her sister Anne: to the Victor Hugo, in downtown Los Angeles. It was thrilling. This was a restaurant M.F. had heard her parents talk about, the epitome of grown-up sophistication. She asked for chicken à la king. She could still remember the black-suited waiters—teams of them—and their enormous silver chafing dishes and glittering spoons.

Now, as M.F. and Jones went through the manuscript in Marseille, they sat in the restaurant Centra and ate *loup au fenouil* (sea bass with fennel). The fish was poached, they noticed, which was unusual, but quite good.

M.F. was happy not to be eating alone. She had survived her "solo performance," as she thought of it—the two-plus weeks in Arles and Avignon—and was feeling carefree. She was tired of writing and of her own internal monologue. It was nice to hear someone else talk for a change. M.F. and Jones discussed the menus and cooking techniques at the restaurants they visited, they told each other about their respective Christmas adventures, and Jones led the way through M.F.'s soon-to-be published book. Most of the changes were minor, fixing word repetitions in consecutive sentences, that sort of thing, but she also wanted a new introduction, and so, by the time they were through, M.F. was left with what she cheerfully referred to as a "nasty pile of work." But she didn't mind. They'd had fun, and just as with the Childs, she had great respect and affection for both Judith and Evan, and for the two of them as a couple.

M.F. and Jones had another meal at the Jambon de Parme, one of M.F's local favorites—the most delicate ravioli she'd ever had, she declared—and then they had to part company. Judith and Evan took the train to Paris, where they discovered that their flight to New York had also been canceled. It took a few days more to get home. M.F., meanwhile, stayed on at the Beauvau a few days longer, waiting for her flight to California. She was looking forward to home. For one thing, she'd had enough of eating in restaurants. She was *bored* of restaurants. She wanted to cook for herself.

❖ ❖ ❖

M.F.'s thirteen-hour flight from Marseille to San Francisco turned into a journey of five days. The weather was still bad—there was terrible fog in England, and an unplanned stopover in Iceland.

Beck and her husband drove from Provence to Neuilly, the quiet town where they lived on the outskirts of Paris, once the roads had been cleared. It took ten hours of slow, tense, dangerous driving.

Judith and Evan arrived in New York several days later than expected. No one at home had paid any attention to Europe's winter storms, and when Jones finally made it into her office at Knopf and gave her excuses, people only said, "Oh yeah, *Gay Paree*," and laughed.

The Childs remained in Provence, enjoying a few weeks of solitude before their own return home. "The captains and kings have departed," Julia said, "every one." Julia was paying her bills, which she'd ignored over the holidays. The weather was cold— there were even a few snow showers, highly unusual in Plascassier. She and Paul returned to Cambridge in mid-January. Julia worked on recipes for the TV show; filming would begin again later that month, and she needed to be ready.

Olney had spent the holidays in Italy, visiting his younger brother, Byron, and family in Vicenza. Byron was a doctor, and stationed there with the U.S. Army. Olney's pre-Christmas flight, like every other flight that season, it seemed, had been a disaster— landing him in Genoa instead of Venice. He hated Alitalia without reservation—"the rudest and most incompetent of national airlines," he declared. He took a train from Genoa and arrived the next day. White truffles were still in season, and he and his brother and sister-in-law admired the piles of them in local shops, "grayish-white, stone-like objects, which, when cut into, presented a pearly flesh veined with feathers of faded lilac," Olney wrote; "the perfume was explosive." He returned to Solliès-Toucas in early January.

In New York, Beard landed in the hospital in the New Year. His legs were worse, not better—quite swollen and painful—and he could barely walk. He had resisted the hospital, but his doctor had insisted, so there he was for six days. "It is annoying and seems unnecessary but nevertheless it happened," he wrote to Child from his hospital bed. But the treatment was apparently working, and the swelling was much reduced.

And so 1971 began: cold, stormy, and with low visibility. It was a year of new beginnings.

⌐16⌐

LAST HOUSE

M.F. MADE IT HOME, EXCEPT THAT SHE HAD no home, really. She had sold her house in St. Helena to longtime acquaintances with the understanding that she would rent it from them until her new house was built. But while she was gone, they had begun to move in—painting the walls, piling her books, papers, and correspondence in the basement. Her telephone had been disconnected, causing all kinds of confusion. Her daughter Anna had tried to call and been told quite firmly by the operator that no one by M.F.'s name had ever been listed in St. Helena. "Murder," M.F. thought, imagining Anna's confusion at being told her mother's listing (and that of her childhood home) had disappeared without a trace. Anna was high strung enough as it was.

Despite her momentarily awkward domestic arrangements, M.F. was happy to be back in California, near her sister, daughters, and grandchildren. For the first few months of the year, she divided her time between her old house during the week, when the new owners were away, and the guesthouse at the Bouverie ranch on the weekends, where she watched her new house being built. As she drove back and forth in her VW, she brought boxes and boxes of books, preparing for the move into Last House. She watched the doorknobs being fitted and the tiles being laid. Though the guesthouse gradually overflowed with cartons of books and papers, she never quite had everything she needed for her work.

"Split living is not for me," she declared. She was looking forward to moving in.

M.F. was working on the new introduction to *Among Friends* for Judith. She was also preparing for the republication of two earlier volumes. Her friend and editor Eleanor Friede at Macmillan would be reissuing *The Art of Eating* in late February. This was the omnibus collection of M.F.'s first five books, for which James Beard had agreed to write an "Appreciation"—a short essay for the new edition, to follow the Clifton Fadiman introduction that was in the first edition. ("Her subject is hunger," Fadiman had written. "But only ostensibly so. Food is her paramount but not obsessive concern. It is the release-catch that sets her mind working.") Originally published in 1954, the collection included *Serve It Forth*, *Consider the Oyster*, *How to Cook a Wolf*, *The Gastronomical Me*, and *An Alphabet for Gourmets*—the books that had made her reputation in the 1930s, '40s, and '50s. Later in the year, Knopf was planning to republish M.F.'s translation of Brillat-Savarin's seminal early-nineteenth-century *Physiology of Taste*, which she had done in 1949.

And so there would be a lot of M. F. K. Fisher in 1971. She had mixed feelings about it. "Except for the new Quaker stuff," she wrote to Gingrich, referring to *Among Friends*, "this is the year that WAS, for Fisher . . . a Voice from the Past. Makes me feel odd . . ."

It felt odd because she was moving in a new direction.

But it was all good for her popular standing: she had reached a new plateau in her career. Her brand of direct, self-revealing writing and her embrace of taste and style as a high-low improvisation fit the mood of the moment. She wrote about oysters and ocean liners and small-town bistros in France, about potato chips and tripe, and about eating alone, being in love, and growing up. She was no Voice from the Past. Indeed, the world seemed only now to be catching up to her.

In his "Appreciation," James Beard described his discovering *How to Cook a Wolf* during World War II and meeting M.F. many years later. He focused on her range, and managed to communicate how very modern—indeed, prescient—these books were:

Mrs. Fisher is a woman who has had many gifts bestowed upon her—beauty, intelligence, heart, a capacity for the pleasures of the flesh, of which the art of eating is no small part, and the art of language as well. Though she can write with a silver attelet dipped in a sauce of Carême or Montagne, her palate goes beyond ortolans and rare vintages. She can also write about eating and drinking with a pure, primitive enjoyment. I think of that intoxicating description, in *Alphabet for Gourmets*, of a family meal in Switzerland, *al fresco*, highlighted by the ritual of eating peas fresh from the garden, cooked right on the spot. This celebration—it could be called nothing else—supports my thesis that good simple food, even rudimentary food, can give the same delight as the most elaborately prepared dishes.

As soon as it came out, Paul and Julia Child each wrote to congratulate M.F. on *The Art of Eating*. "We are re-reading it with pleasure—re-pleasure!" Paul wrote. "We are delighted to re-have it," said Julia, "and just love that appreciation by Jim Beard. I think that is one of the most charming bits of J. A. B. I've read, full of love and warmth and so deftly said." She asked how the construction of Last House was coming along, and described the renovations underway at their house in Cambridge—"dust, disorder, and stacked up furniture."

Last House was being built without a hitch, M.F. said. Bouverie had told her with cautious astonishment that he'd never seen a house go up with fewer complications—and he'd built a number of them on his ranch already. M.F. might be in by Easter.

◆ ◆ ◆

And so she was: in the spring of 1971, M.F. moved into Last House. It was beautiful, set back a long distance from the country road that ran through Sonoma's Valley of the Moon and surrounded by pasture land. The cows took some getting used to, roaming in lumbering fashion across the land, the calves stopping in the shade of the house to lick the stucco walls. M.F. wondered if they would walk in through one of the open doorways to her terrace, but they never did. There were wildflowers growing in the fields, and stands of live oak and walnut trees. Across the valley in the distance were rolling hills planted with wine grapes.

The house had thick walls and high, vaulted ceilings, built-in floor-to-ceiling bookshelves, and black tile floors. There were two large, spacious rooms, each with a Franklin stove, and a luxuriously large bathroom with a claw-foot tub. One of the walls and the ceiling of the bathroom were painted a dark, rich Pompeian red, and the same color backed the bookshelves and cupboards throughout the house.

M.F. unpacked her thousands of books and arranged them according to subject. She put down her slightly threadbare but newly cleaned Persian carpets. On the walls were numerous paintings by Dillwyn Parrish and a few hand-painted posters advertising an agricultural fair, which she'd bought in Dijon in the 1930s, when she was living there with Al Fisher. She hung small paintings and reproductions in the bathroom, too. The simple kitchen lined one wall of the living room; the cabinets were white—she'd fended off the currently fashionable avocado and harvest gold colors. Facing west was a large covered veranda with wicker furniture and some old wicker trunks from Provence.

Her sister Norah came to visit frequently—she had bought a house on the Sonoma coast a few years earlier, in Jenner, just over an hour's drive away. Her daughter Anna, who was living in Oregon, called and wrote; her daughter Kennedy and her family came to visit from Oakland now and then. And in June, Arnold Gingrich flew in from New York for a weekend. She met him in San Francisco for a crab lunch, and then they drove to Glen Ellen, where he admired her new house and the views of the Bouverie ranch from her windows.

M.F. was home.

She wrote at her desk in her bedroom, and drank vermouth and gin cocktails on the terrace, with one of her two cats at her feet.

✦ ✦ ✦

The reviews of her various books later that year were good: in the *Times,* Raymond Sokolov, the young one-time foreign correspondent who had taken over Craig Claiborne's food editor position, described her translation of *The Physiology of Taste* as "a work of skill and devotion. Mrs. Fisher, the doyenne of American food writers, has not only translated well but has also contributed extensive notes on the text that will be valued for themselves as well as for the contemporary counterpoint they add to Brillat-Savarin's august yet flippant 'meditations.' " In *Vogue,* the eminent—and in this case rather florid—Jean Stafford reviewed *Among Friends:* "This memoir of M. F. K. Fisher is a needle in the arm filled with nectar and ichor, and distillations of irony and wondrous corn and sassy razzmatazz and tempered temper tantrums and tolerance." *The New Yorker* highlighted the book's thematic connection with the contemporary civil rights movement, calling the religious divisions M.F. observed as a child in Quaker-dominated Whittier an "almost impalpable Jim Crow arrangement," and concluding: "Her account of her family's evolution and her own growing up is, in one sense, proof that 'belonging' is not everything, and, in another, an indictment of every form of exclusiveness that has ever been attempted in this country."

Most important to M.F. was her sister's reaction.

The trip to France had brought them closer than ever: "At this stage in our lives as sisters we enjoy many of the same things," M.F. wrote of Norah.

M.F.'s success as a writer was one of the things seldom discussed in the family—her parents, when they were alive, had never felt it necessary to comment on any of her books. "Any publication of mine was treated as if I had just developed a recurrence of my old syphilis," M.F. wrote, only half-jokingly, to Gingrich. But now Norah chose to speak out: she had read *Among Friends,* she wrote

M.F., "and at the grave risk of breaking the long tradition of utter silence will indicate to you that I like it very much—it is a very warm, genial record."

M.F. was much gratified to hear that. "Dearest N.," she wrote, ". . . yes, it was pretty reckless of you to break the Embarrassed Family Hush! Thank you, though . . . what you think and do not think matters very much to me . . . perhaps even more than it *should* . . . or is that possible?"

In the same letter in which Norah commented on M.F.'s memoir, she told her that she had begun to contemplate retirement from her counseling position in the Berkeley schools. Norah, then in her early fifties, wrote:

> I suppose that I really believe I will *fall into* a delightful useful
> way to spend the next 10 or 15 years, which is not very realistic.
> I too would prefer not to be so well-cushioned, but every
> alternative I think of seems goody-goody and/or sanctimonious.
> I love the water and the garden and Jenner but am far from
> ready to sit and snooze forever—well Doc?

M.F. responded that "it does seem strange to me that you are getting out of a 'career' you have devoted yourself to, at a really young age . . . I like to think of you as a vigorous and eminently *sane* (Mens sano etc) woman well into the 70s and still stamping about life . . . But doing what?" She didn't have an answer, but she was encouraging. "Only you can know that, and I feel absolutely sure that you do know."

✦ ✦ ✦

M.F. had begun a new chapter in Glen Ellen, a relaxed and socia-
ble one. David Bouverie entertained a stream of visitors, and she
found herself in the role of hostess at many of these gatherings.
He called M.F. his "writer-in-residence" or sometimes his "resident
recluse"—"R.R." for short. She, in turn, referred to him as "Squire
Bouverie" or, in letters to him while he was traveling, as her "ab-
sentee landlord." She mockingly addressed one envelope with a
numbered list of names:

1. David P. Bouverie
2. David Pleydell Bouverie
3. David Pleydell-Bouverie

He returned it with annotations in red ink—an "Explanation
for Mary Frances!" "This I reject whenever possible," he wrote of
number 1. "This is the 'take it or leave it' compromise," he wrote
of number 2. "This is mandatory for social columns *and* at the
Knickerbocker Club *and* in England. It is also incomprehensible
to genealogical illiterates and I am tired of *explaining* something
so *irrelevant*," he wrote of number 3. "Q.E.D., D.P-B." he wrote
at the bottom of the envelope.

They had developed an affectionate, teasing repartee, something
like a flirtation. Gingrich jealously wondered if she had "turned
into Madame Butterfly," to which M.F. scoffingly replied that she
and Bouverie were "as amiably sexless as two bulbs in a flower-bed,
two potatoes in a bin." In any event, Bouverie's sexuality was a
veiled affair. It was understood but unspoken that he was gay.

They talked about art, news, and gossip; when he was away,
M.F. sent amusing reports about local goings-on, how the trees

and plantings were holding up, what she was working on at the moment—she had an assignment from *Travel + Leisure* to write about oysters, and *Playboy* might send her off to explore the restaurants of New Orleans. Bouverie sent notes describing his glamorous travels, taking evident delight in his good fortune while also winking at the madness of it all. Scrawled on the back of a postcard from Hotel Las Brisas in Acapulco: "Flew direct from New York in a fast private jet. Ann & Edgar Bronfman have two larger houses further along from the little ones shown on this card. Edgar quite rightly tries to prevent [the staff] from dropping hibiscus buds in the swimming pools every morning!"

Bouverie and M.F. shared an American sense of humor and irreverence about society, taste, and the inflexible certitudes of European snobbery. Her recent trip to France had only reinforced the sentiment.

From London that fall, on letterhead bearing the address 45 Park Lane, Bouverie wrote:

My dear RR,

The above address is a pseudonym for the London Playboy Club apartments. The Ritz was full . . . The lobby is a riot, for the girls come simpering in and go whimpering out day and night. The rooms (which are as costly as the Ritz) are five or six feet wide and twelve feet long. If there were not a kitchenette (two feet from the bed and *in* the room), radio, TV, and suggestive paintings, one would consider it, in old fashioned parlance, a servant's room!

With the top of my head I admire English fortitude and England's "cultural heritage," but with my solar plexus I detest it all, and the horrors of my youth well up in me and fester. At least I have achieved enough detachment to come here, do a little Samaritan "turn," and split.

Bouverie had found liberation of sorts in comparatively free-wheeling California. And at Last House, M.F., too, felt rejuvenated. "I am no longer the woman whose children have grown up and whose husbands have died, dusting the corners now and then and trying to write," she wrote. She had settled into a "new pattern of life." She was happy, serene—and more productive than she'd been in a long time.

+ + +

In December 1971, the Childs came to visit M.F. at Last House. They stayed for the weekend, sleeping in the Bouverie ranch guest-house. Bouverie was away for the season, in New York.

Julia and Paul adored M.F.'s small house, and the open, rural Sonoma landscape. At the end of her long, unpaved driveway, they had stopped to admire the tongue-in-cheek sign on the fence: TRES-PASSERS WILL BE VIOLATED.

"I hope you won't collapse like balloons in the quiet," M.F. said, laughing. "Sometimes people turn and toss the first night here, because the air is so sweet and the silence so silent."

Last House was charming, cozy, *Provençal,* Julia declared—it suited M.F. perfectly. They had brought her a gift: a large wreath made of herbs and fruits. M.F. served bread and cheese and ver-mouth cocktails, and they sat in her book-filled living room and talked. Beard had recently suffered a heart attack, which sent him to the hospital for nearly a month. But now he was doing well, Julia reported—so well, in fact, that he was planning to go to France for the holidays. The Childs had lent him La Pitchoune; they were staying home.

They marveled at Beard's fortitude. M.F. had last seen him in New York the previous spring—they'd had tea and croissants in his town house on West Tenth Street, and he'd been in great form. He planned to visit M.F. soon in California, he said, and tour the local vineyards.

The next day, M.F. took the Childs to the nearby town of Sonoma. It was a pleasantly sleepy place, set around a tree-filled plaza and home to the Sonoma Mission, a whitewashed adobe complex built by the Spanish in the 1820s and now a historic site. The buildings had a somber, mysterious beauty about them, and the walls were decorated with Native American patterns.

Everywhere Julia went, people stopped her. "*Juuuulia,*" they would say, delighted to see the French Chef in person, their dear friend from television. It wasn't just that she was famous: Child's TV persona was sui generis, combining passionate instruction; a theatrical, at times comic sensibility; and real human warmth. It all served to make her both supremely fascinating and supremely approachable. Indeed, the Child on television and the Child in person were one and the same.

"She is unfailingly gentle and warm," M.F. observed, as three different fans in downtown Sonoma expressed their admiration, "and always knows somebody's maiden aunt or something." Child connected with people, embracing her role as a pop culture icon.

Just around the corner from the mission was the Swiss Hotel, where they went for a midday drink after touring the mission. The restaurant and bar at the Swiss were regular stops for M.F.—she'd taken Judith and Evan Jones there a few weeks earlier when they had come to visit. It was a family-run place, unchanged for generations. They ordered Bear Hair sherry, the house label, as Child greeted yet more well-wishers. The sherry was delicious, they all agreed. They ordered another round.

✦ ✦ ✦

That afternoon, after the Childs retreated to the guesthouse for a nap, M.F. blanched pieces of a cauliflower, small zucchini, tiny rosy potatoes in their skins, and green, stringless beans. She cooled the vegetables briefly in a bowl of ice water and then arranged them in piles on a long, narrow fish platter. The beans she placed in an orderly stack, followed by the cauliflowerets, the potatoes, and a row of zucchini. She put the platter in the refrigerator. Then she minced a clove of garlic and anchovies from a tin, with which she made a strongly flavored vinaigrette. She stewed plums with water and sugar to make a sauce for the dessert, pureeing it afterward. In the refrigerator were two boxes of ravioli she had bought for the occasion. The simple dinner was more or less ready to serve, as soon as her guests arrived.

FRESH RAVIOLI

BLANCHED, CHILLED VEGETABLES WITH AN ANCHOVY SAUCE

ICE CREAM WITH PUREED PLUMS

M.F. had invited her neighbors, Genie and Ranieri di San Faustino, to join them. The San Faustinos were a genial San Francisco couple—she was American; he was an Italian prince—and they stayed in one of Bouverie's houses on many weekends.

They drank cocktails and set the table. They talked about Sonoma—how much the Childs had liked the mission—and about news of the food world. Elizabeth David was having a sad, difficult time in London, M.F. had heard in a letter from Lord—David's sister had committed suicide, leaving her to care for the orphaned children. They discussed the sudden death of Michael Field, earlier in the year. "We last saw him at a party when our *Vol. II* came out," Julia said, "and he was like a wild man. Pale, greenish gray, thin to emaciation, eyes darting. It was as though he was driving himself to breakdown and death." Field had personified the sped-up, big-money metabolism of the modern food world, and now he was gone. "He seems to have dropped into a well—boom-plop, and that was the end of him," Julia continued. "I somehow thought there would be more talk, or writings, or something. But no. Silence." It was strange when people died, how quickly they were forgotten.

On a happier note, Beck was as robust and forceful as ever, Child reported; she was already nearly done with her book.

M.F. served the ravioli with butter and sage, and Paul opened a bottle of wine. The cold vegetables were set in the middle of the table, accompanied by the vinaigrette. They raised their glasses and toasted M.F. and her new house.

As they ate, they talked about southern France. The Childs had been back at La Pitchoune in the spring—"enjoying life and being totally relaxed, even incognito," Julia said. She relished her anonymity there. She loved the fact that the phone never rang. Paul said the old olive trees had survived the winter well, but the darling, scrawny tree he'd planted on the terrace had looked as scrawny as ever.

The dishwasher had finally been installed.

M.F. loved hearing about Provence, and La Pitchoune. "I cannot even think of Plascassier," she said, "without a strange twinge, and kind of generalized *pinggg* that goes from just above my heart down to my pelvis. I suppose it is incurable." Still, she no longer had any doubt that this was where she belonged, at Last House. She felt settled.

They ended the evening with ice cream and the still-warm plum sauce, happy to be in Sonoma, among friends.

✦ ✦ ✦

The Childs left the next morning before dawn. M.F., still in bed, heard their car creeping away and had a sudden, childish urge to rush to the window and wave. She adored them both.

The following week they sent a letter of thanks, and it captured all the beauty of her new house, and her new life in Glen Ellen.

Dec 12, 1971

Dear M*F*
This cannot be construed as a "bread and butter letter" because so much more than B&B runneth over from your generous cup: The food had to be splendid and interesting, naturally. But only you have Charlie-the-cat, a cow-barrier at your front door which, happily, allows people to pass in, an extravagant dressing table mirror facing a Queen-of-Egypt tub, a view into

the embracing arms of a live oak growing up from a baroque pedestal of moss-covered boulders, thousands of readable books, a black and white fresco of grapes framed in an arch, a very special vermouth, a four-painting-decorated skylight, a tile floor glittering like black ice, the odor of wet eucalyptus trees hovering over the house . . . in short, your special personal creation, satisfying, filled with delights and beauties, a pleasure to know.

While writing this letter, I see you there, like the Tibetan "jewel in the center of the lotus"—a memory full of pleasure for us both.

Paul & Julia

~17~

NEW BEGINNINGS

IN THE SPRING OF 1971, BEARD FINALLY FIN-
ished *American Cookery*, his magnum opus. It had taken six years.
Little, Brown planned to publish the book the following year.

Beard was soon back to his relentless schedule—writing his
column, teaching classes, consulting for restaurants, appearing in
commercials for Spice Islands and Heckers Flour. He remained
somewhat hobbled by his various ailments, but forged ahead anyway. He wore long compression stockings to prevent swelling,
and his doctors outfitted him with special shoes. They were enormously comfortable, Beard declared. He thought they looked like
eighteenth-century boots—quite dashing.

His friends continued to worry about his health, but he was
in good spirits. One reason was his latest acolyte, Felipe Rojas-
Lombardi, a beautiful young Peruvian chef working as an assistant
for Beard's cooking classes. He had wavy hair and a beard and an
angelic smile. It was not a sexual relationship, but it was romantic
in its way—the eager young student flattered and enlivened Beard.

Beard began losing weight. At Rojas-Lombardi's urging, he had stopped drinking liquor, and bought some new clothes.

Jones had been taking Beard to lunch with some regularity, trying to convince him to write a book about bread. Bread was having its countercultural moment: everyone, it seemed, was baking "hearth bread." And Beard had been complaining for years about the poor quality of American bread. Jones figured the iconic Beard could write the definitive book on the topic. *Beard on Bread*, they would call it.

Beard had resisted while writing *American Cookery*, but now that it was done he agreed to take on the bread book. The narrow focus and modest ambition of the project was a relief after the monumentalism of the American book.

Jones enlisted junior staffers at Knopf to test the bread recipes, and Beard would stop by the office to examine and judge the results. It was remarkable how different the loaves turned out, even though they were all following the same recipes, and starting with the same ingredients. Breadmaking was not about the recipe; it was about technique. Beard was a brilliant teacher, but when it came to sitting down to work, Jones discovered, he found it hard to focus. If the phone rang while they were working together, he would inevitably take the call and end up talking at great length to some woman in Iowa about her macaroons. Beard kept his phone number listed, and loved hearing from his fans and readers.

◆ ◆ ◆

In Cambridge, meanwhile, in 1971 and 1972, Child was immersed in her television show. It was stressful, but she loved it. *The French Chef* was filmed twice a week at a dedicated studio on Western Avenue in Boston. Each shooting day was preceded by a rehearsal day, and the days were long. There was now a thirty-five-person crew at work on the show, assembling ingredients, filming close-ups, washing dishes. The program had been in reruns in the late 1960s, while Child was working on *Mastering II*, but it had remained popular. Now in color, Child was seen on 134 public television stations nationwide. She was bigger than ever.

People stopped her on the street to tell her they loved her—Paul called them "JWs," short for "Julia Watchers." Newspapers and magazines profiled her and the show, lauding her unflappable, entertaining way around the kitchen and her belief that anyone could cook, and cook well, if they were willing to learn. This was the democratization that she believed in, and that Beck had disdained. It was part of her American-ness, just as Beck's attitude had been part of her French-ness.

In early 1971, Child wrote to M.F.:

We are engulfed in our TV and just finished taping our second
show of French bread Thursday—a horrendous experience,
with bowls of dough rising and falling all over the set, hot irons
on the stove, the oven panting, and the whole story to be done in
28 minutes or bust . . .

In fact Child found the chaos of the show energizing, and she defused all tension with her laughter. She also counted on Paul, who was with her every step of the way, working on scripts, managing logistics, and shooting publicity stills on set. They continued to be full partners, as they had always been.

Later that year, Julia and Paul embarked on a national tour to promote the paperback boxed-set edition of *Mastering*. Julia did cooking demonstrations and answered questions from St. Louis to Denver to Seattle and everywhere in between. It was important to get out there, she realized—her large audiences in these cities "could care less about the East Coast and the *New York Times*," she wrote to Beard. "They have their own good lives and own good papers, and we're not reaching them *atallatall* if we stay put." Beck stayed at home in France; she had disengaged from the *Mastering* books, which were seen as Child's, in any case, and was hard at work on her own *Simca's Cuisine*.

Child made omelets in department stores (frequent stops on her paperback book tour) and staged more elaborate demonstrations at larger venues. She traveled with two assistant cooks in addition to Paul, and signed books for hours wherever she went, an evangelist of cooking.

And thanks in considerable part to her, American food in the early 1970s was indeed changing. But it was a slow process. Yes, there were fashionable dinner parties where *pâté en croûte* and asparagus soup were being served; and yes, there were also community gardens and hippie bakers and natural food co-ops, and large and enthusiastic audiences for books such as *The Whole Earth Cookbook*, *The Commune Cookbook*, and *The Vegetarian Epicure*, all of which were published in the early 1970s. But there were still many places where it was hard to find good fresh produce, much less the more rarified ingredients in some of Child's recipes—many places where the culinary 1950s seemed to live on.

Beard described one of those places in a letter to M.F., when he went on a trip to Plainfield, Indiana, for a cooking demonstration in the spring of 1972. The church group that invited him had served lunch:

The lunch was prepared by the good ladies of the church who do this sort of thing semi-demi and it was true Indiana food via ladies magazines. It turned out to be a piece of iceberg lettuce on each plate with a sad little mound of a mixture of chicken, mandarins, pineapple, chopped pecans, celery and what seemed to me like Aunt Laura's boiled dressing. This was garnished by a cinnamon apple ring and centered with a pimento stuffed olive. The rest of the plate was occupied by an enormous cinnamon bun. This bounty was followed by a large dessert which turned out to be chunks of torn angel food topped with lemon pie filling (from a package, of course) and garnished with something I haven't seen for years—marshmallow cream!

◆ ◆ ◆

Beck was hard at work on her new cookbook in 1971, and had finished writing it by early 1972. Before she began, she and Jones continued their discussion about possible collaborators—that was the first order of business. Jones took charge; she knew that Beck's strength was her creativity and intensity, and that she needed to work with someone who could corral and streamline her ideas. They needed more than simply a translator, in other words.

Jones asked around. One candidate was apparently not very systematic or careful about writing down recipes. That wouldn't work. Another did not want to play second fiddle to the imperious Beck. And then she found Patricia Simon, a well-regarded free-lance food writer based in Pennsylvania.

Simca's Cuisine would be truly French. Although the recipes would not be strictly classical, they would be deeply rooted in Normandy, Alsace, and Provence, and would include recipes from her own family as well as traditional regional preparations. Many were quite elaborate—they were for times, she said, when "one wants to be a little bit special, a little festive."

The first recipe in the book would be Porc Braisé au Whiskey— the very dish that she and Child had fought over when completing the pork chapter the previous year for *Mastering II*. It was a slowly simmered dish (with mustard and brown sugar, in addition to the whiskey) that Beck liked because it was excellent hot or cold. It would be served with timbales of lettuce pureed with shallots and cream, and followed by a green salad and a frozen chocolate mousse. The dessert was a favorite of Jean's—he loved chocolate.

✦ ✦ ✦

As M.F. worked on various magazine assignments and wrote a few book reviews, she was thinking about France. She had come to new terms with the place during her time in Provence, and she wanted to put her thoughts in writing. The natural starting point was the diary she had kept in Arles and Avignon. She showed it to Norah, who encouraged her to send it to Rachel MacKenzie, M.F.'s editor at *The New Yorker*. MacKenzie, one of the few women editors at the magazine, was brilliant, dry, and affectionate, all at the same time. Her advice was that it might work as part of a book, and to send it to Judith Jones at Knopf. And thus began a conversation about a new Provence book. It would have darker shadings than *Map of Another Town*, M.F.'s early sixties book on Aix. It would take the measure of how France had changed, and how M.F. had changed, too. Maybe it would center on Marseille, a port town, a place of comings and goings, a place where she had come and gone countless times.

The book would be called *A Considerable Town* and, though she didn't know it then, would take many years to write.

◆ ◆ ◆

In Solliès-Toucas, Richard Olney was working on his next cookbook, *Simple French Food*. This would be his reaction to the changing times, a fuller expression of the purist food philosophy he'd begun to articulate in the *French Menu Cookbook*, with a greater emphasis on rustic and regional dishes. It would be a cookbook of *la cuisine de bonne femme*, with a strong Provençal influence: stuffed braised cabbages, *daubes à la provençale*, rabbit civets, and terrines.

If Child was finding her voice as a newly liberated American cook, making curries and chowders, Olney was setting the stage for a new view of French cooking, no longer beholden to the litany of four-star restaurant classics. His next book would be based on something more elemental than training or tradition (neither of which he could really claim, being a self-taught American); it would be an expression of his lifestyle. He shopped at the local open-air markets, he cooked whatever was fresh, he improvised freely. Olney lived in rustic seclusion, and this book would represent his brand of "simple" country cooking. Unlike his previous book, which included very elaborate, formal menus and preparations, the new book would emphasize roasts, braises, stews, ragouts, terrines, and grilled dishes; there would be much discussion of tripe, kidneys, livers, and hearts. There would be lots of lamb and rabbit.

For Olney, simple cooking was not necessarily simple. In fact, it was quite difficult. The idea was to create dishes that were what he called "pure in effect": presented without artifice or unnecessary decoration; possessing pure, uncomplicated flavors; celebrating traditional techniques. The recipes would all be for just the sort of effortless-seeming yet transcendent dishes he prepared for guests in his house in Solliès-Toucas. (Needless to say, it took enormous effort to achieve this "pure" effect.)

Olney compared cooking to art—to painting. He would attempt to teach improvisation by laying out basic preparations and then pointing to possible variations. Blindly following step-by-step instructions, a paint-by-numbers approach, was not the way to learn to cook, he felt. He wrote:

> You, the cook, must also be the artist, bringing understanding to mechanical formulas, transforming each into an uncomplicated statement that will surprise or soothe a gifted palate, or from your knowledge drawing elements from many to formulate a new harmony—for such is creativity, be it in the kitchen or in the studio: the application of personal expression to an intimate understanding of the rules.

He planned to include an entire chapter in *Simple French Food* on improvisation, but it proved difficult to set out in any convincing way: "Improvisation is at war with the printed word. It either defies analysis or, in accepting it, finds its wings clipped. The classroom facilitates things; with one's hands deep in the mixing bowl, eliminating a chosen ingredient, deciding to add another, tasting, altering, discussing, the spontaneity is alive and contagious and the result is there to be tasted."

Olney began teaching summer cooking classes in Avignon, mostly to Americans, during which he demonstrated his improvisatory technique. He was busy, though he had never really done much to promote *The French Menu Cookbook*. "He won't do anything to make himself known," Child wrote to M.F. Olney maintained a standoffish distance from the so-called food establishment.

◆ ◆ ◆

Over the coming months and upcoming publishing seasons, their latest books were released, each in its way signaling what was a new direction in American cooking. It was as if the subterranean currents of the fall and winter of 1970 in Provence had sprung forth, shifting the culinary landscape, making way for a fresh and energetic confidence. It was a moment of liberation and experimentation, of discovery and growth. There were ever more cookbooks being published, including some of the first rigorous surveys of international gastronomy, such as Diana Kennedy's *The Cuisines of Mexico* and Claudia Roden's *A Book of Middle Eastern Food*. At Knopf, Jones was instrumental in launching many of these books.

Some of the books sold well, some did not. Beard's *American Cookery* received mixed reviews and modest sales. Nika Hazelton declared it "a marvelous book," but Raymond Sokolov was skeptical of Beard's attempt at a grand theory of American food. He wrote:

> The real problem with Mr. Beard's approach is that it is synthetic, it homogenizes an apparently orderly food heritage for Americans out of the most heterogeneous possible pool of recipes . . . It feels, somehow, too "invented," too much born of a desire to delineate a national cuisine in one volume, to show that America has a cooking style of its own.

The trouble is, America is not a homogenous nation-state like France. And American cooking, when it is good, is a federation of recipes that has grown up with local roots.

Beard took the criticism personally. "What can he have against me?" he asked soon after the review was published in the *New York Times*. "It still hurts and humiliates me very much." He wrote to Sokolov to protest what he considered an unfair attack. Sokolov stood his ground, explaining that he had only the greatest respect for Beard, and had written "in the spirit of a zealous acolyte."

Simca's Cuisine, likewise, did not resonate. "It was a very French book," Child later wrote, "with ambitious menus that demanded a lot from the American cook." There were far fewer detailed, step-by-step instructions, like the ones in the *Mastering* books, and the American audience probably found it intimidating. Child found it charming but wasn't surprised when it didn't sell so well. In the *Times*, Hazelton revered the book as an artifact of the old, disappearing, *douce France*. "They don't make them (or rather, her, Simca) anymore," she wrote, "and her kind of life, the essence of civilized French life, is being swept away by superhighways and supermarkets and the new skyscrapers that have ruined the Paris skyline."

It was *From Julia Child's Kitchen, Beard on Bread*, and Olney's *Simple French Food* that best reflected the shape of things to come, setting the terms and the tone of a new American cooking.

Child's book was an immediate success, powered by her celebrity and her approachable, commonsense instruction. Unlike the *Mastering* books, this one listed all ingredients at the beginning of each recipe, and recounted many amusing anecdotes of her cooking experiences, including near-disasters and close calls on the set of *The French Chef*. She also addressed her readers personally, offering money-saving advice and shopping tips—how to tell the butcher exactly what you need, for example. As she'd planned, she had moved beyond purely French recipes, and her confidence and verve anticipated that of her increasingly sophisticated audience. "The great lesson embedded in the book," she said, "is that no one is *born* a great cook, one learns by *doing* . . . try new recipes, learn from your mistakes, be fearless, and above all have fun!"

In his review, Sokolov remarked on the book's personal tone and broader scope:

> It is a pleasure to read Julia Child's reminiscences about great meals: glimpsing Colette in Monaco's Hôtel de Paris dining room in the 1950s over a bowl of consommé George Sand (a clear fish soup with crayfish quenelles and morels as garnish) and sensing that an era was creeping to a close, but grandly creeping. Julia (great stars are properly known by their first names) discourses with easy learning on the lore of peeling hard-cooked eggs, on turkeys, on all manner of edible subjects large and small, French and non-French.

For Child, the book represented what she called her "great liberation"—from France, from Beck. Perhaps for that very reason, Beck hated it, and so did Olney. They scorned both its detailed explanations of the obvious (seven pages alone on how to boil an egg) and its sometimes playful, intimate tone. "What a problem for cookery bookery writers," Child wrote. "How are we to know the extent of our reader's experience? I, for one, have solved that riddle by deciding to tell all." Experienced cooks could skip ahead, she figured. She also made a point of emphasizing the idea that cooking *well* did not mean cooking *fancy*.

"Now tell me, Richard, very frankly, *what* do you think of Julia's book?" Simca asked Olney when *From Julia Child's Kitchen* came out.

"Very frankly," he said, "it is without interest."

"Yes," she agreed. "I think so too—and those cartoons—*such* bad taste!" (The book contained reproductions of a couple of cooking-related *New Yorker* cartoons by George Price.)

The term *cookery bookery* was also in questionable taste, Olney replied—too "quackery-wackery." He was referring to Child's casual, joking style. Not quite knowing what he meant, Beck agreed wholeheartedly: The book was unsophisticated. It was *American*.

Beard's bread book was also a huge success, and hugely gratifying for him after the dismal *American Cookery* experience. The book was just the sort of definitive, accessible guide that home bakers wanted. *Beard on Bread* brought to America the techniques, textures, and flavors of European baking, translating them for use with American flours and yeast. The book jacket, too, spoke to the cultural moment: a hand-drawn and painted sketch of Beard in his kitchen, with an enormous loaf of bread in the foreground. The cover was printed on light brown paper and wasn't flashy in the least; it looked almost homemade, the aesthetic more Berkeley than New York, resonating with the same audience that was buying titles such as *The Whole Earth Cookbook*. In the *Times*, John Hess reported on the new interest in home-baked bread:

A kitchen revolt is underway, against what the venerable James Beard in *Beard on Bread* calls "spongy, plasticized, tasteless breads, pre-sliced, doctored with nutrients and preservatives, and with about as much gastronomic importance as cotton wool."

Olney's book, *Simple French Food*, was decidedly French, but he, too, had managed to find an informal, personable style that worked for an American audience, presenting authentic dishes in great detail, infusing the recipes with an almost palpable sense of place. Beard had written a brief foreword: "The dishes are not those found in posh restaurants but those one enjoys in comfortable little country restaurants, less prevalent since the Second World War, and in well-run homes where the traditions of good eating have been maintained." Olney's authority and depth of knowledge were rooted in his passionate connection to the land, the markets, flavors, and fragrances of southern France. He made this world accessible, connecting it in spirit to the growing American interest in natural, seasonal ingredients. He had also made consistent efforts to address the American availability of all the ingredients he used, specialty products, herbs and spices. He gave mail-order information for his favorite olive oil. He gave advice and instruction on growing herbs, brining olives, and making vinegar.

Simple French Food was more than a cookbook; it was a treatise of sorts on what he called the "sensuous-sensual-spiritual elements" of cooking. It was also beautifully written. In the *Times*, Hazelton raved:

The book's greatest virtue, I think, is that the author, in his preface on a number of subjects including herbs, wine, improvisation, practicals (oven temperatures, etc.) and in the way he writes the recipes, really teaches you to cook French in a way I've never seen before. Here, you don't learn to cook a set dish, the way an actor acts a set role, but you acquire the methods, the *tour de main*, the tricks that are the heart and essence of French food.

To promote her book, Child traveled far and wide, and made high-profile appearances, including on Barbara Walters's *Not for Women Only* interview program and on the cover of *People* magazine. Beard, too, was frequently on the road, performing cooking demonstrations. And even Olney agreed to come to the United States to promote his new book.

✦ ✦ ✦

On September 4, 1974, Olney arrived in New York on the SS *France*, the same ship M.F. and Norah had taken to France four years earlier. It was the ship's last westbound voyage, as the French Line was finally going out of business. Olney planned to stay for six months, touring the country to teach cooking classes (his publisher, Atheneum, had organized numerous appearances) and visiting his parents in Marathon, Iowa.

Beard had recently moved a few blocks, from Tenth Street to Twelfth Street in Greenwich Village, into a large town house. He had offered to host a launch party for *Simple French Food,* and Olney would be teaching a week's worth of classes in the downstairs demonstration kitchen.

Beard's house was the teeming epicenter of the New York food world, crowded with writers, cooks, students, and acolytes at all hours. Gino Cofacci had launched a small cake and pastry business, and spent all his time in the third-floor kitchen, assembling disks of meringue and layers of butter cream. Beard held court in his jovial manner; Olney arrived to find him surrounded by a group of women, watching a demonstration of how to fry meat on the newly installed CorningWare glass stovetop, a smooth surface embedded with electric burners. Beard asked him about his trip on the *France*, and professed to be shocked when Olney said he'd traveled tourist class.

"If things are done right," Beard said, "one never pays one's way, and one always goes first class."

Olney laughed. *And one didn't pay for one's CorningWare stovetop, either,* he thought. (Beard had indeed received the equipment for free, in exchange for promotional considerations.) Olney said nothing. Free or not, the CorningWare was a far cry from his beautiful La Cornue, as troublesome and prone to repair as it sometimes was.

The party was a blur of new faces. Olney had prepared hundreds of *caillettes*—baked, caul-wrapped morsels of chopped pork, innards, spinach, and chard. For his cooking classes, he led students through a litany of stews, roasts, fresh pastas, truffled scrambled eggs, crêpes, and gratinés. He maintained his superior, sometimes contemptuous attitude toward many in Beard's inner circle, including Cofacci and Rojas-Lombardi—the "Peruvian Adonis," in Olney's words. But he also found himself warmly embraced by a new group of friends and admirers, including the *Times* food writer Nika Hazelton, the Associated Press food editor Cecily Brownstone, and the food writer Irena Chalmers. They went out drinking together in the evenings.

All anyone ever talked about was food and cooking. They discussed recipes and restaurants, the proper way to make *pâte brisée*. ("What's the secret of your pastry?" Beard asked Olney. "Lots of butter, very cold, diced," he replied; "cross two knives, like our grandmothers, to cut it into the flour—work fast, don't over-work.") There was the inevitable, perennial gossip about Craig Claiborne, who had thrown in the towel on his newsletter and was returning to the *Times*. He'd apparently agreed to return only if he did not have to write restaurant reviews.

As Olney traveled from Philadelphia to Washington, D.C., and from St. Louis to Dallas, he found eager audiences, including a number of his former students from Avignon. He could feel the energy of the moment in American food. It was remarkable to him how much had changed so quickly.

In Boston, Olney stayed with the Childs, at their house in Cambridge. Paul was recovering from a recent stroke, but Julia graciously insisted Olney come anyway. He stayed in their guest bedroom.

They had seen each other a few times in France in the years since the winter of 1970, over lunches, and usually accompanied also by Beard. Olney had always felt on edge on such occasions, embittered and superior. But now he had a different perspective. He could see, for one thing, what an enormous impact Child had managed to achieve, even if it was mostly due to television. The sheer numbers of people; the interest in cooking, in baking bread, in new recipes and cookbooks, owed much to her, and Beard's, pio-neering work. And perhaps more important, Olney felt for the first time that he had made a place for himself in the American food establishment. His brand of culinary purism was catching on.

Part of the routine in Boston, as in many other cities, was to perform a five-minute spot at the end of the local newscast. Olney traveled with a frying pan with rounded edges that allowed him to sauté chopped onion and zucchini and ham and then theatrically toss the food high in the air and catch it in the pan. Then he'd talk a bit, add some garlic and parsley, talk a bit more, squeeze a bit of lemon juice over the dish, and he was done.

He and Child commiserated about the miserable hot plates to be found in television studios. He'd had a bad experience in New York (the hot plate never got more than warm) and now brought his own wherever he went. Child had long been doing the same thing. They talked about their mutual contempt for the newly emerging nouvelle cuisine, which they considered faddish and artificial. All those dainty, overly fussy dishes that looked like the chef's hands had been all over the food. And they talked about their French ovens—the La Cornue in La Pitchoune had begun to release great clouds of black smoke every time it was used. Olney had the same model, and he had the same troubles. They laughed.

Olney's stay with the Childs in Cambridge in the winter of 1974–1975 was a moment of détente, a reflection of their respective shifts in outlook. Child had half-turned away from France, while Olney had half-turned toward America. Child had expanded and deepened the American food conversation, while Olney had planted the seeds of an artisanal and purist cooking philosophy. Both had found their inspiration in France, and were now reinventing the shape and style of modern American cooking.

It had all started during those few weeks in Provence in 1970, when the primacy of France, of French taste, had come into serious question, at least in the minds of several of its greatest champions. Who knows how the story of American cooking would have turned out if Child, Beard, and M.F. hadn't lost their patience for snobbery, thanks in part to the snobbery they were exposed to during that time. Child had been battling Beck all year about what was and wasn't authentically French (*"Ce n'est pas français!"* was the refrain that had echoed in her head); Beard had been struggling for over half a decade to articulate, in the writing of his book, the evolution of American cookery as a distinct and worthy cuisine; M.F. had come to France with the question of "France" on her mind— what it had meant to her in the past, and how it might figure in her future.

Olney, too, had changed. Not his personality, which remained as prickly and judgmental as ever. But he had become a teacher, first in Avignon and now as he toured the United States. He could see that his book was reaching people, Americans, and changing how they cooked.

That was never clearer than when he arrived on the West Coast for the last leg of his promotional tour, where he was giving demonstrations in Williams-Sonoma kitchen supply shops in Beverly Hills, Palo Alto, and San Francisco. (The company and its catalogues were expanding rapidly, another sign of the times.) At the end of his demonstration in San Francisco (split chicken, stuffed beneath the skin) he was approached by two admirers, Alice Waters and Jeremiah Tower. Waters had opened Chez Panisse, in Berkeley, a few years earlier, and Tower was now a chef and partner at the restaurant.

Chez Panisse was the ground zero of the emerging organic, bohemian-utopian, locally sourced food movement. It represented, in many ways, the future of American cooking, combining culinary influences in an easygoing way—the menu was French-inflected, but not exclusively so—and highlighting the freshest ingredients. The ambiance was casual; the food was seriously ambitious.

Waters and Tower had both been inspired by Olney's first book, and they adored his new one. Waters invited him to dinner that night at Chez Panisse, and had arranged for a surprise guest—Olney's old friend Kenneth Anger, the avant-garde filmmaker. He and Olney had known each other in the bohemian Paris of the early 1950s. A new strain of bohemianism, a culinary bohemianism, had taken root in California at Chez Panisse.

✦ ✦ ✦

At Last House, over the coming years, M.F. worked on her Marseille book. It was a highly personal account of the city, weaving recollections of earlier visits with recent observations. She had spent four months there in 1973, for the purpose of gathering material. Norah came, too. They'd rented a small apartment near the harbor, and hired Raymond Gatti for periodic excursions out of town—to Aix and Nice. Gatti brought them slices of his wife's homemade lemon tart, which M.F. declared to be the best she'd ever tasted.

They found Marseille much the same as they always had—it was a rough, tough place in parts, long a hub of smuggling. The port city had a vitality M.F. admired.

But it was changing, too, wicked in new ways. There were drugs and crime everywhere; there were shootings. She wrote about how four people had been gunned down in the port: "Nobody seemed to be much annoyed by anything except the fact that the act was one of petty revenge carried out by amateurs. Where was the old spit and polish in crime?" There were countless identical bars in the arcades under the quai, with names such as La Lune Bleue and

Bébé-à-Go-Go. She observed the young dandies in coffee shops—
Pinball Boys, she called them—and the prostitutes lingering outside
the seafood restaurants on Bouillabaisse Row. She noted the layers
of development and overdevelopment.

She also described the tomatoes of Provence, her favorite restaurants, and the sights and sounds and smells of the fish market:

> Often, in a window opening onto the street, as crown of the dis-
> play inside, there will be a kind of *pièce montée,* a Dalí or Carême
> sculpture of one stunningly graceful *loup,* posed for an endless
> second with a great pink shrimp in its mouth, as it leaps from a
> high wave of smaller red and blue and silver fishes over the piles
> of oysters, mussels, urchins, clams . . .

She wrote about meals she'd eaten in Marseille in 1932, and
about walking home from a movie (*Last Tango in Paris*) late at
night with Norah in 1973, and about "sitting in cafés drinking de-
generate apéritifs before lunch." She had found a new tone in this
book—it was vintage M.F., but it was also less elegiac and tougher,
more rooted in the present. Her experiences in Arles and Avignon
in 1970 and her refusal to sentimentalize the glamour of France
could be felt on every page.

A Considerable Town took her until 1977 to finish. Arnold Gingrich had died in 1976, of cancer. It was another blow, but it had
happened quickly, and she was glad of that. The book would turn
out to be her last of entirely new material. There would be essays
and anthologies and magazine stories in the coming years, but this
was her final book.

Jan Morris reviewed the work in the *New York Times Book*

Review: "Nobody who reads this book, I swear, will ever think of the place in the same way again."

M.F.K. Fisher stands to so many of us, wherever we live, in the office of an endlessly entertaining and slightly mysterious aunt. She has written one such book before, about Aix, but in "A Considerable Town" she develops the genre much further, and weaves a meditative, discursive, and sometimes enigmatic spell about that Chicago of European seaports, Marseille.

Anatole Broyard reviewed the book in the daily *Times*. He noted M.F.'s focus on Marseille's contemporary changes.

Inevitably, Marseilles is now going the way of all old cities. There is talk of high rise apartments to house the fishermen's families near the port, and of moving the auction house for the day's catches to a suburb. Good restaurants are being replaced by snack bars with electric organs and "oriental bistros." But that may simply be the way of the world in our time.

In the summer of 1978, shortly after the book was published and on the occasion of M.F.'s seventieth birthday, Alice Waters proposed a celebratory dinner at Chez Panisse, and M.F. accepted. The women had met earlier in the year, when M.F. invited Waters and cookbook author Marion Cunningham to lunch at Last House. They'd hit it off.

The dinner at Chez Panisse was playfully organized around the titles of some of M.F.'s books—quantities of oysters, of course, in honor of *Consider the Oyster*. Four dishes inspired by Marseille and *A Considerable Town:* snails in Pernod, tomatoes and garlic; charcoal-grilled rockfish with wild herbs and anchovies; spit-roasted pheasant; and bitter lettuces with goat cheese croutons. For dessert there were three plum sorbets and a Muscat de Beaumes-de-Venise, inspired by *A Cordiall Water.*

All of the San Francisco food world was in attendance, and so was James Beard, who'd traveled from New York. The food was incredible—the best M.F. had ever had at an American restaurant, she said. She had come with Norah, and they sat together enjoying the valedictory moment, the toasts, the laughter, and it was clear to both sisters that Waters and her generation of cooks had found a new idiom, an entirely original continuation of the legacy of the winter of 1970, a modern art of American eating.

It made a certain, perfect sense that Waters had embraced both Olney and M.F., as different as they were. For Waters, avatar of the new American cooking, was rooted both immediately as a cook in Olney's bohemian purism, and culturally in M.F.'s groundbreaking literary sensuality. Cooking was for Waters about more than food, it was a philosophy. The same had always been true for M.F., and for Olney, too.

M.F. had come full circle: She could see that the seeds she had planted were blooming. She saw it at Chez Panisse; she saw it in Glen Ellen. "In the Sonoma Valley I see young people growing their own food and making their own bread," she said. "And of course the American people seem to be demanding so much more and, with exposure, choosing more wisely what they put in their stomachs."

It was true: Americans had tuned in to food, and to the possibility of good, simple cooking, the sort of cooking M.F. had always embodied: the primacy of flavor over all else, the astringent luxury of the oyster, the explosive sweetness of the tangerine. M.F. would live more than another decade before being struck by Parkinson's disease, and would see her gimlet-eyed philosophy of food and living adopted and celebrated. Like Julia Child, she had become an icon of sorts, presiding over a renaissance in American cooking.

AFTERWORD

PROVENCE NOW

THE ROAD UP TO LA PITCHOUNE IS A NAR-
row, unpaved driveway, winding up a steep hill. It's narrow enough
that if you happen to encounter a car coming the other way, someone is going to have to back up, or pull into one of the turnoffs for
the other houses in the immediate area. Each house has a name;
small signs with dark green lettering and arrows point to the left,
toward Le Vieux Mas, the eighteenth-century farmhouse where
Simca and Jean lived, and to the right toward La Campanette, La
Pitchouline, and Le Mas de Levandre, all built by the Beck family over the years. La Campanette is where Beck taught cooking
classes in the 1970s. The Childs' La Pitchoune is at the top, at the
end of the road.

I arrived on a Saturday in early July 2010. The weather was hot,
the cicadas singing a gale-force barrage of noise, a wall of sound
of summer. The horses in the fields below La Pitchoune stood in
whatever shade they could find, and they all looked up and watched,
diffidently, as we passed by. I was here with my family: my wife and

six-year-old daughter, my father and my grandmother Norah. The last time she had been here was to visit the Childs with her sister, in 1978—M.F.'s last trip to Europe. M.F. died in 1992. Now here I was writing about their 1970 trip, and what better place to do that, to research, think, write, and cook, and sit on the terrace with afternoon cocktails with my grandmother and ask her about that time, than La Pitchoune? I had rented the house for a good part of the summer.

It was something of a miracle that my grandmother had made it over—she still lives in Sonoma County, a long way from the Côte d'Azur for a woman in her nineties. She was sure this would be her last trip to Europe, her last Provençal hurrah.

Norah was shocked at how much the area had changed since she was last here. She could hardly recognize the landscape and the towns as we drove to Plascassier from Nice and through Cannes, a half hour away. There were new buildings everywhere, American-style big-box stores and car dealerships, highways crowded with traffic.

In 1971, Paul Child had written in a letter to his brother, from La Pitchoune:

Everywhere around us the horridly inevitable up-building and despoliation of this terrain goes forward relentlessly. Little box-like villas and large Hollywood-style stucco mansions are mushrooming everywhere. The concomitant roads, concrete telephone and lightpoles too, of course now spatter across the once pristine landscape, and noise, people, and smoke add to my sense that our lovely earth is being plundered by the human race.

The statement is just as true—*more true*—today. By the time we got to the house, however, the rush and noise of the Côte d'Azur had long receded. Standing on the terrace, looking across the little valley at the village of Plascassier, set on a hilltop a mile away, the view was more or less identical to the one I'd seen in photographs from the 1960s and '70s.

I was looking for these views, looking to catch glimpses of the past, to find the Provence that had inspired Child, M.F., Beard, and Olney—to see it, however refracted, through their eyes. I planned to travel in their footsteps, cook in Julia's kitchen, and sit in the shade of Paul's beloved olive tree. I wanted to see for myself the world I had found in their letters and diaries, and also to gauge the distance between then and now.

Paul's tree looked healthy and robust, its dark, dusty-silvery-green leaves glowing in the sun.

The house was a pale apricot yellow, with light-blue shutters. The screen doors were unusual, with tiny latched insets by the door handles, just big enough to reach a hand through in case the inner door was closed.

In the kitchen, outlines of the utensils on the walls had survived multiple repaintings more or less intact. Many of the objects were original to the kitchen, and some were now admittedly more decorative than functional, but this was no museum; it was a fully functional kitchen. The knives were all extremely sharp.

The house belongs to Kathie Alex, a former student of Beck's who bought the property from the Beck family in the mid-nineties, and who teaches cooking classes in its well-pedigreed kitchen. She had repainted the kitchen pale yellow; put in a new, state-of-the-art stove and oven; and more fundamentally modernized the place, updating the electrical system, adding bathrooms in every bedroom, and putting in a pool in the garden below the terrace.

I wondered what Paul and Julia would make of their one-time house done up so luxuriously—all those "en suite" baths and the pool. Then there was the construction zone for a new addition next door, at Le Vieux Mas. There was a looming tower crane, one of those right-angle types with huge cement counterbalancing weights high up in the air. The Becks had sold the old farmhouse for well over a million euros to the daughter of a French industrialist and her husband, to be their vacation villa.

Indeed, as I sat at my desk in what was once Paul Child's study, and paged through my great-aunt's diary—the pale green spiral-bound notebook in which she had inscribed the words "Where was I?"—I thought about what had changed, but also what hadn't.

◆ ◆ ◆

One of the first things I found at La Pitchoune was a binder with a set of instructions for houseguests, written by the Childs in the 1970s, with advice about everything, from where best to buy fresh fish to which electrician to call if the power went out. It was now of course largely out of date, but it provided a vivid introduction to the house—and to the personalities of its inhabitants—nonetheless. The label on the front read:

THIS IS:
"THE BLACK BOOK"
LA PITCHOUNE
GENERAL INFORMATION

The first line, on the first page, was underlined for emphasis: "PLUMBING IS FRAGILE. Nothing but paper in toilets. Pipes are narrow and can clog up as it backs around the house—awful smell!!"

There followed warnings about the stove ("a fine object, but re-calcitrant . . . close the door carefully or you will blow out the gas"), the laundry machine ("be sure closing drum is securely locked, or clothes fall out and motor breaks"), the furnace ("pump will pick up sludge in bottom of tank, and furnace burner will clog"), the sum-mer furniture ("if it stays out in the sun it disintegrates"), and what to do if the plumbing stopped up ("the Fischbachers have a long flexible length of wire, and that worked once—Jean Fischbacher managed the operation), followed by the exclamation: "This only happens if some nutty person throws something into the toilet." A few pages had Paul's beautifully detailed drawings of the various mechanical systems, as well as of the property as a whole, showing where the water pipes were buried.

But more than an instruction manual, the Black Book was a love letter to Provence, describing all their neighbors, and the impor-tant people and businesses in the local community. There were two electricians: Mr. Carrenta, "a fat jolly man . . . but he takes days and weeks to come"; and Mr. Barla and his workers—"nice people, and eventually come (but don't call them if you've already called Carrenta!)" The painter, plumber, carpenter, and firewood man were listed (along with helpful French phrases—*bois d'allumage* for "kindling"); Dr. Michel Biondi was excellent, made house calls, and spoke only French; the best chauffeur was Raymond Gatti ("A very nice man, we have all used him—not cheap!").

Closer to home, there were descriptions of the Becks' house-keepers, Jeanne Villa and Marie-Thérèse; the gardeners; and the En-glishwoman who lived down the hill. Everyone had pets: "A brown dog belongs to Marie Therese. A friendly black Labrador named Ursus belongs to Simca. An old poodle belongs to Jean, Iota. Black and white poussiequette is partly ours: we call her Minoir, they call her Whiskey; she will happily adopt you if you feed her, especially chopped raw beef, but she will eat canned cat food." A small photograph of a very contented-looking cat (Minoir, a.k.a. Whiskey) was stuck to the bottom of the page.

The long list of food shops—butchers, bakers, fishmongers, fruit and vegetable stands—came with notes about when they were open, where to park, which was the best, who was improving, or overcrowded, or simply "OK." It was remarkable how personal it all was—these were more than shops, they were proprietors and purveyors with whom the Childs had real relationships. Everyone was listed by name.

Today, the closest food shop was the local Super U, one of a chain of large, boxy supermarkets, just off the main road through town. It was a useful if charmless place, good for basic provisions. In fact, all the shops in town were on this same fast road: there were no longer any shops at all among the narrow streets of the old walled, medieval section of Plascassier, up on the hill.

But even if the setting was no longer quite so romantic, there were excellent shops to be found, hidden among the gas stations, strip malls, and real estate broker offices: two bakeries, a tiny butcher, and a magnificent fruit and vegetable shop.

Dumanois Primeurs didn't look like much, just a storefront with crates of peaches, tomatoes, and apricots out front, in a modern and nondescript single-story building off the main roundabout in town. Inside, however, was an astounding collection of fresh fruits and vegetables. There were green beans in shallow wooden crates—three varieties, each a bit thinner than the last. There were tiny, flowering zucchini and brilliant orange-yellow chanterelle mushrooms. The strawberries were small, the leeks long and thin, the cabbages dense and heavy. There were soft green raw almonds, and figs and cherries. And there were tomatoes and peaches in multivarious abundance. Along the back wall was a small collection of wine, honey, and jam.

And so I went about putting together my own Black Book, even if it was just in my head, gathering bits of information that gradually assembled themselves into some ad hoc sense of expertise. Within a few days, I knew that the local butcher was open Sunday morning but closed Mondays (whereas the larger butcher in the next village over was closed Sundays but open the rest of the week), that finding a parking spot in nearby Valbonne on Fridays (which was market day) was more trouble than it was worth, and that both local bakeries ran out of croissants by midmorning. I did not learn the shopkeepers' and proprietors' names, but as the weeks went by I knew them by sight—the large, talkative butcher, the elegant middle-aged couple at the fruit and vegetable stand, the harried young women behind the counter at the bakery.

We cooked together, my grandmother, my wife, and I, gathering around the tall square table in the kitchen to chop eggplants, onions, and red peppers for ratatouille, or to prepare a chicken for roasting. For lunches we didn't really cook, but just turned our beautiful groceries into salads—leeks, tomatoes, cucumbers, potatoes, green beans, and more tomatoes—and ate them with torn-up baguettes and some cheese. There was a small herb garden along one side of the house, for basil and tarragon, and a row of rosemary bushes along another. We ate all our meals outside, at a round metal table on the terrace.

During the hottest part of the afternoon, we closed the shutters to keep the house cool, and I would read various cookbooks, thinking about dinner, or planning ahead for tomorrow's dinner. A group of old friends had joined us for a time, some staying at La Pitchoune, others at the Becks' La Campanette, next door. With the large crowd, the evening meal was a group effort, everyone cooking, shopping, drinking, talking. When we decided to make a bouillabaisse, I consulted *From Julia Child's Kitchen*.

From *bouillabaisse* in the Mediterranean, *marmites* and *chaudrées* in the Atlantic, and fresh-water *meurettes, pauchouses,* and *matelotes* in the interior, France abounds in recipes for hearty fish chowders, any one of which is a meal in itself. Praises be, also, for our own New England fish chowder.

"Bouillabaisse à la marseillaise" was the first show of our new color series, and we'd filmed part of it in Marseille itself, at the open public market, and at the Criée aux Poissons, the wholesale market in the old port—fishwives screaming, the stands teeming with the morning's catch . . . You cannot, of course, expect to transport all the essences of Marseille to a *bouillabaisse* made in Birmingham, Boston, Buffalo, Boise, or San Bernadino because the fish are different. But you do have those hearty flavors of Provence that give the soup its particular character—the tomatoes, onions, garlic, saffron, olive oil, and herbs. Using these and strong fish stock, which you can make out of bottled clam juice if you've no fresh trimmings, you can produce a marvelous dish, and rather quickly, too. It doesn't have to be a fancy production; remember that it originated as a simple fisherman's soup and not a high priced restaurant fantasy.

Whatever fish you choose, whether fresh or frozen, it must smell absolutely fresh, as though it had just swum in from the sea; your nose is the best indicator of this.

Her recipe was straightforward: you make a soup with fish trimmings (or bottled clam juice) and tomatoes, leeks, and onion, then strain it and add a wide selection of fish. Olney's recipe, from *The French Menu Cookbook,* was more complex, involving marinating the fish in olive oil, saffron, and pastis; brewing a fish stock with wild fennel, among other things; and then cooking leeks and tomatoes, adding the stock and finally the fish. The recipe was preceded by a brief discussion:

Bouillabaisse is, to tell the truth, more a philosophy than a culinary preparation. More gastronomic literature—and quarrels—have centered around it than any other dish (with *cassoulet* running a close second). If most of the recipes for it were to be followed, however, the result could only be the most banal of fish soups (I am thinking of those in French—some that I have seen in American and English cookbooks would make the hair of the most indifferent Marseillais stand on end).

It is not a delicate dish; to be good, it must be highly seasoned, and it is terrifyingly soporific, but it embodies and engenders the warmth, the excitement, and the imagination which, perhaps, of all the Mediterranean peoples, the Provençaux exude in the highest degree. At best, it belongs to the realm of divine things. . . .

It should be the main dish—and plentiful; it should be shared with friends in a relaxed and informal atmosphere . . . the wine should be kept generously flowing throughout the meal. I, personally, have many sublime memories of entire days devoted to shopping (early in the morning to the fish market to find the freshest fish of the greatest variety), everyone preparing fish and vegetables together (accompanied by a few more pastis than wisdom would ordinarily dictate), followed by euphoric hours spent at table.

We didn't follow either recipe, exactly, but looked to them for inspiration. From Child we took to heart the idea that the soup could be simple: we skipped making a fish stock and bought some instead. It came in jars, but it was a far cry from bottled clam juice—this was a rich Provençal fish stock sold by the fishmonger. We also did not belabor our choice of fish, and bought whatever seemed most fresh.

From Olney we embraced the idea of bouillabaisse as a divine thing, a cause for euphoria.

One of my visiting friends was the Zurich restaurateur Cello Rohr, and he took charge of the kitchen in an easygoing and precise way. We had bought a couple of medium-size *loups de mer,* a large silver snapper, salmon fillets, squid, and mussels. The *loups de mer* and snapper were cleaned but whole, with doleful, accusing eyes and unfriendly mouths.

Cello filleted the fish while I chopped vegetables. We stopped to search the wall of kitchen utensils for a pair of pliers to pull out some of the larger bones in the snapper. Following Olney, we drizzled olive oil and pastis over the fish, and then started the soup in a large Le Creuset pot: chopped onion, tomatoes, fennel, and celery. Wine and pastis. Garlic, saffron, and thyme. Later, we added the fish stock and some small potatoes, and much later the fish itself, when the table was already set. We also made a garlicky rouille and a large green salad with cucumbers and shallots.

Our soup was not a bouillabaisse, technically speaking—it had potatoes in it, for one thing, and squid and salmon are also not traditional ingredients. It was simply a fish soup, but it, too, belonged to "the realm of divine things." We served it with a dry Sancerre and bread.

As we sat outside, under the olive tree in the gentle evening air, I thought about how little had changed in forty years, when it came to making and eating fish stew in Provence with friends. This was where it had all started, for Child, Olney, M.F., Beard, and Beck—not their love of France, or of cooking, but their embrace of casual, improvised meals, outdoor eating, and the primacy of fresh herbs and seasonal ingredients. They had found in Provence in the late 1960s and early '70s a more freewheeling, modern style of cooking, one in which the rules and formalities of haute cuisine had been loosened, in which more ancient traditions—the simple fisherman's stew, for example—were revered.

Whatever their differences, this was where they cooked for each other, and together. I had spoken with Judith Jones in New York, and one thing she emphasized every time we met was "the sheer joy of home cooking," and how important that was to Child and the others. "It is not about showing off, and never was. There is love and care that is expressed in cooking for someone else." In her mid-eighties and semiretired from Knopf, she still came into the office every day; her husband, Evan, had died years earlier. She went on to say that she would be eating dinner with friends that evening, and they were making her a simple, midwestern chicken pot pie.

As I cooked in the kitchen at La Pitchoune, I could sense their presence, all of them—Julia at the stove; Paul opening wine; Beard, M.F., Beck, Jones, and Olney gathered around, offering advice and opinions and judgments. They spoke to me through their books and recipes, in the same way that my mother's voice accompanies me in the kitchen. It was my mother, who died a few years ago, who taught me how to cook. And when I make something she made for me, or with me, I feel her presence—not in any literal or even ghostly way, but in the form of an atmospheric shift, an emotional warmth. It is striking how cooking binds us to the past, and to the people we love, even when they're gone.

Child, M.F., Beard, Olney, and Beck are gone now, too, leaving behind a cacophonous, booming food culture—from celebrity chefs and the Food Network to organic, locally sourced restaurant menus and artisanal sausages and pickles for sale at the farmers' market. There is more good food and cooking than ever in America, and more hype, spectacle, money, moralizing, and pontificating, too—much of the discussion still circling around the same undying questions of authenticity, elitism, and taste that divided Child, Olney, and the others.

All that seemed far away now, though, in the kitchen at La Pitchoune. Their real legacy was that very kitchen—the way that, metaphorically speaking, they had thrown open the doors to a welcoming, unintimidating, casual cooking.

◆ ◆ ◆

Raymond Gatti, the driver, still lived in Plascassier. He was a garrulous, sharply dressed man, and these days he no longer drove a Mercedes but rather a sporty VW coup. He had retired in 1986 and written a memoir, *Taxi de guerre, taxi de paix,* about his experiences during World War II and his career as a chauffeur.

We drove around together as he told me his stories. He'd never worn a chauffeur's cap, he said, just a suit and tie. "Always spic and span, like they say in Texas." He had developed long-term arrangements with many of his clients—people who came to the Côte d'Azur every year and hired him for weeks at a time. He had driven the Duke of Windsor for fifteen years. He remembered Elizabeth Taylor and her twenty-five pieces of luggage. The Childs and their friends had also been regular customers. "Julia is one of those people you remember," he said. "Very friendly; she treated me like a brother." Paul was trickier. Gatti described picking up Julia and Paul one morning: "We were packing the car and I said to him that perhaps he should bring a coat, in case it got cold, and the look he gave me! 'It's cool,' I said. 'You should wear a jacket.' He looked at me like I killed my mother!"

Mostly, though, he wanted to talk about the war. He was the most unabashedly pro-American Frenchman I'd ever met, his car decorated with numerous U.S. Army and U.S. special forces decals. I was reminded of M.F.'s cynical take on her taxi driver's pro-American "spiel" in Arles in 1970 ("some Frenchmen have forgotten the American help in 1944 but not *this* one"), but Gatti was perfectly sincere. He is the head of a group whose mission is to erect memorials to the sacrifices and achievements of the American forces in southern France. They were his heroes, the men he had served alongside in 1944. On the way to Grasse one day, to take me to the site of Dr. Pathé's diet clinic, he told me he wanted to show me one of his memorials, not far away. The clinic, Villa Fressinet, was long gone, replaced by the local police headquarters, a massive concrete edifice.

We drove farther, up into the foothills of the Alpes-Maritimes, and then Gatti pulled to the side of the road. To the right was a valley; to the left a sheer stone wall. In between were cars driving at highway speeds, coming fast around the blind curve up ahead. We stood next to the car and Gatti pointed at the wall, which rose at least a hundred feet above us. "Do you see?" he asked. There was a modest marble plaque, inscribed in English and French. It read:

IN MEMORIAM

On the night of 24 August, 1944, after an intensive attack by the U.S.-Canadian First Special Service Force, the city of Grasse-Provence was liberated.

In the course of the glorious operations by the force to free southern France, 66 of our comrades died and over 200 were wounded.

This memorial is dedicated to the memory of our companions in arms who died in this campaign and to the citizens of Grasse who fell in the liberation of their beautiful city.

FIRST SPECIAL SERVICE FORCE ASSOCIATION

24 August, 1991

I took his picture, standing below the plaque.

Back at La Pitchoune, Gatti and my grandmother remembered each other and reminisced. We discussed his wife's famous lemon tart, the recipe for which had nearly found its way into *From Julia Child's Kitchen*. Julia had heard about the tart from M.F., as she explained in the note preceding the recipe for Tarte au Citron, La Pitchoune:

> While I was finishing up this book in the south of France, Mary Frances (M. F. K.) Fisher wrote one of her elliptically charming letters, recalling Marseille, and Aix, and our own region around Grasse. And she spoke of lemon tarts; that the one she remembered in Saint-Remy hadn't the appealing homey quality of a certain Mme. Gatti's lemon tart from our region. I know Mme. Gatti, and Mme. Gatti was delighted to be so praised by Mme. Fisher. Mme. Gatti said she'd bring me her tart and her recipe for it, but so far I've had neither one nor the other.

> Mme. Gatti's lemon tart recipe would remain a secret.

✦ ✦ ✦

It wasn't just Mme. Gatti's lemon tart or Pathé's now-vanished diet clinic—the past is a seemingly always elusive thing. When I peered at Paul Child's photographs or read my great-aunt M.F.'s diaries, the truth was somewhere between the lines, or just out of camera range. Similarly, when I went with my grandmother in search of Les Bastides, Allanah Harper's former estate in La Roquette-sur-Siagne, where Eda Lord and Sybille Bedford stayed and where M.F. rented an apartment in 1970, we could find no trace of it.

La Roquette was a short drive from La Pitchoune, through Mouans-Sartoux and then along a country road winding through roundabouts and narrowing to squeeze past a cluster of yellow and pale orange buildings—the town center, such as it was. La Roquette was tiny. It was also stubbornly unfamiliar.

My grandmother sat in the front seat, wearing sunglasses. My wife and daughter were in the back. We were all on the lookout for something, anything, a sign. Google Maps said there was a rue des Bastides. Was that a clue? The official address in 1970 (to which Arnold Gingrich had addressed his numerous letters) was simply "Les Bastides, 06 La Roquette-sur-Siagne, France." We drove some more.

"I remember the villa as dark and cool," my grandmother said. The apartment they'd rented was just across a very narrow lane. It had no garden, but there was a second-story terrace on one side of the building. Where were they now, these houses? I had sent inquiries to the mayor's office and to a local historical society, but hadn't received a reply.

Driving along the main road, we slowed down to read the signs announcing the names of the houses and estates to be found along each side street. I took one turnoff and then another, crawling past one property after the next, stopping to examine some of the older ones.

We circled back to the town square. It was a beautiful if slightly desolate place—the too-quiet town square surrounded by a proliferation of villas everywhere, just as Paul Child had prophesied. A similar withering had happened in Plascassier, in the old village center on the hill. Nevertheless, we enjoyed the slow rhythm of the square under the shadows of the tall plane trees. Our pleasantly fruitless search had come to an end.

Another day, I made my way to Solliès-Toucas, to visit Richard Olney's house. Here was a place where nothing had changed—

Olney's books and paintings and pots and pans were still in place, the wine in his cellar continued to age. The property is now owned by his two brothers, Byron and James, who vacation there during the summer. The rest of the year, a young family takes care of the place—Marc Lanza and his wife and children. Lanza was about forty years old, a cook who runs a small catering business. He wore his hair in a small ponytail the day I met him.

He showed me the house, a solid two-story stone building with an open kitchen. Outside was the vegetable and herb garden; off to the left, an aviary with small, colorful parakeets; and beyond that, a chicken coop. We walked up the hill, a steep climb to a stunning rock swimming pool, carved out of the side of the cliff. We could see down to the village and the valley beyond, and like everywhere else in Provence, there were new buildings going up in every direction. "He would have hated this," said Lanza, pointing at a construction site off in the distance. "Richard believed in preserving the old Provençal traditions, ways of life. He did not drive, he had no television."

In the wine cellar, he showed me Olney's remarkable collection—wines going back to the teens in some cases, the bulk of them from the 1950s through the 1980s. Each bottle was marked in heavy white pen with its year, in Olney's handwriting. (The labels were in many cases illegible.)

The house and the landscape were beautiful, a self-contained world on a Provençal hillside. But it was the food Lanza cooked in Olney's kitchen that revealed the spirit of the place.

There is a heartbreaking scene described in the afterword of Olney's autobiography, *Reflexions*, written by his brother James. James and Byron arrive at the house just after Richard has died, in August 1999. They find a "picture of perfect order":

A dish with traces of tomatoed pilaf on it, the pan in which the pilaf was warmed, and a wine glass, all placed next to the sink for washing (the remains of the pilaf neatly stored in the refrigerator); on the table an open book with Richard's glasses alongside.

He had been struck by a heart attack in his sleep. A few days later, the brothers ate dinner.

Byron to James at table on the terrace in Solliès (Menu: brochettes of lamb's hearts and kidneys, the remains of the pilaf found in the refrigerator, a bottle of Château de Beaucastel 1986 from the cellar): "Do you realize what we're doing?—eating the last meal Richard will ever cook for us."

Silence.

Lanza had prepared *pieds et paquets,* a quintessential Olney dish: lowly tripe, cooked very slowly to transcendent tenderness. It was a meal that encapsulated Olney's Provence, the rustic sophistication more than a way of cooking and indeed a philosophy of life, not unlike the tomatoed rice pilaf and lamb brochettes the Olney brothers ate in silence in 1999.

OLIVES

PIEDS ET PAQUETS

STEAMED POTATOES

GOAT CHEESE SALAD

The rolled, stuffed tripe had simmered with tomatoes for twelve hours. Lanza served it directly from a shallow, heavy cooking dish. The potatoes tasted like the essence of potato, and the goat cheese had been piled on top of bread and put under the broiler. We ate on the terrace, drinking a Domaine Tempier red wine from 1987. It was a pale and dusty color, the best wine I'd ever tasted.

◆ ◆ ◆

Child's final visit to La Pitchoune was in the summer of 1992. She knew it was a farewell, for she had decided to return the house, as agreed, to the Beck family. Beck had died the previous year, and Beard, who visited so often, had died in 1985. His larger-than-life spirit lived on in the kitchen, where they had cooked together so happily, but the "Gigis" were no more. And Paul, after suffering a series of strokes, was now living in a nursing home. He would die two years later. Julia wrote:

> And I came to a decision. Without Paul to share the house with, or my *grande chérie* Simca, or all of our other favorite friends and family, it had come time to relinquish La Pitchoune.
>
> People seemed surprised when I told them that it wasn't an especially difficult or emotional decision. But I have never been very sentimental. La Pitchoune was a special place, but the heart had gone out of it for me now. It was the people I shared it with, more than the physical property, that I would miss.
>
> Besides, Provence was no longer the quiet refuge we had all loved. It had become hideously expensive (a head of lettuce cost twice as much in Cannes as in Cambridge), and the coastline was

more jammed than ever. Houses were multiplying on the hillsides, and the winding country roads were clogged with streams of cars and enormous trucks. Our little village of Plascassier, which had always had a butcher, baker, vegetable shops, and electrician, now had no little businesses left at all; everyone went to the big supermarket down the hill. As Paul had accurately predicted years earlier, the place was turning into southern California. And *that* I could walk away from *sans regret*.

Child would live another dozen years, never returning to Provence before her death in 2004.

I thought of her words as we prepared our final dinner at La Pitchoune. It would be a feast, a celebration, in honor not only of our time there with family and friends, but of our connection to the place and to the past. Like Julia and Paul, M.F., Beard, Beck, and Olney— and despite the possible Southern California-ization of Provence, as Paul described it—we would rejoice in cooking together, for one another.

For me, this was a meal that would also recapture the leisurely formality of the meals of my childhood, at Last House and at my grandmother's house, meals that were themselves rooted in a kind of Provençal ideal. We would gather at the long, narrow wooden table in Jenner (which my grandmother had bought in France in the 1950s and shipped home) or on the balcony in Glen Ellen, the adults drinking wine and children putting out the silverware. By the time I knew them, M.F. and my grandmother were both imposing, matriarchal figures, demanding a measure of seriousness about food, eating, and manners. My mother was young (twenty-two when I was born in 1968), but she, too, was an opinionated cook. She was from Switzerland, and believed in homemade bread, whole grains, and fresh vegetables. In terms of cooking, she was a child of both Europe and of Berkeley in the 1970s. My culinary inheritance came from these three women.

We had shopped for groceries with abandon—at the butcher and charcuterie in the neighboring town of Valbonne, and at the Dumanois Primeurs greenmarket. We bought a large slice of fresh foie gras, escargots in garlic butter, and pâté. We bought tomatoes, cucumbers, and onions for a gazpacho. Potatoes, celery root, and Gruyère for a gratin. Leeks for a leek vinaigrette. Two rabbits, and mushrooms, and handfuls of tiny red, yellow, and orange peppers for a *gibelotte*. Lemon sorbet and raspberries. And plenty of wine.

In the spirit of M.F., Bedford, and Lord's 1970 "collaboration dinner," we each planned to be responsible for one dish. The kitchen at La Pitchoune was a large, accommodating room, and soon we were unpacking our ingredients and spreading them out on cutting boards.

Cello took charge of the rabbit, browning the pieces in olive oil before adding white wine, mushrooms, and the colorful peppers. It was a simple recipe, the *gibelotte*, celebrated by Olney as *"un plat canaille"*—a rakish dish: rabbit and white wine stew, he wrote in *Simple French Food*, was "thought of as vulgar, popular, unrefined (in this context, all considered to be positive virtues)."

I sliced and cleaned the leeks and let them simmer with the rabbit, and began making the gratin. I was following Beck's method, cooking the sliced celery root in water and lemon juice, and the sliced potatoes in milk, then layering them with cheese, cream, and nutmeg in a shallow dish. It went into the oven.

My wife made a vinaigrette for the leeks, and I toasted some hazelnuts to put on top—a combination we'd discovered at a New York City bistro.

Across the kitchen, two more friends, brother and sister, were making the gazpacho in a Cuisinart, chopping tomatoes and onion, and also watching a small saucepan of boiling eggs. They had decided to devil them. Beard would have approved: he had a deep affinity for hors d'oeuvres, and considered deviled eggs a real delicacy: "If you have taken care to observe at a cocktail party, nothing disappears as quickly as the eggs," he noted in *American Cookery*. When the eggs were done, the siblings turned the yolks into three fillings, one plain, one spicy, one with olives.

Yet another old friend—we had a full house, even after my father and grandmother had departed the previous week—joined us in the kitchen and announced that he would be making a cocktail, a new invention, in fact. It would be called "The Plascassier." Into the blender went a basket of raspberries, fresh mint, lemon juice, and vodka. This liquid was poured judiciously into the bottoms of glasses, and then topped with Laurent-Perrier champagne.

We all raised our glasses, and continued to cook and talk. The mood in the kitchen was purposeful but also intoxicating, alluring smells radiating from the oven and stove. We were amateurs (except for Cello, of course), but we had each found a spot in the kitchen, like line chefs at an exceptionally casual restaurant.

I took the leeks out of the stewpot and let them cool in the vinaigrette.

The escargots were in the oven, turned up high to brown the gratin. We had leftover whole peppers and put them in the oven to char briefly and serve as another side dish.

The pâté and the stuffed eggs were arranged on plates. We eyed the foie gras with a certain amount of awe: the pale goose liver had been sliced thickly from a terrine at the charcuterie, and it cost a fortune. It was the purest decadence.

In *Simple French Food*, Olney describes foie gras as a luxury fit for special occasions—which this was—and touches on the ethics of foie gras production in an unforgettable parenthetical remark:

(I once listened in amazement to a Périgord farmwife describing— in what was intended to be a vehement denial that the raising of geese destined to produce foie gras involves cruelty to animals— the tenderness and gentleness with which the birds are treated and, with mounting enthusiasm and in the most extraordinarily sensuous language, the suspense and the excitement experienced as the moment arrives to delicately slit the abdomen, to lovingly—ever so gently—pry it open, exposing finally the huge, glorious, and tender blond treasure, fragile object of so many months of solicitous care and of present adoration. One sensed vividly the goose's plenary participation, actively sharing in the orgasmic beauty of the sublime moment for which her life had been lived.)

Olney left it at that, then discussed a complicated recipe for preserving geese in their own fat.

We paid our silent respects to this goose, divided its liver onto rounds of toasted baguette, and prepared to serve dinner.

ESCARGOTS

FOIE GRAS

PÂTÉ AND CORNICHONS

DEVILED EGGS THREE WAYS

GAZPACHO

RABBIT *EN GIBELOTTE*

ROASTED PEPPERS

POTATO AND CELERY ROOT GRATIN

LEEKS VINAIGRETTE WITH TOASTED HAZELNUTS

LEMON SORBET WITH RASPBERRY SAUCE

We ate outside on the terrace, at two tables set beneath the mulberry tree. There had been a brief thunderstorm that afternoon, and the air and light seemed especially clear, the late afternoon sun slanting over the hilltops. We opened wines, corralled children, and passed plates.

It was all transcendently wonderful—the melting foie gras; the quickly disappearing deviled eggs (just as Beard had predicted); the spicy gazpacho; the tender, dense rabbit in its light, fragrant broth;

the rich gratin—the dinner was an extravaganza, and it lasted for hours. When the sun went down we lit candles, and someone went to the kitchen to make an instant raspberry sauce—cooking the berries with sugar and lemon juice. We spooned it over the sorbet. It was the final touch.

I thought of Child, and how she'd left Provence behind, *sans regret,* and yet how the legacy of the place—*her* Provence—lived on. The intimate intertwining of food, life, love, and friendship, the simple pleasure of cooking that seemed so natural and rooted here, had been joined to the democratizing, culture-changing force of her personality and her TV show. The shift that had occurred in the fall and winter of 1970, when Child, M.F., Beard, Beck, and Olney had come together, finding new directions for themselves and for American cooking, lived on, too. It could be felt in home kitchens, restaurants, and farmers' markets.

Our last meal in Plascassier was a dinner that, for me, embodied not only the continuing seductions of Provence—traffic, mega-supermarkets, and all—and the still-vital, inspiring power of Child, M.F., Beard, Beck, and Olney through their recipes and writing, but also our own role in their story. We had cooked with an eye on the past, on what they had transmitted to us, but having absorbed that legacy, we had remade it in the present—in a way that I felt sure would have been approved of by M.F. and Child.

"One reason we are friends," M.F. had written so memorably to Child in 1970, "is that we both understand the acceptance of NOW. There is all the imprisonment of nostalgia, but with so many wide windows." We had found our windows, in the kitchen at La Pitchoune.

On her last night at La Pitchoune, in 1992, Child had stood in this very spot, barefoot, looking out into the dark:

> Just before going to bed that night, I stood on the terrace in the dappled shadows of the mulberry tree. A pale moon hung in the sky over the red-tiled roof. A cool breeze brushed my face and rustled the trees on the hillside across the valley. I inhaled the sweet scent of flowers, listened to the nightingale-and-frog chorus, and felt the familiar rough stones under my bare feet. What a lovely place.

ACKNOWLEDGMENTS

I would like to thank, most of all, my grandmother Norah Barr, for her help in telling this story. Her memories of the events and the people described in this book were invaluable, and so were her notes and comments on the manuscript along the way. My agent and friend, David Kuhn, made this book possible in the first place. Doris Cooper, Emily Takoudes, and Beth Rashbaum were brilliant, patient editors. Nancy Novogrod's wisdom, support, and advice were essential. I thank Judith Jones, Raymond Gatti, James and Byron Olney, Marc Lanza, Alex Prud'homme, Kathie Alex, Christian Beck, Robert Lescher, Joan Reardon, John Petersen, John Martin, Clark Wolf, and Kermit Lynch for their insights and recollections. Marvin Taylor and the Fales Library at New York University, the staff at the Schlesinger Library at Harvard, and Jay Barksdale and the New York Public Library provided important research help. For their generosity and editorial assistance of all kinds, I thank my friends Adam Lehner, Benoît Peverelli, Mark Leyner, Bruno Maddox, Suzanne Petren-Moritz, Ocean MacAdams, Chris and Vicky D'Annunzio, Mariana Hoppin, Adrian Erni, Deborah Burkart, Cello Rohr, Gernot Jörgler, and Adi Schultheiss. My cousin Kennedy Golden guided me through our family archives, for which I am deeply grateful. Finally, I could not have written this book without the help, inspiration, and love of my parents, John and Catrine Barr, and my wife and daughters, Yumi, Sachi, and Emi.

NOTES AND SOURCES

The following pages catalogue my sources for the material in this book. I was
fortunate to be writing about a group of people who sent each other wonderful
letters (and saved them), who kept diaries, and wrote memoirs. M. F. K. Fisher's
daily letters during this period to Arnold Gingrich provided a detailed, sometimes hour-by-hour record of events. I was also able to speak at length with
three of the people I was writing about: my grandmother Norah Barr, Knopf
editor Judith Jones, and chauffeur Raymond Gatti, and with many others familiar with the characters and time period I describe. All the events, meals, menus,
conversations, and arguments described in this book originate in these documents and interviews. In creating a narrative—to bring scenes to life—I have
incorporated quotes from contemporaneous letters and diaries as dialogue; the
source for each quotation is listed here. In chapter 1 ("All Alone") and chapter
13 ("The Ghost of Arles and Avignon"), I made use of extensive quotes and
scenes from M.F.'s 1970 diary. (Parts of this diary were published in the chapter
"About Looking Alone at a Place: Arles" in M.F.'s *As They Were*, in 1982. It
was in the manila folder containing page proofs and edits of that book that I
found the 1970 diary among her personal papers.) I have also relied on—among
many other books and newspaper articles—Julia Child's *My Life in France*, Judith Jones's *The Tenth Muse*, and Richard Olney's posthumous autobiography,
Reflexions, much of which is a compendium of his correspondence. All quotes
and references are listed below, and in the case of letters and unpublished material, the library or collection is listed: the private Fisher and Olney papers, the
Beard papers at NYU's Fales Library (Fales), and the Fisher, Child, and Beck
papers catalogued at the Schlesinger Library at Harvard (Schlesinger).

PROLOGUE

9 "books about eating": Fisher, *Serve It Forth*, p. 5.

10 "you sit, pompously nonchalant": Ibid.

10 "firm authority": Ibid., p. 6.

10 "I am not old and famous": Ibid.

11 "It was then that I discovered": Ibid., p. 27.

11 "The sections of tangerine": Ibid., p. 28.

12 "You are known, my dear!": Ibid., p. 67.

14 "Why is it that each year": Beard editorial for the *National Premium Beer Journal* (Fall 1952), as quoted in *James Beard: A Biography*, by Robert Clark, p. 148.

14 "Station Wagon Way of Life": *House Beautiful*, June 1950, discussed in *James Beard: A Biography*, p. 138.

15 "We have purposely omitted cobwebbed bottles": Child, Bertholle, Beck, *Mastering the Art of French Cooking*, p. vii.

16 "One of the main reasons": Ibid., p. viii.

16 "the year of curry": Nora Ephron, "Critics in the World of the Rising Soufflé (or Is It the Rising Meringue?)" *New York*, September 30, 1968.

CHAPTER ONE: ALL ALONE

23 M. F. K. Fisher walked into the lobby: All the scenes and quotes in this chapter are from M.F.'s 1970 journal, Fisher papers.

CHAPTER TWO: TEN WEEKS EARLIER . . .

32 "too dreamily sensitive": Fisher, *The Gastronomical Me*, p. 389, in *The Art of Eating*.

33 "I do not know of anyone": W. H. Auden introduction to *The Art of Eating*, 1963.

33 "Gastronomy Recalled": *The New Yorker*, 1968 and 1969.

33 "I'm about to make a real break": M.F. to Eleanor Friede, July 2, 1970, Schlesinger.

34 "Say we shall not miss again!": Julia Child to M.F., August 4, 1970, Schlesinger.

34 "The main thing is to see you both": M.F. to Childs, September 16, 1970, Schlesinger.

35 "lucid and enlightened": Craig Claiborne, "Debut for a Series of International Cookbooks," *New York Times*, February 19, 1968.

35 "Such a time we've been having": Paul Child to M.F., September 6, 1970, Schlesinger.

36 "while a lady": M.F. to David Bouverie, August 29, 1970, Fisher papers.

36 "Shades of my great aunts!": Ibid.

37 "Excuse me": M.F. to Arnold Gingrich, October 11, 1970, Schlesinger. I have changed a few words and tenses for clarity. The full quote is: "Well—just as we got to the elevator the other couple came running after us and to my real amazement asked if I was M. F. K. Fisher. Of course I said I was—but how did *they* know?"

38 "the finest French restaurant": Craig Claiborne, "The Finest Restaurant in the World: S.S. France," *New York Times,* January 2, 1969.

39 "You don't see chervil": Norah Barr, interview with author.

40 Hôtel de France et de Choiseul: The hotel is described in a letter, M.F. to Gingrich, October 15, 1970, Schlesinger. (Years later, the hotel was renovated and reopened as the fashionable Hôtel Costes.)

41 "stopped in a small bar": Ibid.

41 "watery spree": Joan Reardon, *Poet of the Appetites,* p. 377.

41 "relaxed philosopher": M.F. to Gingrich, October 15, 1970, Schlesinger.

42 Hôtel Terminus: M.F. had been to the hotel before, and described it (and its wine faucets) in "A Mission Accomplished," written in 1970 and published in *As They Were,* in 1982.

42 They saw the tiny owl: Norah Barr, interview with author.

42 "One has to be a real nut": M.F. to Gingrich, October 19, 1970, Schlesinger.

43 fat ducks, fish, veal stews: Ibid. M.F. described the meals on board: "The food is delicious, with lots of vegetables—everything fresh—this morning cook Michel was plucking two fat ducks off the aft bow—last night we had quenelles made from two brochet he caught—with a perfect crayfish sauce, then a *sauté de veau* with mushrooms, sauce Marchego, and a *jardinier de légumes—plateau de fromages de la région* (magnifique!), fruits, café—we drank a delicious Pouilly Fumé and then a local Tammay Rouge. Oh my."

44 "Norah and I did our secret trick": M.F. to Gingrich, October 30, 1970, Schlesinger.

44 The girls wore midi or maxi skirts: Aix and inhabitants described in a letter, M.F. to Gingrich, October 31, 1970, Schlesinger.

45 "You and Norah are officially forbidden": Paul Child to M.F., September 6, 1970, Schlesinger.

CHAPTER THREE: EN ROUTE TO PROVENCE

47 "invaded by telephone": Paul Child to William Krauss, March 18, 1971, Schlesinger.

50 "I am not an entertainer": Child to Beard, December 21, 1971, Schlesinger.

50 "It is hard to conceive of a cookbook": Raymond Sokolov, *Newsweek,* November 9, 1970.

50 "heralded like the Second Coming": Nika Hazelton, "Genghis Khan's Sauerkraut and Other Edibles," *New York Times,* December 6, 1970.

51 "Wonderful job": M.F. to Child, November 23, 1970, Schlesinger.

51 "*Tant pis!*": The book party is described in a letter, Child to Simone Beck, September 26, 1970, Schlesinger.

52 "Nobody's looking": Child on TV, quoted in Calvin Tomkins's Child profile, "Good Cooking," *The New Yorker,* December 23, 1974.

52 "Never apologize": Ibid.

53 "such an integral part": Judith Jones, *The Tenth Muse*, p. 83.

54 "obediently": Richard Olney, *Reflexions*, p. 125.

54 "He is, by his own definition": Craig Claiborne, " 'Hermit' Treats Guests to His Lavish Cooking," *New York Times*, November 14, 1970.

55 "It is high time": Child to Beard, June 7, 1970, Schlesinger.

55 "Offhand": Beard, "American Writes a French Cookbook," *Los Angeles Times*, September 17, 1970.

56 "If rare or medium-rare": Olney, *The French Menu Cookbook*, p. 113.

56 "a rave": Olney to his brother James, November 1970, Olney papers.

56 "Things seem to be stirring": Ibid.

57 "wicked thrill": Beard, "Appreciation," *The Art of Eating*, p. xx.

58 "Designing hors d'oeuvre": Quoted in Evan Jones, *Epicurean Delight*, p. 105.

58 "biggest whore": Quoted in Noel Riley Fitch, *Appetite for Life*, p. 351.

59 "Dear James Beard": Olney to Beard, October 1, 1970, Fales.

CHAPTER FOUR: AN EPIC DINNER WITH RICHARD OLNEY

61 small, pointy knife: This and all other cooking details in this chapter are derived from Olney's *The French Menu Cookbook* and *Simple French Food*.

66 "Apéritif: Morey-Saint-Denis": Menu from Olney, *Reflexions*, p. 125. He also published the menu in *Cuisine et Vins de France*.

67 "It killed both the Sauternes": Olney to James Olney, November 1970, Olney papers.

70 it tasted a bit off: Ibid.

70 "real radiance": M.F. to Childs, December 11, 1970, Schlesinger.

71 "We enjoyed a few minutes": Olney, *Reflexions*, p. 123.

72 "All the articles I have seen": Olney to James Olney, fall 1970, Olney papers.

72 Olney had found an old villa: M.F. described the evening in a letter to Gingrich, November 20, 1970, Schlesinger.

73 Bedford was testy: Ibid.

74 "Richard's house is fantastic": Ibid.

74 "The M. F. K Fisher visit": Olney to James Olney, November 1970, Olney papers.

CHAPTER FIVE: FIRST MEALS IN FRANCE

76 "This has become our ritual": Paul Child to M.F., May 8, 1971, Schlesinger.

76 "While we are in the grip": Ibid.

77 lunch at La Couronne: Described in Child, *My Life in France*, p. 15.

77 sometimes the sole was a duck: Laura Shapiro, *Julia Child: A Life*, p. 28.

78 best bread she'd ever tasted: "The Most Important Meal I Ever Ate," *Napa Valley Tables* (Spring/Summer 1990), described in Reardon, *Poet of the Appetites*, p. 45.

78 "It sounds almost disrespectful": Ibid.

79 pot-au-feu: Beard, *Delights and Prejudices*, p. 131.

79 "It was a dinner I have never forgotten": Ibid., p. 132.

80 stuffed eggplant: Ibid, p. 202.

80 "a glum little dining room": Olney, *Reflexions*, p. 11.

81 "I am no longer content": Jones, *The Tenth Muse*, p. 20.

81 "mostly with cakes": Beck, *Simca's Cuisine*, p. 4.

CHAPTER SIX: LA PITCHOUNE, COUNTRY RETREAT

83 "perfect": Paul Child to M.F., May 8, 1971, Schlesinger.

83 rapid gear-shifting: Ibid.

84 "as tied down by television": Paul Child to M.F., October 18, 1971, Schlesinger.

85 "I keep thinking THANK GAWD": Child to Beard, June 29, 1970, Schlesinger.

85 "primetime": Paul Child to M.F., September 6, 1970, Schlesinger.

87 "I have only 5 weeks": Child to Beck, February 5, 1970, Schlesinger.

88 "say to Julia": Beck to Jones, February 9, 1970, Schlesinger. Translated from the original French: ". . . vous dites à Julia que vous trouvez que ce chapitre est un peu court, et vous lui demandez si par hasard, elle n'aurait pas une autre recette pour compléter ce chapitre? Vous verrez sa réaction."

88 "The recipe I must say": Jones to Beck, February 16, 1970, Schlesinger.

88 "How does ½ cup": Ibid.

89 "parfaitement": Beck to Jones, February 24, 1970, Schlesinger.

89 "Ma chérie": Child to Beck, February 18, 1970, Schlesinger.

90 "not really temples": Child to M.F., August 4, 1970, Schlesinger.

91 "best bread": M.F. to Childs, August 27, 1970, Schlesinger.

91 "re-imprisoned by nostalgia": Child to M.F., August 4, 1970, Schlesinger.

91 "And that dear Mary Frances": Child to Beard, June 7, 1970, Schlesinger.

91 "Indeed, Jim Beard adored you": Child to M.F., July 23, 1967, Schlesinger.

92 "We who do not live in France": Fisher, *Cooking of Provincial France*, p. 53.

92 "an overall feeling": Child to M.F., October 26, 1966, Schlesinger.

92 "One reason we are friends": M.F. to Child, August 27, 1970, Schlesinger.

93 "Every Frenchman": Child to M.F., September 1, 1969, quoted in Noel Riley Fitch, *Appetite for Life*, p. 348.

93 "exactly what has been bugging me": Ibid.

94 "Sorry about the pencil": M.F. to Childs, December 11, 1970, Schlesinger.

CHAPTER SEVEN: JAMES BEARD'S DOOMED DIET

98 "To Whom It May Concern": From Dr. Sullivan, October 28, 1970, Fales.

98 He weighed 138 kilograms: This and all other medical details are contained in Beard's file from the Pathé clinic, Fales.

98 "moral victory": Ibid.

99 "Prudent Diet": Ibid.

99 "Breakfast: 70 grams fruit": Ibid.

101 "Polynesian school of cookery": Beard, *American Cookery*, p. 6.

102 "the goal of every amateur": Ibid., p. 4.

103 "grotesqueries of American cooking": Ibid, p. 7.

105 "Heavenly": M.F. to Gingrich, November 16, 1970, Schlesinger.

105 "If you don't like being alone": Lord to M.F., July 29, 1970, Schlesinger.

105 "general handyman": M.F. to Gingrich, November 16, 1970, Schlesinger.

106 Bert Greene: Norah Barr, interview with author.

106 "adjoining studios": Sybille Bedford, *Quicksands*, p. 359.

107 "If I believed": M.F. to Lord, November 18, 1959, Fisher papers, quoted in Reardon, *Poet of the Appetites*, p. 30.

107 "like a bear": Quoted in Olney, *Reflexions*, p. 133.

107 "With breathless casualness": Richard Plant, "A Family Scandal or Two," *New York Times*, February 3, 1957.

108 "strange and withdrawn": Child to M.F., July 23, 1967, Schlesinger.

108 "closed cooking circle": Lord to M.F., July 29, 1970, Schlesinger.

109 "We had two dinners": Ibid.

110 It was odd to be alone: Described in a letter, M.F. to Gingrich, November 20, 1970, Schlesinger.

110 "I almost never see Eda": M.F. to Gingrich, November 22, 1970, Schlesinger.

111 His clients included celebrities: Described by Gatti, interview with author.

112 "On a clear day": Ibid.

112 "glamorous aristocrats": Jones, *Epicurean Delight*, p. 283.

113 "Few potatoes": Beard, *American Cookery*, p. 569.

113 "It was a fine moment": Fisher, *Gastronomical Me*, p. 395, in *The Art of Eating*.

114 "one of the most beautiful": M.F. to Gingrich, November 22, 1970, Schlesinger.

114 "What a wonderful way": M.F. to Gingrich, December 13, 1970, Schlesinger.

CHAPTER EIGHT: PARIS INTERLUDE

118 "emotional climates": Norah Barr to M.F., December 1971, Schlesinger.

118 "a dream": M.F. to Gingrich, October 15, 1970, Schlesinger.

119 "Belon oysters and Palourde clams": Meal described in a letter, M.F. to Gingrich, December 6, 1970, Schlesinger.

120 "Cream of pheasant soup": Menu described in Olney, *Reflexions*, p. 127.

122 "sublime": Ibid.

122 "There exists a bastard cuisine": Olney, *The French Menu Cookbook*, p. 18.

123 "I prepared an oxtail pot-au-feu": Olney, *Reflexions*, p. 70.

123 "rags": Ibid., p. 83.

CHAPTER NINE: A DINNER PARTY AT THE CHILDS'

125 Boussageon: Boussageon and other local purveyors described in a letter, Child to Beard, January 1971, Schlesinger.

128 "Soupe Barbue": Ibid.

128 "Put it to the test": Jones, interview with author.

128 "Will Julia approve": Ibid.

128 Pâté de campagne and smoked salmon: Ibid.

129 "You'd think": Ibid.

130 "We worry about him": Child to M.F., December, 1970, Schlesinger.

130 "Our dear fat friend": Paul Child to M.F., February 24, 1971, Schlesinger.

130 "zipping deftly here and there": M.F. to Childs, October 25, 1971, Schlesinger.

131 "I thought of you today": Elizabeth David to Beard, October 16, 1970, Fales.

131 "a squalid little book": Ibid.

131 "I'm very pleased": David to Beard, January 8, 1971, Fales.

132 "I have eaten every bit as well": Child to M.F., August 4, 1970, Schlesinger.

133 "widely reputed to have a predilection": Craig Claiborne, "The 1960's: Haute Cuisine in America," *New York Times,* January 1, 1970.

133 "doing his best": Childs to Claiborne, January 2, 1970, Schlesinger.

134 "Simca: *quelle femme!*": M.F. to Gingrich, November 20, 1970, Schlesinger.

134 "I liked her": Ibid.

136 "sad, grim No": M.F. to Gingrich, November 6, 1970, Schlesinger.

136 "amazing, quite beautiful": M.F. to Gingrich, December 13, 1970, Schlesinger.

136 "cinema sycophants": Paul Child to Charlie Child, May 28, 1971, and copy sent to M.F., Schlesinger.

137 "It's very enheartening": Ibid.

138 "For my own meals": Fisher, *Serve It Forth,* p. 51.

138 "*le parking*": Child to Beard, January 5, 1971, Schlesinger.

138 "*le deesvashaire*": Paul Child to M.F., May 8, 1971, Schlesinger.

138 "Everyone has been splendid": Child to M.F., January 1971, Schlesinger.

CHAPTER TEN: SEXUAL POLITICS

139 "I wonder if you've heard": M.F. to Gingrich, November 20, 1970, Schlesinger.

139 "The Greening of America": Charles Reich, "The Greening of America," *The New Yorker,* September 26, 1970.

140 "more of the same": M.F. to Gingrich, November 6, 1970, Schlesinger.

140 "It seems to me": Fisher, *The Gastronomical Me,* p. ix.

141 "There was a bottle of smooth potent gin": Ibid., p. 167.

141 "In 1935 or 1936": Ibid., p. 128.

142 *How to Cook in Bed:* M.F. to Eleanor Friede, February 13, 1971, Schlesinger.

142 "M. F. K. Fisher writes about food": Clifton Fadiman, "Books," *The New Yorker,* May 30, 1942.

142 "the past-mistress": M.F. to Eleanor Friede, February 13, 1971, Schlesinger.

142 Eleanor Friede: Eleanor Kask Friede had married Donald Friede after he and M.F. divorced in 1950. She worked in publishing in New York, and became a

good friend of M.F.'s and stepmother to her children. Donald Friede died in 1965.

142 "Perhaps Kip Fadiman": M.F. to Eleanor Friede, February 13, 1971, Schlesinger.

144 "As for Beard": M.F. to Gingrich, December 31, 1970, Schlesinger.

145 "as for talking about 'us as us'": Ibid.

CHAPTER ELEVEN: TWILIGHT OF THE SNOBS

149 "caught in unmentionable locations": Fisher, *With Bold Knife and Fork*, p. 59.

149 There were stern dissertations: Described in M.F.'s 1970 journal, Fisher papers.

152 "valuable innovation": Olney to James Olney, December 1970, Olney papers.

152 "I immediately tried it": Ibid.

152 "nasty, vicious old cow": Olney, *Reflexions*, p. 127.

153 "Simon-pure French": Hazelton, "Genghis Khan's Sauerkraut and Other Edibles," *New York Times*, December 6, 1970.

153 "I am completely puzzled": Olney to James Olney, December 1970, Olney papers.

155 "huge, gentle and benign": Olney, *Reflexions*, p. 127.

155 "salt-free, alcohol-free": Ibid.

156 "I have no idea": Olney to James Olney, December 1970, Olney papers.

157 "He had arrived at the oracular period": Olney, *Reflexions*, p. 139.

157 "selfishness and willingness to use friends": Ibid., p. 136.

157 "I continue to moon around": Olney to Beard, April 1972, Fales.

157 "Of course, I would teach him": Olney, *Reflexions*, p. 178.

157 "deeply introspective": Beard to M.F., July 28, 1972, Schlesinger.

159 "small and crisp": M.F. to Gingrich, December 15, 1970, Schlesinger.

159 "Picasso was a happy man": M.F. to Gingrich, December 13, 1970, Schlesinger.

160 "not into breaking up friends' love relationships": Olney, *Reflexions*, p. 128.

160 "Shrimp tails": The menu described, ibid., p. 127.

161 "Some pleasant wines": Bedford described the trip in a letter to Child, February 16, 1977, Schlesinger.

162 "We were living": Bedford, *Quicksands*, p. 359.

162 Harper had attended the masquerade: The costumes were described in a letter, M.F. to Norah Barr, October 12, 1980, Schlesinger.

163 "admirable": Olney, *Reflexions*, p. 127.

164 "do more than stand here": M.F. journal, September 15, 1963, Fisher papers, quoted in Reardon, *Poet of the Appetites*, p. 302.

164 "We all sat there in the living room": M.F. to Gingrich, September 2, 1970, Schlesinger.

165 "black as coal," Ibid.

166 "The fact that she's a television star": Olney, *Reflexions*, p. 225.

166 "She remains sweet": Ibid., p. 127.

166 "A pompous buffoon": Ibid., p. 140.

166 "A pathetic creature": Olney to James Olney, December 18, 1970, Olney papers.
166 "Bitter . . . irrationally anti-French": Olney, *Reflexions*, p. 196.
166 "I came away feeling rather unclean": Olney to James Olney, December 18, 1970, Olney papers.
166 "mad old Sybille": Ibid.
166 "critical, negative, destructive": Olney, *Reflexions*, p. 128.
167 "interminable and pointless": Ibid.
167 "Very nice": Ibid., p. 127.
167 "Trash": Ibid.
168 "In Escoffier's *Guide Culinaire*": Olney, *The French Menu Cookbook*, p. 18.
168 "I have a feeling": Olney to James Olney, December 18, 1970, Olney papers.
171 "Eda and Sybille were also there": Olney to Beard, fall 1972, Fales.
171 "You don't *r-e-a-l-l-y*": Olney, *Reflexions*, p. 145.
172 "Her observations": Ibid.
172 "Of course I am not supposed to say this": Ibid., p. 240.

CHAPTER TWELVE: ESCAPE
174 avoiding any prickly remarks: Described in M.F.'s 1970 journal, Fisher papers.
174 the prospect of seeming sneaky: Ibid.
174 "I should be packing": M.F. to Gingrich, December 16, 1970, Schlesinger.
175 like trying to find another Sheila Hibben: This scene is described in a letter, M.F. to Gingrich, December 16, 1970, Schlesinger.
176 "Dear Julia and Paul and Jim": M.F. to Childs and Beard, December 16, 1970, Schlesinger.
177 "The Making of a Masterpiece": *McCall's*, October 1970.
177 "I am finished working": Quotes and details from this scene are from Child, *My Life in France*, pp. 309–310.
179 "Now I don't have to be": Quoted in Shapiro, *Julia Child: A Life*, p. 93.

CHAPTER THIRTEEN: THE GHOST OF ARLES AND AVIGNON
181 The restaurants were closed: All of the scenes and quotes in this chapter, except where noted, are from M.F.'s 1970 journal, Fisher papers.
182 "I know, at this far date": M.F. to Gingrich, November 6, 1970, Schlesinger.
187 "It's not the weather": M.F. to Gingrich, December 21, 1970, Schlesinger.
190 "To hell with Noël": M.F.'s 1971 journal, Fisher papers.
191 "All I did was cook": M.F. to Hal Bieler, December 9, 1969, Schlesinger, quoted in Reardon, *Poet of the Appetites*, p. 367.

CHAPTER FOURTEEN: CHRISTMAS AND *RÉVEILLON*
197 "Do come!": Childs to M.F., late December 1970, Schlesinger.
198 "gossipy profession": Child to Beard, September 28, 1968, Schlesinger.

198 "I am certain Pan Am": Beard to Childs, December 28, 1970, Schlesinger.

198 "red gout chair": Ibid.

198 "Some progress": Ibid.

199 "*Soupe de l'enfant Barbue*": Ibid.

200 "thump-thump-thump": Jones, *The Tenth Muse*, p. 83.

200 "What a dear pair": Child to Beard, January 5, 1971, Schlesinger.

200 "The *pâté de bécasse*": Jones, *The Tenth Muse*, p. 86.

201 "Just like pulling the cork": Ibid., p. 87.

202 "Precise measures bore me": Olney, *Reflexions*, p. 219.

203 "The implication was": Jones, *The Tenth Muse*, p. 58.

203 "Although a pint of water": Child, *From Julia Child's Kitchen*, p. 673.

203 "Poor old Julia": Olney, *Reflexions*, p. 219.

203 "After all": Child, *From Julia Child's Kitchen*, p. ix.

204 "My fowl": Ibid., p. 227.

206 "Apéritif: vermouth, Dubonnet": Menu described in Jones, *The Tenth Muse*, p. 87.

206 "They seem much less fat": Child to Beard, January 1971, Schlesinger.

207 "Simone Beck: The Cookbook Author without a Show on TV": *New York Times*, November 12, 1970.

207 "It seems to me": Jones to Beck, November 13, 1970, Schlesinger.

208 "*You* were the one": Jones, interview with author.

208 "Well, let's just settle this": Ibid.

209 "Of course, dear": Ibid.

209 "It is a fact": Child, *My Life in France*, p. 317.

210 "Caviar": Menu described in Jones, *The Tenth Muse*, p. 87.

211 "Autumn in Normandy": Beck, *Simca's Cuisine*, p. ix.

212 "Certainly I am able to read": Jones to Beck, November 13, 1970, Schlesinger.

212 "who adore to cook": Beck, *Simca's Cuisine*, p. xiii.

212 "There was no need to": Child, *My Life in France*, p. 318.

212 "41 minutes into 1971": M.F. to Gingrich, December 31, 1970, Schlesinger.

213 "I came to think of him": Fisher, *A Considerable Town*, p. 185.

CHAPTER FIFTEEN: GOING HOME

215 "Helicopters dropped food": Associated Press, January 4, 1971.

216 "I think this way of life": Fisher, interviewed by *Publishers Weekly*, March 29, 1971, excerpted in David Lazar, *Conversations with M. F. K. Fisher*, p. 10.

217 "latent sensuality": Fisher, *Among Friends*, p. 283.

217 "It made me feel creative": Ibid., p. 291.

218 "solo performance": M.F.'s 1970 journal, Fisher papers.

218 "nasty pile of work": M.F. to Childs, January 6, 1971, Schlesinger.

219 she'd had enough of eating in restaurants: Described in a letter, M.F. to Gingrich,

December 26, 1970. After this period of "living in restaurants," she wrote, "I am consummately bored—ugh, I say, even at the thought of Prunier!"

219 "Oh yeah, *Gay Paree*": M.F. to Gingrich, February 6, 1971, Fisher papers.

219 "The captains and kings": Child to Beard, January 5, 1971, Schlesinger.

220 "the rudest and most incompetent": Olney, *Reflexions*, p. 128.

220 "grayish-white, stone-like objects": Ibid.

220 "It is annoying": Beard to Child, January 8, 1971, Schlesinger.

CHAPTER SIXTEEN: LAST HOUSE

221 "Murder": M.F. to Gingrich, January 28, 1971, Fisher papers.

222 "Split living is not for me": M.F. to Gingrich, February 6, 1971, Fisher papers.

222 "Her subject is hunger": Fisher, *Art of Eating*, p. xv.

222 "Except for the new Quaker stuff": M.F. to Gingrich, 1971, Schlesinger.

223 "Mrs. Fisher is a woman": Fisher, *Art of Eating*, p. xix.

224 "We are re-reading": Paul Child to M.F., February 24, 1971, Schlesinger.

224 "We are delighted": Child to M.F., February 28, 1971, Schlesinger.

226 "a work of skill": Sokolov, "In Literature of Food, Two Books to Satisfy a Reader's Appetite," *New York Times*, December 30, 1971.

226 "This memoir of M. F. K. Fisher": Jean Stafford, "Love Match of Pleasures," *Vogue*, January 1972, quoted in Reardon, *Poet of the Appetites*, p. 390.

226 "almost impalpable Jim Crow arrangement": "Books," *The New Yorker*, November 13, 1971.

226 "At this stage in our lives": M.F. to Mary Kennedy Wright, April 2, 1972, Schlesinger.

226 "Any publication of mine": M.F. to Gingrich, December 31, 1970, Schlesinger.

227 "and at the grave risk": Norah Barr to M.F., fall 1971, Schlesinger.

227 "Dearest N.": M.F. to Norah Barr, December 17, 1971, Schlesinger.

227 "I suppose that I really believe": Norah Barr to M.F., fall 1971, Schlesinger.

227 "it does seem strange": M.F. to Norah Barr, December 17, 1971, Schlesinger.

228 "Explanation for Mary Frances!": David Bouverie to M.F., 1971, Fisher papers.

228 "turned into Madame Butterfly": M.F. to Gingrich, September 28, 1971, Schlesinger.

228 "as amiably sexless": Ibid.

229 "Flew direct from New York": David Bouverie to M.F., December 19, 1971, Fisher papers.

229 "My dear RR": David Bouverie to M.F., October 10, 1971, Fisher papers.

230 "I am no longer the woman": M.F. to Gingrich, September 28, 1971, Schlesinger.

230 "I hope you won't collapse": M.F. to Childs, October 11, 1971, Schlesinger.

231 "She is unfailingly gentle": M.F. to Bouverie, December 6, 1971, Fisher papers.

232 "Fresh ravioli": Menu described in letter, M.F. to Bouverie, December 1971, Fisher papers.

233 "We last saw him at a party": Child to M.F., May 28, 1971, Schlesinger.

233 "enjoying life": Ibid.

234 "I cannot even think of Plascassier": M.F. to Childs, September 10, 1971, Schlesinger.

234 "This cannot be construed": Childs to M.F., December 12, 1971, Schlesinger.

CHAPTER SEVENTEEN: NEW BEGINNINGS

237 they looked like eighteenth-century boots: Described in a letter, Beard to Childs, June 10, 1974, Schlesinger.

239 "We are engulfed in our TV": Child to M.F., February 28, 1971, Schlesinger.

240 "could care less about the East Coast": Child to Beard, May 11, 1972, Schlesinger.

241 "The lunch was prepared": Beard to M.F., March 11, 1972, Schlesinger.

242 "one wants to be a little bit special": Beck, *Simca's Cuisine*, p. xv.

243 "pure in effect": Olney, *Simple French Food*, p. 10.

244 "You, the cook": Ibid., p. 11.

244 "Improvisation is at war with the printed word": Ibid., p. 17.

245 "He won't do anything": Child to M.F., quoted in Fitch, *Appetite for Life*, p. 366.

245 "a marvelous book": Hazelton, "Cooking by the Book," *New York Times*, December 3, 1972.

245 "The real problem with Mr. Beard's approach": Sokolov, "America in the Kitchen," *New York Times*, May 25, 1972.

246 "What can he have against me?": Beard to John Ferrone, quoted in Clark, *James Beard, A Biography*, p. 257.

246 "in the spirit of a zealous acolyte": Ibid., p. 258.

246 "It was a very French book": Child, *My Life in France*, p. 319.

246 "They don't make them": Hazelton, "Cooking by the Book," *New York Times*, December 3, 1972.

247 "The great lesson": Child, *My Life in France*, p. 328.

247 "It is a pleasure to read": Sokolov, "Cooking by the Book," *New York Times*, December 7, 1975.

247 "great liberation": Child, *My Life in France*, p. 328.

247 "What a problem": Child, *From Julia Child's Kitchen*, p. x.

248 "Now tell me, Richard": Olney, *Reflexions*, p. 196.

248 "A kitchen revolt is underway": John Hess, " 'Plasticized, Tasteless Breads' Give Rise to Kitchen Revolt," *New York Times*, October 4, 1973.

249 "The dishes are not those found in posh restaurants": Olney, *Simple French Food*, p. xi.

249 "sensuous-sensual-spiritual": Ibid., p. 6.

249 "The book's greatest virtue": Hazelton, "Cooking and Eating and Reading about It," *New York Times*, December 1, 1974.

251 "If things are done right": Quoted in Olney, *Reflexions*, p. 177.

251 "Peruvian Adonis": Ibid., p. 129.

252 "What's the secret of your pastry?": Ibid., p. 181.

255 "Nobody seemed to be much annoyed": Fisher, *A Considerable Town*, p. 47.

256 "Often, in a window": Ibid., p. 122.

256 "sitting in cafés": Ibid., p. 43.

257 "Nobody who reads this book": Jan Morris, "Marseille Ramble," *New York Times*, June 4, 1978.

257 "Inevitably, Marseilles is now": Anatole Broyard, "Books of the Times," *New York Times*, May 10, 1978.

258 "In the Sonoma Valley": From an interview with James Villas in 1978, in David Lazar, *Conversations with M. F. K. Fisher*, p. 32.

AFTERWORD: PROVENCE NOW

262 "Everywhere around us": Paul Child to Charlie Child, June 12, 1971, and copy sent to M.F., Schlesinger.

264 "The Black Book": Courtesy of Kathie Alex.

268 "From *bouillabaisse* in the Mediterranean": Child, *From Julia Child's Kitchen*, p. 28.

269 "*Bouillabaisse* is, to tell the truth": Olney, *The French Menu Cookbook*, p. 398.

271 "the sheer joy": Jones, interview with author.

275 "While I was finishing up this book": Child, *From Julia Child's Kitchen*, p. 507.

277 "picture of perfect order": Olney, *Reflexions*, p. 395.

279 "And I came to a decision": Child, *My Life in France*, p. 330.

281 "*un plat canaille*": Olney, *Simple French Food*, p. 356.

282 "If you have taken care to observe": Beard, *American Cookery*, p. 17.

283 "(I once listened in amazement": Olney, *Simple French Food*, p. 389.

285 "One reason we are friends": M.F. to Childs, August 27, 1970.

286 "Just before going to bed that night": Child, *My Life in France*, p. 332.

BIBLIOGRAPHY

Barr, Norah K., Marsha Moran, and Patrick Moran, eds. *M. F. K. Fisher, A Life in Letters: Correspondence 1929–1991.* Washington, DC: Counterpoint, 1998.

Beard, James. *American Cookery.* New York: Little, Brown and Company, 2010.

———. *Beard on Bread.* New York: Alfred A. Knopf, 1973.

———. *Beard on Food: The Best Recipes and Kitchen Wisdom from the Dean of American Cooking.* New York: Bloomsbury USA, 2012.

———. *Delights and Prejudices.* Philadelphia, PA: Running Press Book Publishers, 1992.

Beard, James, and Alexander Watt. *Paris Cuisine.* Boston, MA: Little, Brown, 1952.

Beck, Simone "Simca." *Simca's Cuisine.* New York: Alfred A. Knopf, 1973.

Beck, Simone, with Suzy Patterson. *Food and Friends: A Memoir with Recipes.* New York: Viking, 1991.

Child, Julia. *From Julia Child's Kitchen.* New York: Alfred A. Knopf, 1982.

Child, Julia, and Simone Beck. *Mastering the Art of French Cooking, Vol. II.* New York: Alfred A. Knopf, 1970.

Child, Julia, Louisette Bertholle, and Simone Beck. *Mastering the Art of French Cooking.* New York: Alfred A. Knopf, 1966.

Child, Julia, with Alex Prud'homme. *My Life in France.* New York: Anchor Books, 2007.

Claiborne, Craig. *A Feast Made for Laughter.* New York: Doubleday, 1982.

Clark, Robert. *James Beard: A Biography.* New York: HarperCollins, 1993.

Ephron, Nora. "The Food Establishment: Life in the Land of the Rising Soufflé." *Wallflower at the Orgy.* New York: Bantam, 2007.

Escoffier, G. A. *A Guide to Modern Cookery.* London: Heinemann, 1966.

Ferrary, Jeannette. *M. F. K. Fisher and Me: A Memoir of Food and Friendship.* New York: St. Martin's Griffin, 1998.

Fisher, M. F. K. *Among Friends.* New York: North Point Press, 2000.

———. *The Art of Eating.* New York: Collier Books, 1990.

———. *As They Were.* New York: Alfred A. Knopf, 1982.

———. *Two Towns in Provence.* New York, Vintage Books, 1983.

———. *With Bold Knife and Fork.* Berkeley, CA: Counterpoint Press, 1969.

Fisher, M. F. K., and the Editors of Time-Life Books. *The Cooking of Provincial France.* New York: Time Inc., 1968.

Fitch, Noel Riley. *Appetite for Life: The Biography of Julia Child.* New York: Anchor Books, 1999.

Gatti, Raymond. *Taxi de guerre, taxi de paix.* Cannes, France: S.E.D.A.IN., 1988.

Jones, Evan. *Epicurean Delight: The Life and Times of James Beard*. New York: Simon and Schuster Fireside, 1992.

Jones, Judith. *The Tenth Muse: My Life in Food*. New York: Alfred A. Knopf, 2007.

Kamp, David. *The United States of Arugula: The Sun-Dried, Cold-Pressed, Dark-Roasted, Extra Virgin Story of the American Food Revolution*. New York: Broadway Books, 2006.

Lazar, David. *Conversations with M. F. K. Fisher*. Jackson: University Press of Mississippi, 1992.

Le Huédé, Henri. *Dining on the France*. New York: Vendome Press, 1981.

McNamee, Thomas. *The Man Who Changed the Way We Eat: Craig Claiborne and the American Food Renaissance*. New York: Free Press, 2012.

Olney, Richard. *The French Menu Cookbook*. Berkeley, CA: Ten Speed Press, 2002.

———. *Lulu's Provençal Table*. Berkeley, CA: Ten Speed Press, 2002.

———. *Reflexions*. New York: Brick Tower Press, 1999.

———. *Simple French Food*. Hoboken, NJ: Wiley Publishing, 1992.

Reardon, Joan. *Poet of the Appetites: The Lives and Loves of M. F. K. Fisher*. New York: North Point Press, 2004.

———, ed. *A Stew or a Story: An Assortment of Short Works by M. F. K. Fisher*. Emeryville, CA: Shoemaker and Hoard, 2006.

Shapiro, Laura. *Julia Child: A Life*. New York: Penguin Books, 2009.

Spitz, Bob. *Dearie: The Remarkable Life of Julia Child*. New York: Alfred A. Knopf, 2012.

Zimmerman, Anne. *An Extravagant Hunger: The Passionate Years of M. F. K. Fisher*. Berkeley, CA: Counterpoint, 2011.

INDEX